EXTINCTIONS

EXTINCTIONS

Edited by
Matthew H. Nitecki

The University of Chicago Press
Chicago and London

MATTHEW H. NITECKI is curator of fossil invertebrates in the Department of Geology at the Field Museum of Natural History and is a member of the Committee on Evolutionary Biology at the University of Chicago.

The University of Chicago Press, Chicago 60637
The University of Chicago Press, Ltd., London
©1984 by The University of Chicago
All rights reserved. Published 1984
Printed in the United States of America

93 92 91 90 89 88 87 86   5 4 3 2

Library of Congress Catalog Card Number: 84-40253

CONTENTS

Contributors   vii

Preface   ix

Death of Species
    David M. Raup   1

Patterns of Extinction in the Fossil
Record of Vascular Plants
    Andrew H. Knoll   21

Marine Mass Extinctions: A Dominant
Role for Temperatures
    Steven M. Stanley   69

Extinction in Hominid Evolution
    Alan Walker   119

Catastrophic Extinctions and Late Pleistocene Blitzkrieg: Two Radiocarbon Tests
    Paul S. Martin   153

"Normal" Extinctions of Isolated Populations
    Jared M. Diamond   191

Mammalian Extinction and Biogeography in
the Southern Rocky Mountains
    Bruce D. Patterson   247

Ecosystem Decay of Amazon Forest Remnants
    Thomas E. Lovejoy, Judy M. Rankin, R. O.
    Bierregaard, Jr., Keith S. Brown, Jr.,
    Louise H. Emmons, and Martha E.
    Van der Voort   295

Appendix -- Abstracts of Papers   327

Author Index   337

Subject Index   345

CONTRIBUTORS

Numbers in parentheses indicate the pages on which authors contributions begin.

R. O. BIERREGAARD, JR (295). World Wildlife Fund -- U.S., 1601 Connecticut Avenue N.W., Washington, D. C.   20009

KEITH S. BROWN, JR (295). Departamento de Zoologia, Instituto de Biologia, Universidade Estadual de Campinas, C.P. 1170, Campinas, Sao Paulo 13.100 Brasil

JARED M. DIAMOND (191). Department of Physiology, University of California at Los Angeles School of Medicine, Los Angeles, California
    90024

LOUISE H. EMMONS (295). National Museum of Natural History, Smithsonian Institution, Washington, D. C.   20560

ANDREW H. KNOLL (21). Department of Organismic and Evolutionary Biology, Harvard University, Cambridge, Massachusetts 02138

THOMAS E. LOVEJOY (295). World Wildlife Fund -- U.S., 1601 Connecticut Avenue N.W., Washington, D. C.   20009

PAUL S. MARTIN (153). Department of Geosciences, University of Arizona, Tucson, Arizona   85721

BRUCE D. PATTERSON (247). Department of Zoology, Field Museum of Natural History, Chicago, Illinois   60605

JUDY M. RANKIN (295). Instituto Nacional de Pesquisas da Amazonia (INPA), Caixa Postal 478, Manaus, 69.000 AM Brasil

DAVID M. RAUP (1). Department of the Geophysical Sciences, University of Chicago, Chicago, Illinois   60637

STEVEN M. STANLEY (69). Department of Earth and Planetary Sciences, The Johns Hopkins University, Baltimore, Maryland 21218

MARTHA E. VAN DER VOORT (295). World Wildlife Fund -- U. S., 1601 Connecticut Avenue N.W., Washington, D. C.   20009

ALAN WALKER (119). Department of Cell Biology and Anatomy, The Johns Hopkins University School of Medicine, Baltimore, Maryland   21205

PREFACE

The Sixth Annual Spring Systematics Symposium, Extinctions, was held in Chicago on May 13-14, 1983. The Field Museum of Natural History hosted the meetings with support from the National Science Foundation. More than 400 evolutionary biologists attended the meeting, which stimulated immediate debate and notice (see for example, J. M. Diamond, 1983, Nature 304:396-397, R. Lewin, 1983, Science, 220:1140-1141, and R. Lewin, 1984, Science, 223:383-385).

This volume includes chapters based on all of the papers that were presented at the meeting except one. The book deals with extinctions both large and small, but it concentrates on mass extinctions. There are many documented extinctions, and rates and patterns of mass extinctions are important aspects of the evolution and organization of ecological systems. Waves of extinctions in the geological past have been recently interpreted as due to the meteoritic (or cometary) impact, and the present volume is greatly influenced by, and in many ways centers around, this hypothesis. Rates and demography of extinctions in local living and fossil populations, and extinctions caused by human activities are also actively investigated.

There are many answers -- and in the future even more will be found -- but today extinctions are a fertile ground of new inquiries, and we are now posing questions that tomorrow will lead to new evolutionary postulates and new evolutionary models.

I would like to thank those who helped with organizational matters, reviewed manuscripts, and made valuable suggestions: David M. Armstrong, James S. Ashe, James H. Brown, William C. Burger, Peter R. Crane, John W. Fitzpatrick, Karl W. Flessa, Robert F. Inger, Richard G. Klein, Ernest L. Lundelius, Jr., Karl J. Niklas, Timothy Plowman, David M. Raup, J. John Sepkoski, Jr., Russell H. Tuttle, S. David Webb, and Glen E. Woolfenden.

Financial support was given by the Field Museum of Natural History and the National Science Foundation, DEB 83-01236; Zbigniew Jastrzebski assisted with text figures and Martha Bryant patiently typed the camera-ready copy, and cheerfully helped with endless book-making chores.

DEATH OF SPECIES

David M. Raup

The extinction of plants and animals has long been an
object of public fascination and of serious scientific inquiry.
The extinction of the dinosaurs was perhaps the most spectacular, whether it occurred gradually, as some people believe, or
whether it happened literally over a weekend as has been
recently suggested. But the demise of the dinosaurs was neither the largest nor the most profound of the extinctions.
Virtually all species that have ever lived on earth are now
extinct, and many of the mass extinctions have involved far
larger and more successful groups than the large reptiles we
call dinosaurs. Furthermore, it is apparent that extinction
continues today partly as a spontaneous biological process and
partly as a result of human activities. We are all familiar
with the most celebrated of these recent cases: the elimination of the Passenger Pigeon, the Great Auk, the Dodo, and so
on. And this raises the possibility that through human activities we may be entering into a new kind of mass extinction.

In just the last few years, new attention has been
directed at extinction because of two quite different developments. One is the increasing concern and debate about the

possibility of contemporary and future extinctions caused by
man, especially in the tropical rain forests of the world, and
the other stems from the proposal made in 1980 by a group at
Berkeley headed by Louis Alvarez and his son Walter Alvarez.
They suggested that dinosaurs and other groups that went
extinct at the end of the Cretaceous, 65 m.y. ago, were the
victims of the impact of a large asteroid. I will consider
both topics in more detail later in this introduction. First,
however, I would like to attempt to put the phenomenon of
extinction in a larger biological and geological context.

In spite of the obvious importance of extinction, and in
Since most species that have ever lived are extinct, the
number of species extinctions has been only slightly smaller
than the number of species originations, just as in human populations over several thousand years, the number of deaths is
only slightly smaller than the number of births. Thus extinction clearly is an important force in evolution. To study evolution without considering or understanding extinction would be
as difficult as to study demography without looking at mortality.

In spite of the obvious importance of extinction, and in
spite of the fact that hundreds of thousands of extinctions in
the geologic past have been documented, we know surprisingly
little about the process itself and surprisingly little about
its actual role in evolution. With regard to the process, our
textbooks contain a fair variety of statements about how
extinction occurs, but many of these are tautological to say
the least. We read, for example, that a species will go
extinct if environments change more rapidly than the organism
can adapt. This really doesn't tell us very much, except that
an organism has to be able to live in order to survive. We
also read that in sexual organisms extinction is often preceded
by a reduction in population size to the point where effective
interbreeding among members of the species cannot take place.

This is also tautological to the point of not being very useful, especially since there have been very few serious attempts
to place actual numbers on the threshold population sizes below
which extinction is either assured or highly probable. It is
clear that if most members of a species are killed or if their
habitats are destroyed, then there is a good likelihood of
extinction. But documented cases on some reasonable geographic
scale are few and far between. Perhaps the best analysis is to
be found in the work Jared Diamond presents in this volume.

Our knowledge of the importance of extinction in the total
process of organic evolution is also surprisingly limited. It
is conventionally assumed that extinction is a good thing in
the long run. That is, it is generally assumed that extinction
is part of a sorting or selection process similar to Darwinian
natural selection but operating on a different time scale and
involving selection between species or groups of species.
Extinction at this level is generally assumed to be a good
thing because it is expected that the better adapted types survive and the others die, thus leading to overall improvement in
the general fitness or adaptive level of the entire biota. But
documenting this constructive aspect of extinction has proved
to be difficult. The main evidence for superiority is the fact
of survival, and this does little more than restate the question unless there is independent evidence that, for example,
the mammals of the latest Cretaceous were in fact superior to
the large reptiles that went extinct. In this context, the
noted satirist, Will Cuppy (1941) wrote many years ago that
"the Age of Reptiles ended because it had gone on long enough
and it was all a mistake in the first place." (p. 93). Cuppy
went on to suggest that the bats "are going to flop too and
everybody knows it except the bats themselves." While presented
in a humorous vein, these and other Cuppy statements capture
the conventional wisdom on the role of extinction in evolution.

But this is often more a matter of faith than demonstrated fact.

The pace of extinction is also subject to considerable uncertainty. On the one hand we have a view of extinction as a rather slow, gradual process that capitalizes on very slight advantages of one species over another and often relates to gradual changes in the environment. This general point of view is to be found in a number of the chapters in this volume. On the other hand, we have the mass extinctions, some of which appear to have been quite sudden. These range from the dinosaur and related extinctions that I have already mentioned, to extinctions of large mammals a few thousand years ago. Clearly, if we had more precise knowledge about rates -- whether of mass extinctions or of normal "background" extinc- tion -- we would be in a far better position to understand the causes of extinction and we would have a better appreciation for the role of extinction in evolution.

The problems just cited prompted Field Museum to plan and organize the symposium on extinctions on which this volume is based. The contributors address an extraordinary range time scales and of points of view and I will introduce each of the contributors and their topics briefly here. But first, some- thing more should be said about the meteorite proposal of the Alvarez group (Alvarez et al. 1980). Although this volume does not contain a paper on extinction by meteorite impact, Walter Alvarez gave a detailed presentation at the symposium and the impact hypothesis was referred to in several of the other papers as well. It is a topic very much on the minds of all students of extinction.

Walter Alvarez is a geologist at Berkeley who got into the extinction game by a curious route. His research interests over the past few years have included depositional rates in sedimentary rocks. In working on these problems, he needed an

effective means of measuring the rate of accumulation of
ancient limestones and was led by this need to make analyses of
the rather rare element iridium. His hope was that the continuous rain of iridium-bearing meteoritic dust would provide
him with the means to assess rates of sedimentation after the
fact. That is, knowing that the influx of iridium from meteoritic dust is fairly constant, Alvarez reasoned that the concentration of iridium in limestone would provide the basic information he needed on depositional rates. In testing this scheme
with Cretaceous limestones near Gubio in northern Italy,
Alvarez found unusually high levels of iridium, higher than
could possibly have accumulated as a result of the normal input
from meteoritic dust. To make a long story short, this led to
the interpretation that the anomalously high levels of iridium
resulted from the impact of a large meteorite, large enough to
contain enough iridium to explain the anomalies at Gubio. In
the few years since the original discovery, similar iridium
anomalies have been found at about 50 sites of the same age
around the world, most of them in marine sequences but some in
nonmarine and terrestrial sediments. The synchroneity of these
anomalies is striking and the Alvarez group has interpreted
this to mean that the collision of the earth and a large
meteorite (estimated to have been about 10 km in diameter) produced a heavy load of iridium-bearing dust that settled out as
a thin clay layer on a world-wide basis. Because the impact
event is dated as being very close to the time of the dinosaur
and other extinctions at the end of the Cretaceous, it is not
surprising that cause and effect have been postulated.

Shortly after the original discovery of iridium anomalies
at the end of the Cretaceous, another quite persistent iridium
anomaly was found near an extinction event at the end of the
Eocene about 30 m.y. after the terminal Cretaceous event. This
clearly adds to the circumstantial argument for a causal

relationship between impacts and extinctions. In addition,
both iridium anomalies are often associated with microtektites
which are known to be byproducts of large body impacts.

It is difficult to exaggerate the effect that the Alvarez
finding and their hypothesis have had on thinking about extinction, but the question is by no means settled in the minds of
many geologists and paleontologists. As of this writing, arguments are raging over the robustness of this hypothesis. Did
the dinosaurs actually go extinct at the precise time of the
large body impact, or had they been in decline for several million years and perhaps were already dead when the impact
occurred? Were the other extinctions that occurred as part of
the same mass extinction strictly contemporaneous with the
large body impact, or did some extinctions occur before and
some after? And were these other animal groups already in
decline before the impact? It should be expected, of course,
that groups already weakened by other environmental stresses
would be the most likely to suffer as a result of any sudden,
extreme stress. This makes the analysis and interpretation yet
more difficult. Along with these problems is the persistent
suggestion that there may be other phenomena that could produce
a high concentration of a trace metal such as iridium. Some
geologists even doubt that the meteorite impact took place.

This short summary barely scratches the surface of a complex and intriguing scientific problem. Interested readers
should consult the extensive report of the "Snowbird meeting"
(Silver and Schultz, 1982) which contains about 50 papers on
the topic. The subject of impacts and extinctions is clearly a
fascinating and important one, and my hunch is that many of the
basic questions will be resolved one way or another in the next
two or three years. In the meantime, the argument is bringing
paleobiologists and geophysicists and astronomers in closer
communication than they have enjoyed for many generations.

The first paper in this volume concerns the role of
extinction in the evolution of plants over very long spans of
geologic time. Andrew Knoll is a paleobotanist best known for
his work with some of the earliest microorganisms (Precambrian:
1-3 b.y. old) but, as can be seen from his contribution to this
volume, Knoll is an accomplished student of the fossil record
of younger plants as well. Within this framework, Knoll
describes the botanical record as one of rather persistently
increasing variety and diversity accompanied by exploitation of
new environments and new ways of functioning. These trends are
interrupted only by two or three major extinction setbacks. At
the risk of oversimplification, I would characterize Knoll's
description of the plant record as one in which major extinction played an important role only occasionally.

The second two papers, those by Steven Stanley and Allen
Walker, fall at an intermediate point in the time scale of
extinction. Both involve events that happened a long time ago
by human standards, that is 1-4 m.y., but almost yesterday in
terms of the vastness of the geologic time scale. Stanley is a
paleontologist at Johns Hopkins specializing in fossil marine
invertebrates and molluscs in particular. In his contribution
to the present volume he is concerned with the very substantial
extinctions that occurred among shallow water marine organisms
in the Pliocene epoch shortly before the beginning of the most
recent ice age. In his work, Stanley is particularly concerned
with analyzing the similarities and differences between species
that survived and those that did not. In particular he has
found rather close correspondence between the life habits and
geographic distribution of certain species and their susceptibility to extinction, and he has related this correspondence to
climatic change and to the geographic distribution of climatic
change. Stanley concludes that climatic deterioration, fairly
gradual over fairly long periods of time, is often the key

factor in producing extinctions. Although his main research
area is in the youngest parts of the fossil record, he makes
the argument that comparable climatic deterioration was responsible for some of the most celebrated of mass extinctions in
the more distant geologic past, including that of the terminal
Cretaceous. In particular, Stanley develops the argument that
climatic change is more important in the extinction mechanism
than is sea level change, which has been a favored causal
mechanism in many studies of extinction. Whereas Stanley makes
little direct reference to the Alvarez model of meteorite
impacts, it is very clear in his chapter that he strongly
favors the more gradual, more long-term climatic mechanism over
the Alvarez scenario. A comparison of the Stanley and Alvarez
theses illustrates and emphasizes the strong differences in
viewpoint that exist about extinction.

     In quite a different context, though at approximately the
same time scale, Walker is concerned with two probable extinctions in the history of the evolution of the human species.
Walker is a paleontologist and anatomist at Johns Hopkins and
has been concerned for many years with that small but important
lineage that leads to man. He considers two basically different extinction situations. One is the rather sudden disappearance of the robust Australopithecus in Africa about a million years ago, and the other is the much more recent disappearance of Neanderthal Man in northern Europe. The Neanderthal extinction illustrates a particular problem in any
small-scale analysis of extinction, usually referred to as
"pseudoextinction." In the late Pleistocene, evidence of Neanderthal Man is replaced very quickly by evidence of quite
modern-looking people. This leaves several alternative explanations: perhaps the Neanderthals died out quite independently
of the evolution in the lineage leading to man; or perhaps
there were two lineages in competition with each other and that

early man in fact caused the extinction of Neanderthal; or
finally there is the possibility (more interesting in the
present context) that Neanderthal Man simply evolved so rapidly
into modern man that we cannot see the change in the fossil
record. After the fact, a very rapid change in a species may
look like nearly simultaneous extinction and origination. The
term "pseudoextinction" is used for cases where evolution is
extremely rapid, but where true extinction, in the sense of
death without issue, does not take place.

     The contribution by Paul Martin brings us closer to man's
influence. Martin is a paleontologist at the University of
Arizona and for many years has been a central figure in studies
of the rather sudden extinction, 8-12,000 years ago, of a great
many of large land animals, including the American mammoth,
large ground sloths, and saber-toothed tigers. Geologists of
the future may see this as a mass extinction, although much
will depend upon how much importance future geologists place on
the history of mammals in the total range of evolutionary
phenomena. But, by any standard, it was a spectacular event
and one that could be attributed to a singular event, a catastrophe of some sort. In Martin's analysis, an especially
important element is his contention that the extinctions were
not actually simultaneous on a world-wide basis, but occurred
at different times in different regions and continents. He
concludes that "no worlds collided". Martin argues that the
extinction of large mammals during this time resulted from an
extremely complex set of events in which man's activities
played a role, but do not represent a single cause. By the
same token, Martin down plays the general effect of climate and
does not favor the sort of catastrophic cause suggested by the
Alvarez model, unless that catastrophic event is a "blitzkrieg"
produced by severe human impact in the form of rapid habitat
destruction and introduction of alien species.

Jared Diamond's contribution also deals with the events of
the last few thousand or few tens of thousands of years, but in
contrast to Martin's work, Diamond is primarily concerned with
living populations, mostly of birds, in small island archipelagoes. Diamond is a physiologist and ecologist at University of California at Los Angeles and has for many years been
concerned with the ecology and biogeography of southern Pacific
insular communities. For Diamond, a central cause of extinctions is changing sea level. The raising and lowering of sea
level during the last glacial epoch has had dramatic effects on
the geography of the southern Pacific Islands. As sea level
goes down, the islands become more exposed until they become
connected to each other by dry land. Conversely, as sea level
rises, large islands become broken into fragments or into
smaller islands. And from this develops a wide body of observation and theory concerned with the relationship between
species and their habitable area. Diamond sees the sorts of
extinctions produced by sea level changes as gradual, at least
in human time scales, and closely related to physical change in
geography and landscape. His work bears directly on problems
of habitable area of species living throughout the world today.

Bruce Patterson's contribution differs in scale and subject matter from that of Diamond, although it also addresses
the effects of recent changes in the physical environment on
species distribution patterns. Patterson is on the curatorial
staff of Field Museum and he is a mammalogist and evolutionary
ecologist of wide experience with montane and intermontane mammalian distributions in the American southwest. Working with
present distributional patterns, evidence from Pleistocene fossils of past distributions, and the climatic history of the
southern Rockies, Patterson pieces together a picture of origination and extinction of small mammals. He argues that the
process is driven ultimately by climatic change. Here again we

have an example of climatic change being suggested as the primary driving force in the extinction process.

   With the contribution of Thomas Lovejoy and his colleagues
we come fully to the present and look into the future. Thomas
Lovejoy is an ornithologist who does research for the World
Wildlife Fund. He concentrates on the general problem of
actual or impending extinction, particularly in Neotropical
rain forests. The concern here is, of course, with the effects
of human activity, particularly in land clearing and other
aspects of habitat destruction. Obviously any rigorous predictions in the context depend heavily on our knowledge and understanding of extinction process. For Lovejoy, questions of
long-term changes in climate or in sea level are not as important as the immediate effects of human activity, primarily
because the latter is presumed to operate on an infinitely
shorter time scale than the natural changes in the physical
environment considered by other contributors to this volume.
Also, it is tacitly assumed (and one hopes with good reason)
that impacts by large objects from outer space are sufficiently
rare that the probability of an impact over a few years or
thousands of years is so low as to be considered negligible.

   In summary, the several papers in this volume present an
almost frightening array of conceptual frameworks and interpretations of extinction. It is clear that there is little agreement on the basics. An event as close to us in time as the
extinction of large mammals a few thousand years ago or an
event so massive and well-documented as the terminal Cretaceous
extinction have an array of explanations varying from gradual
deterioration of conditions over millions of years to events
lasting but an instant in time. Whereas there is always controversy in science, I submit that the range of views presented
in this volume shows a level of disparity or downright confu-
sion which is offscale. In this context I suggest that

evolutionary studies, as well as many of the other natural sciences, are in a period of transition. Conventional dogma is
being questioned and in some cases discarded. We are seeing a
change from dominantly gradualist interpretations of natural
phenomena to those that emphasize strongly chaotic events.

Something should be said here about "catastrophe" as a
word and as a concept. The word "catastrophe" is highly
charged, and its use in geological contexts is almost
guaranteed to start arguments. According to my dictionary, the
geological definition is quite clear: any significant event,
such as a flood or an earthquake, that causes sudden changes in
the configuration or composition of parts of the earth. The
only real problem in applying this definition is to decide what
constitutes "sudden". The impact of a large meteorite (a la
Alvarez) is certainly sudden but was the collision of India
with the Asian continent through continental drift also sudden?
Rates of continental drift are measured in centimeters per year
and whether this is sudden depends on one´s perspective. The
collision of two continents may take a long time in terms of
human time scales but may be considered instantaneous in geologic time.

Far more troublesome are some of the connotations of the
word "catastrophe" that go beyond the dictionary definition or
that involve legitimate but nongeological uses of the term.
For many people, catastrophe implies some sort of supernatural
intervention and therefore, they assume that working with
models based on catastrophe is unscientific. Many geologists
seem to equate "extraterrestrial" with "supernatural" and this
just makes matters worse. The word "catastrophe" is often used
generally to imply that an event is tragic, disastrous, or
ruinous. In fact, my dictionary gives "disaster" as the only
synonym of "catastrophe." Thus, any discussion of seemingly
catastrophic explanations of geological events is made more

difficult by the differing perceptions of a single word. We
probably should use another, less loaded term for rare events
of significance in geologic or biologic history. Lacking a
suggestion for such a term, I will continue to use "catastrophe" but must emphasize that it is meant only as a geologically sudden (and usually rare) event -- without implying cause
and without implying tragedy.

It may be useful to review briefly some of the history of
ideas about extinction, particularly those invoking catastrophism. I make no pretense of being an historian of science,
but I will attempt to touch on a few of the highlights.
Extinctions were well-known many years before Darwin developed
his theory of evolution. In fact, extinctions were relied upon
in the early days of the development of the geologic time scale
simply because they provided useful datum planes for the establishment of a chronology and for the correlation of other
events from one region to another. In the late 18th and
throughout much of the 19th Centuries extinction was assumed to
be catastrophic in the sense of involving sudden destruction of
life. The noted anatomist and paleontologist Georges Cuvier
was a particularly effective proponent of the catastrophic view
of extinction. To emphasize this point, let me quote a couple
of passages from Baron Cuvier´s "Essay on the Theory of the
Earth" (1817): "These repeated [advances] and retreats of the
sea have neither been slow nor gradual; most of the catastrophes which have occasioned them have been sudden; and this
is easily proved, especially with regard to the last of them,
the traces of which are most conspicuous." In this passage,
Cuvier was not only emphasizing the suddenness of the change,
but also he invoked sea level change as an explanation of
extinction. With regard to extinction itself, he said: "Life,
therefore, has been often disturbed on this earth by terrible
events -- calamities which, at their commencement, have perhaps

moved and overturned to a great depth the entire outer crust of
the globe... numberless living beings have been the victims of
these catastrophes; some have been destroyed by some sudden
inundations, others have been laid dry in consequence of the
bottom of the sea being instantaneously elevated. Their races
even have become extinct, and have left no memorial of them
except some small fragments which the naturalist can scarcely
recognize."

The general set of attitudes exemplified by Cuvier came to
an abrupt end with the rise to prominence of the ideas of
Charles Lyell in the mid-19th century. Preceding Darwin, Lyell
developed a far more gradualistic account of earth history that
avoided catastrophe or any significant deviation from "business
as usual". In the first edition of Lyell's Principles of
Geology (1833), for example, he said: "We hear of sudden and
violent revolutions of the globe, of the instantaneous elevation of mountain chains, of paroxysms of volcanic energy, declining according to some, and according to others increasing in
violence from the earliest to the latest ages. We are also
told of general catastrophes and a succession of deluges, of
the alternations of periods of repose and disorder, of the
refrigeration of the globe, of the sudden annihilation of whole
races of animals and plants, and other hypotheses, in which we
see the ancient spirit of speculation revived, and the desire
manifested to cut, rather than patiently to untie, the Gordian
knot." Lyell clearly considered suggestions of sudden or
catastrophic changes as speculative, probably wrong, and possibly immoral. In the same passage, he goes on: "In our attempt
to unravel these difficult questions, we shall adopt a different course, restricting ourselves to the known or possible
operations of existing causes; feeling assured that we have not
yet exhausted the resources which the study of the present
course of nature may provide, and therefore, that we are not

authorized in the infancy of our science, to recur to extraordinary agents. We shall adhere to this plan ... because ...
history informs us that this method has always put geologists
on the road that leads to truth." In other words, if you work
hard enough, you can find a noncatastrophic solution to any
problem in geology. I wonder, in passing, whether the evolu-
tionists who complain about contemporary fundamentalists having
an allegiance to a certain world view are possibly in the position of the pot calling the kettle black.

The conventional wisdom of the present day regarding
extinction is a direct descendant of and strongly influenced by
the Lyellian attitude. In what is generally known as the
Modern Synthesis in evolutionary theory (a set of generalizations that developed in the 1930´s and 1940´s) extinction is
seen as a rather ordinary phenomenon, but one that is complex
and not amenable to simple explanations. Species are seen as
intricately interacting with each other and occasionally
replacing each other through a complex set of adaptive and competitive factors. Physical environmental change is seen as
important but only as one component. Extinction is seen as
relatively easy and a general fact of evolutionary life. When
the extinction process has been modelled mathematically, the
mathematical framework is that of a process continuous through
time, though the rate may vary occasionally, producing what we
call mass extinctions. It is a staunchly Lyellian and
Darwinian view.

The conventional wisdom about extinction that I have just
described explains why there has been so much negative reaction
to the Alvarez hypothesis. But in a way, it does not explain
the reaction. Typically, one would have expected the original
Alvarez paper to have received little attention for the simple
reason that it was so completely outside conventional thinking
that it could be discarded as too speculative, too

undocumented, and therefore probably wrong. There is good pre-
cedent for this sort of reaction. In the present context, it
is interesting to look back on similar proposals of extraterrestrial causes of extinction that have been made in the past
20 years. For example, in 1962 Otto Schindewolf suggested that
the yet larger mass extinctions at the end of the Permian might
have been due to a close encounter with an exploding star or
supernova. He suggested this in a paper which contained catastrophism in the title and presented it as a serious proposal.
The paper was never taken seriously, and certainly had no
impact on general thinking. To be sure, Schindewolf had no
documentary evidence; he only had his observation of the suddenness of the Permian extinctions. He suggested the supernova
interpretation more out of desperation at his inability to find
a terrestrial cause than anything else. Then in the early
1970´s, in his Presidential Address to the Paleontological
Society of America, Digby McLaren discussed the mass extinction
in the late Devonian in great detail and concluded that something special must have happened to explain his data. He suggested, as one possibility, the impact of a large meteorite.
This proposal caused hardly a ripple.

McLaren, like Schindewolf, had no documentary evidence and
therefore, his suggestion was really somewhat different from
that of the Alvarez group. But in 1973, the famous Nobel
laureate in chemistry, Harold Urey, published a short paper in
Nature in which he presented what he considered to be strong
statistical evidence for meteorite or comet impacts having
caused extinctions in the last 40-50 m.y.; that is, during the
Cenozoic. He based this conclusion on an observed association
in time between extinctions and the ages of tektites. Tektites
are assumed to be the secondary products of large meteorite
impacts. This was a case of another prominent scientist

presenting the same idea but with some sort of documentary
basis. However, the Urey paper too was hardly noticed.

In contrast, the Alvarez work produced a storm of excite-
ment and reaction, perhaps because the geochemical anomalies
the Alvarez group described had more muscle than anything that
had come before. But I think the difference is more a matter
of a changing set of attitudes toward the basic Lyellian wisdom. In a variety of fields cognate to historical geology and
paleontology, catastrophe has suddenly become respectable. We
have learned that continents drift and collide, that the mag-
netic field of the earth reverses every once in a while, and
that the macromutations and the hopeful monsters of the early
days of evolutionary theory are being reconsidered. Geologists
have recognized impact craters, such as the big ore district in
Sudbury, Ontario as well-documented impact features. Even 20-
30 years ago, such a suggestion for Sudbury would have been
laughed away out of hand. Thus, because of these developments
in cognate fields, the intellectual climate seems to be more
receptive to ideas about catastrophism.

Meetings such as the symposium at the Field Museum are
being held to consider extinction and one factor stimulating
this activity is the possibility that extinction is not just an
example of Lyellian gradualism. About a week before the Field
Museum symposium, several of the participants took part in a
week-long conference in West Berlin which had the working
title, "Earth History: How Smooth, How Spasmodic?" This is
just another example. Of course, the general interest in sudden, nonrecurring phenomena can be found in fields distant from
historical geology. The Big Bang of cosmology, Thom Theory of
mathematical catastrophe, and the role of disturbance in ecology, are a few examples.

A few directions are evident in the extinction debate.
Most important is that we are moving toward what can only be

described as the position of Baron Cuvier. The search is on
for iridium anomalies and tremendous attention is being given
to the details of mass extinctions deep in the geologic past,
in the Pleistocene, and in contemporary rain forests. What of
the future? My own impression is that we may also be seeing
the beginnings of a return to another kind of once popular
interpretation of history. I refer to cycles and periodici-
ties. At an earlier Field Museum symposium, A. G. Fischer
(1981) presented his claim that extinctions occur on a 32-
million year cycle, but few people have paid any attention to
this idea. The identification of cycles in time has been
anathema for the last generation or two. But this, I submit,
is also changing and we may find that we are dealing not only
with sudden events, but events that fall into cycles that have
astronomical or astrophysical causes. The Fischer work has
been followed up recently by an intensive statistical analysis
of the spacing of about ten extinction events in the past 250
million years. The result is a fairly strong case for a 26
million year periodicity and the suggestion that the driving
mechanism is to be found in solar or galactic phenomena (Raup
and Sepkoski 1984).

LITERATURE CITED

ALVAREZ, L. W., ALVAREZ, W., ASARO, F., and H. V. MICHEL.
     1980. Extraterrestrial causes for the Cretaceous-Tertiary
     extinction. Science, 208:1095-1108.
CUPPY, W. 1941. How to Become Extinct. University of Chicago
     Press, reprint 1983.
CUVIER, L. C. F. D. 1817. Essay on the Theory of the Earth,
     translated by R. JAMESON, Edinburgh.
FISCHER, A. G. 1981. Climatic oscillations in the biosphere.
     pp. 103-131. In: M. H. Nitecki (ed.) Biotic Crises in
     Ecological and Evolutionary Time. Academic Press.
LYELL, C. 1833. Principles of Geology, London.
MC LAREN, D. J. 1970. Presidential Address: Time, life and
     boundaries. Journal of Paleontology 44:801-815.

RAUP, D. M. and J. J. SEPKOSKI, JR. 1984. Periodicity of
    extinctions in the geologic past. Proceedings of the
    National Academy of Sciences 81:801-805
SCHINDEWOLF, O. H. 1962. Neokatastrophismus? Deutsche Geolo-
    gische Gesellschaft Zeitschrift 114:430-445.
SILVER, L. T. and P. H. SCHULTZ (eds.). 1982. Geological
    implications of impacts of large asteroids and comets on
    the earth. Geological Society of America Special Paper
    190, 528 p.
UREY, H. C. 1973. Cometary collisions and geological periods.
    Nature, 242:32-33.

PATTERNS OF EXTINCTION IN THE FOSSIL RECORD OF VASCULAR PLANTS

Andrew H. Knoll

INTRODUCTION

The invertebrate paleontological literature contains numerous references to patterns of extinction in the geological record. These range from early anecdotal accounts of the Great Dying at the end of the Permian, to Newell's (1967) classic quantification of extinctions at the family level, Palmer's (1965, 1982) recognition of biomeres in Cambrian shelf sequences, and recent statistical analyses of extinction patterns by Raup and Sepkoski (1982). In contrast, there has been relatively little examination of extinction patterns in the evolutionary history of vascular plants.

To be sure, the plant record presents certain problems of analysis not encountered to the same degree by invertebrate paleontologists. Chief among these is the distribution of fossil plant assemblages in time and space; the record of terrestrial vegetation is, on the whole, somewhat patchier, or less complete, than that of shelf dwelling skeletonized marine invertebrates. Paleobotanists must also face nettlesome problems of plant disarticulation, both during the life of an individual and during post-mortem transportation, as well as those

introduced by varying modes of preservation that record different sets of anatomical and morphological information about
plant organs. All of these problems have been discussed elsewhere (e.g. Knoll and Rothwell 1981); the important point is
that they do not preclude meaningful evaluations of the vascular plant fossil record.

Because the evolutionary record of skeletonized marine
invertebrates is, to a first approximation, so clearly defined,
investigations of tracheophyte history necessarily become comparative studies; and the comparisons are instructive. Comparisons of patterns of total taxonomic diversity through Phanerozoic time tend to highlight the similarities between the
records of plants and marine invertebrates. Both groups show
an initially logistical pattern of diversification that cul-
minated in a short-lived plateau in taxonomic richness. A
second, larger increase in diversity (in plants this
corresponds to the Carboniferous diversification of pteridosperms and ecologically related pteridophyte groups) was followed by an extended period of more or less stable taxonomic
richness; and a third, late Mesozoic and Cenozoic period of
renewed increase brought total diversity to levels well in
excess of those reached in earlier eras (Sepkoski 1981, Niklas
et al. 1983, Knoll et al. 1984). Additionally, just as one can
recognize a small number of "evolutionary faunas" in the marine
invertebrate record (Flessa and Imbrie 1973, Sepkoski 1981),
so, too, can one discern several "evolutionary floras" that
have successively dominated terrestrial vegetation (Niklas et
al. 1983). Indeed, Gothan and Weyland (1954) spoke in terms of
Paleophytic, Mesophytic and Cenophytic floras before computer
analysis of comparative diversity trends was possible. Rather
than pointing to fundamental biological similarities between
plants and animals, this may be telling us something in general

about ecological controls on diversity and the rarity of biological events that enable diversity ceilings to be lifted.

In contrast to diversity studies, comparisons of extinction patterns underscore differences between the evolutionary
records of vascular plants and animals. Indeed, they suggest
that different sets of controls may underlie major features of
the fossil records of the two groups.

WORKING HYPOTHESES OF VASCULAR PLANT EXTINCTIONS

I would like to propose that much of the documentable
record of vascular plant extinctions and most of the differences between the records of tracheophytes and marine invertebrates can be understood in terms of three brief statements:

1. Relative to animals, plant species are extremely
vulnerable to extinction as a result of competition from newly
appearing taxa.

2. Plant species are also vulnerable to extinction as a
consequence of climatic change.

3. Compared to animals, vascular plants may be relatively
invulnerable to extinction following catastrophic mass mortality. That is, mass mortality may be less likely to translate
into mass extinction for plants than it is for animals.

These propositions are not simply ad hoc hypotheses
erected for the explanation of observed patterns in the fossil
record. They can be derived as predictive hypotheses from
several simple but important facts about plant biology.

1. In a very basic sense, plants all do the same thing.
Vascular plants virtually all absorb water and simple nutrients
from their substrate (and to a lesser extent from the atmosphere), fix atmospheric (or dissolved) CO_2 and convert it into
organic compounds via the Calvin cycle, and obtain the energy
necessary to drive the cycle from sunlight. Certainly, there
exist physiological differences among species, but these do not

mask the fundamental trophic homogeneity of the group. This, of course, means that vascular plants cannot be partitioned into tropic guilds comparable to the carnivores, herbivores, detritus feeders, and other trophically differentiated groups of animals (Harper 1969). It also means that should a potential competitor appear on the scene, a plant population cannot avoid or minimize competition by switching food sources. Vascular plants can minimize direct competition by partitioning niches on the basis of growth forms and physiological adaptations to specific habitat conditions. Yet, being rooted to the substrate and, with rare exceptions, unable to shift food resources, plants do not possess the broad repertory of behavioral responses to competition that are available to many animals. These attributes also suggest that within a given neighborhood, all plants potentially compete with one another (Goldberg and Werner 1983).

Particularly significant from the standpoint of competition is a general characteristic of vascular plants that an engineer would regard as a basic design flaw--the fact that CO_2 uptake cannot be divorced from simultaneous water loss. Many patterns of morphological, anatomical, and physiological evolution among tracheophytes can be viewed as attempts at the solution of this problem. Indeed, the ecological distribution and evolutionary longevity of plant species is relatable in large part to their relative success in balancing photosynthetic gain versus water loss under a given set of environmental conditions.

These considerations suggest that competition should be important in determining patterns of tracheophyte evolution and extinction. Supporting evidence can be drawn from the plant ecological literature, particularly from accounts of the introduction of exotic species into new geographical areas. To provide but a single example, until the mid-nineteenth century,

bluebunch wheatgrass (Agropyron spicatum) was the dominant
species in intermountain grasslands of the northern United
States. In the 1850´s or thereabouts, cheatgrass (Bromus
tectorum) was introduced from Europe, and since that time this
species has increased its biomass enormously at the expense of
bluebunch wheatgrass. Cheatgrass´ success stems from its rapid
winter root growth, giving it an increased ability to obtain
water and, therefore, photosynthesize actively during summer
dry periods (Harris 1967).

   2. Plant distributions sensitively reflect climatic
conditions. This fact was recognized as early as 1806 by Alex-
ander von Humboldt. On a global scale, it can easily be confirmed by comparing vegetation and climate maps of the world.
The effects of local climatic heterogeneity can be observed in
the comparison of north and south facing slopes of mountains.
This sensitivity to temperature and precipitation regimes is,
again, a consequence of basic features of plant biology.
Plants are rooted to their substrates and so must adapt to
local conditions. This fact, coupled with the strong requirement for plants to balance photosynthetic CO_2 fixation against
water loss, results in combinations of structure and physiology
that often allow a population to thrive in one area, while pre-
cluding its expansion into neighboring environments having different patterns of temperature and rainfall distribution.

   Whether or not climatic change results in high levels of
extinction probably depends not so much on the absolute values
of mean annual temperature or precipitation changes, but rather
on whether or not migration to more suitable areas is possible.
(Plant populations migrate in successive generations through
the agency of seed or other propagule dispersal.) A good example of the interrelationships between climatic change and the
geography of dispersal is provided by the temperate zone
forests of eastern North America and northwestern Europe. As

little as three million years ago, in the Pliocene Epoch, the
taxonomic compositions of these forests were quite similar at
the generic level. With the expansion of continental ice
sheets in the Pleistocene, temperate forests in eastern North
America were displaced from the regions they previously had
occupied. Because the Appalachian Mountains run in a
north/south direction, it was possible for populations to
migrate to the south and survive full glacial climatic conditions in Gulf Coast and Mexican refugia. This contrasts
strongly with events in Europe, where the Alps run from west to
east. Ice sheets expanded from the north as well as from the
Alps themselves, and species populations in northwestern Europe
were caught in a cul-de-sac, with migration routes difficult or
impossible. As a result, the present day woody flora of
northwestern Europe is quite species-poor relative to that of
eastern North America, even though the two biotas were equally
rich a few million years ago (Reid and Reid 1915, Friis 1975,
Wood 1972, Frenzel 1973).

3. Vascular plants have evolved numerous mechanisms for
coping with environmental stress. The requirement for such
mechanisms can again be seen in the stationary habit of vascular plant sporophytes and in the variability of weather conditions, both seasonally and in unpredictable patterns. Various
plant species have leaves or whole branch systems that wilt or
drop off during periods of drought. In middle and high latitudes many herbaceous species die back to the ground at the end
of the growing season, perenniating as underground stems, or
rhizomes. Other species become dormant during periods of
adverse weather or survive inclement intervals as seeds. The
point is that although stress tolerance varies in mechanism and
degree from species to species, many if not most vascular
plants have the capacity to deal with the imposition of short-
lived environmental perturbations.

The importance of this in the context of extinction patterns lies in my contention that vascular plants should be
relatively invulnerable to mass extinction caused by catastrophic events. (I restrict my use of the word "catastrophe"
to biospheric perturbations that appear instantaneous when
viewed at the level of resolution provided by the geological
record.) One can conceive of a simple experiment (not recom-
mended in practice) to illustrate this point. If one were to
take a hammer to the local zoo and hit all the animals on the
head, that would be the end of the zoo population. Barring the
importation of new specimens, the population could never be
regenerated. In contrast, if one were to defoliate local conservation lands, new photosynthetic activity would be observed
within a relatively short time. Even if one were to take a saw
and scythe and cut back all above-ground biomass, the vegetation would regenerate itself on a time scale of several tens to
hundreds of years. Forest soil can contain thousands of seeds
per square meter and these often remain viable for decades or
even longer. Further, many plant species can regenerate aerial
stems from parenchymatous tissue in roots and rhizomes.

A good example of such vegetative regeneration is provided
by the American chestnut (Castanea dentata). Once a dominant
element of forests in the northeastern United States, this
species was decimated by chestnut blight during the 1930's.
Since that time, few if any chestnuts have reached reproductive
maturity, yet chestnut saplings remain common sights in forests
because of vegetative regeneration. New England forests also
provide an illuminating example of seed viability in soil.
Following disturbance, pin cherries (Prunus pennsylvanica)
often become established, later to be replaced by oaks,
beeches, and other elements of the mature forest. A mature
stand may contain no visible pin cherry sporophytes, but examination of the forest soil reveals up to several hundred

thousand pin cherry seeds per hectare, viable and ready to ger-
minate at the next instance of site disturbance (Bormann and
Likens 1979).

Thus, from the basic biology of plant species, one can
predict that tracheophytes will show less dramatic long term
evolutionary responses to short term catastrophic events than
animals, even though such events may level above ground vegetation over wide geographic areas. I will return to this topic
below, in a discussion of botanical events at the
Cretaceous/Tertiary boundary.

OVERALL PATTERNS OF DIVERSITY AND EXTINCTION

Figure 1 presents a plot of total species richness through
time, based on tabulations of macrofossils from the paleobotanical literature (Niklas et al. 1983). (The time scale used for
this and all other figures is that of Harland et al. 1982.)

The figure shows a diversity increase from the Silurian
through to the Middle Devonian, with a subsequent slight fall-
off prior to a major burst of diversification in the Carboniferous Period. Except for a modest Permo-Triassic dip in
diversity, total species numbers remain more or less constant
until the middle of the Cretaceous Period when angiosperms
begin their dramatic radiation. (In figures 1-3, the dotted
line extending from the Lower Cretaceous to the Pliocene charts
non-angiosperm diversity. Since the solid line marks total
taxon numbers, angiosperm diversity is seen to be the zone
between the two lines.)

Species level compilations of fossil diversity present a
host of procedural problems, the most serious of which concern
sampling (e.g., Signor and Lipps 1982, and references cited
therein). Therefore, although species are biologically the
taxa of choice for compilations of diversity, families have
often been chosen to minimize sampling problems (Valentine

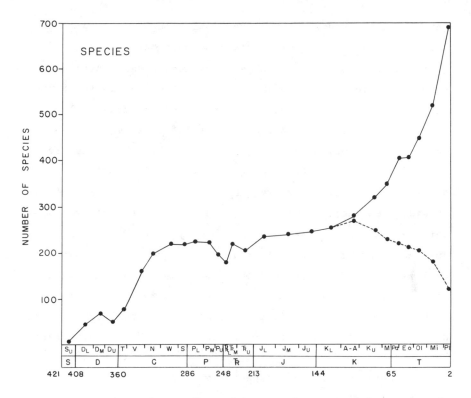

FIGURE 1. Number of vascular plant species recorded per epoch
through Phanaerozoic time (redrawn from Niklas et al. 1983).
The solid line tracks total tracheophyte diversity, while the
dotted line indicates species numbers for non-angiosperm
vascular plants in the Cretaceous and Tertiary. Angiosperm
species richness, then, is the difference between the two
lines. The time scale used in this and all other figures is
that of Harland et al. 1982. The Carboniferous is divided
into the Tournaisian (T), Visean (V), Namurian (N), Westphalian
(W), and Stephanian (S), while the Cretaceous is split into the
Berriasian-Barremian (K_L), Aptian-Albian (A-A), Cenomanian-
Campanian (K_U), and Maastrichtian (M).

1974, Raup and Sepkoski 1982). The use of higher taxa, in

turn, introduces at least two further problems of interpreta-

tion. The less serious one concerns the equivalency of fami-

lies or orders compared across a broad spectrum of organisms.

Without some objective means of defining the level of phylo-

genetic relatedness to be included in a family, it is

impossible to ensure equivalence among groups labelled as families. Perhaps immunological distance or other measures of
macromolecular sequence divergence will eventually provide
rigorous criteria for the definition of families in the living
biota, but even if this occurs, extinct higher taxa will continue to be based on authors' concepts of relative relatedness.
On the other hand, extant and extinct families both represent
groupings of species based on similarities in structure. Thus,
patterns of family diversity can be taken as reflections of
general architectural diversity, and it is reasonable to
believe that this correlates in a highly positive way with
species diversity. For this reason, the question of taxonomic
equivalence need not prevent one from drawing valid qualitative
conclusions from diversity data based on higher taxa. The
second problem is potentially more serious, especially for studies of extinction. Daniel Simberloff (quoted in Lewin, 1983)
has stated that "a family is a mysterious unit to an ecologist". This criticism is especially trenchant when applied to
ecologically diversified groups such as many mammal or angiosperm families; however, it is less worrisome when the subjects
of discussion are Paleozoic and Mesozoic fossil plants. Higher
taxa in these groups as based on commonalities in sporophyte
architecture and reproductive system that suggest a measure of
ecological unity. Sedimentary biases in plant preservation
also impose a degree of ecological uniformity on the paleobotanical record as a whole (Knoll et al. 1979).

     Temporal patterns of diversity for vascular plant families
are illustrated in figure 2. At this taxonomic level, the geological record of plants can be regarded as reasonably well
known. Among non-angiosperm plants, it is likely that a few
new families will be recognized from time to time, but it is
unlikely that the pattern presented in figure 2 will change in
any major aspect. Higher level classification of angiosperms

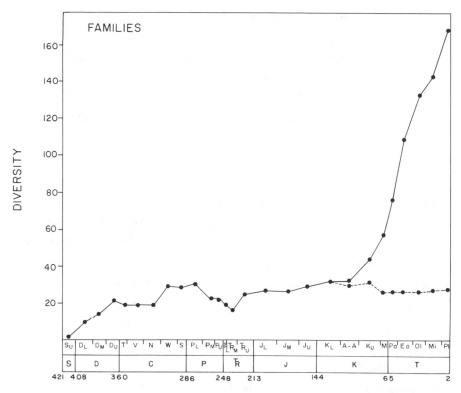

FIGURE 2. Vascular plant diversity per epoch at the family level. Explanation as in figure 1. Various sources were used to compile relevant data; Muller (1981) was the chief source for angiosperm data. The Cretaceous diversification of the angiosperms is underestimated because no extinct angiosperm families have been named.

presents an interesting problem because extinct flowering plant families and orders have not been named by paleobotanists. For this reason, the diversity of Cretaceous angiosperms in figure 2 is underestimated; as the practice of recognizing archaic angiosperm families becomes more widespread, it may be expected that the initial slope of the flowering plant diversification curve will become even steeper than it is in the figure.

Figure 2 shows many of the same features as figure 1, with the following differences. The differences in plant diversity between the Devonian and Carboniferous periods are understated

in the family diagram, a consequence of the fact that late
Paleozoic families had many more differentiable species than
those of the Devonian Period. In figure 2, pre-angiosperm familial diversity reaches its zenith during the early Permian and
then declines until the middle Triassic, following which there
is a recovery in family richness. Most significant, the effect
of the flowering plant radiation is far more pronounced in figure 2. Given that, on the average, a present day angiosperm
family contains about twice as many species as a family of
non-angiosperms, this figure suggests that the present world
flora contains approximately an order of magnitude greater
number of species than were in existence just before the advent
of angiospermy. My feeling is that this relative figure is
about right. Figure 3 presents ordinal diversity figures, cor-
roborating the trends seen in the family curve.

     Of particular interest in the present context are the com-
ings and goings of individual taxa. Again, species constitute
the taxonomic group of greatest biological interest; however,
the longevity of plant species is generally shorter than the
intervals of geological time that can confidently be used in
diversity compilations. Thus, plots of first and last appearances closely reflect total diversity figures. This means that
one cannot approach the question of background extinctions from
this perspective, although it may be possible to do so using
spores and pollen, whose stratigraphic ranges are often more
precisely known.

     Figure 4 shows plots of first and last appearances of fam-
ilies per million years for Phanerozoic epochs. It is clear
that extinctions are not distributed evenly in time, but rather
cluster to form several peaks of varying height. Extinction
maxima occur in the Late Devonian-Tournaisian and, broadly,
during the Permian and Early Triassic. A smaller but significant peak occurs in the Late Cretaceous. A similar plot for

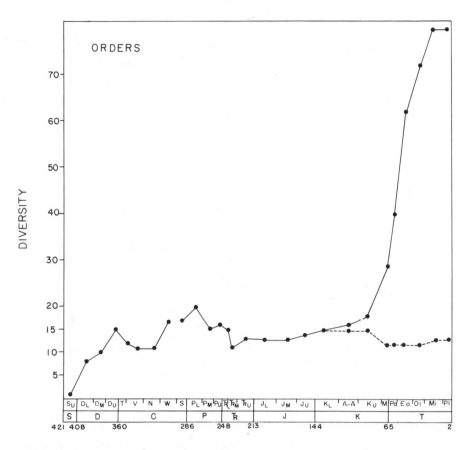

FIGURE 3. Vascular plant diversity per epoch at the ordinal
level. Explanation as in figure 1. Various sources were used
to compile relevant data; Muller (1981) was the chief source
for angiosperm data. The Cretaceous diversification of the
angiosperms is underestimated because no extinct angiosperm
orders have been described.

orders is presented in figure 5. It differs principally in the
sharpness of the Early Triassic peak.

As Raup (1978, 1983) has pointed out, the extinction of a
family is not necessarily a biological event of special significance. Family extinction occurs, by definition, when the
last species belonging to a family disappears, and this may
simply constitute the final event in the diminution of species

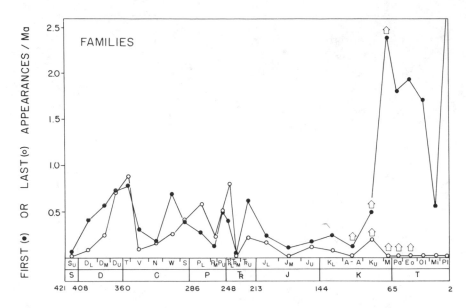

FIGURE 4. Plot of first and last appearances of vascular plant
families per million years through Phanerozoic time; time scale
as in figure 1. Arrows indicate that as more and more extinct
early angiosperm taxa are recognized, both first and last
appearances will increase for the epochs noted.

number through a long time interval. Whether or not the demise
of family is considered interesting must be determined on the
basis of field evidence documenting the importance of the family in floras up to the time of extinction. Such an approach
indicates that indeed many of the higher taxa extinctions used
to compile figures 4 and 5 do involve the relatively rapid
extirpation of groups that were important members of terrestrial communities for significant geological time periods.

     Interestingly, periods marked by relatively high levels of
family and order extinctions among vascular plants correspond
in general to times of major extinction in the marine invertebrate realm: the Late Devonian Permo-Triassic, and Late Cretaceous (Raup and Sepkoski 1982). How well the periods of
biotic change correspond and whether the causes for extinction

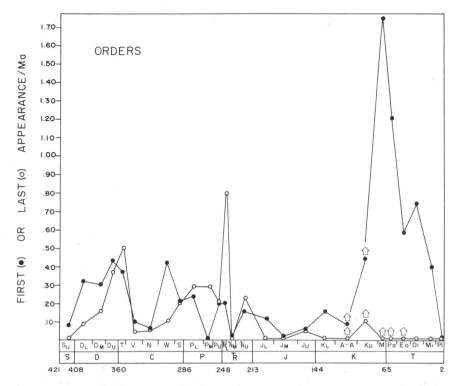

FIGURE 5. Plot of first and last appearances of vascular plant orders per million years through Phanerozoic time; time scale as in figure 1. Arrows indicate that as more and more extinct early angiosperm taxa are recognized, both first and last appearances will increase for the epochs noted.

events are similar requires a closer look at individual time periods.

DEVONIAN EXTINCTIONS: A CASE FOR COMPETITION

The early diversification of vascular plants is plotted in figure 6. Taxonomic richness is presented at the generic level because genera are thought to be relatively well known for this time interval (Banks 1980a, Chaloner and Sheerin 1979). Macrofossil (sporophyte) genera exhibit a diversity pattern similar to that observed for Cambrian marine invertebrates (Sepkoski

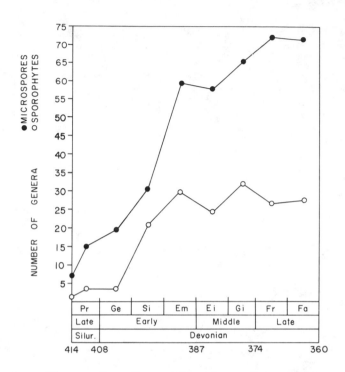

FIGURE 6. The early diversification of vascular plants, plotted as total number of genera per stage for macrofossils, or sporophytes (open circles), and microspores (filled circles). Stage names are as follows: Pridolian (Pr), uppermost Silurian; Gedinnian (Ge), Siegenian (Si), and Emsian (Em), Lower Devonian; Eifelian (Ei) and Givetian (Gi), Middle Devonian; Frasnian (Fr) and Famennian (Fa), Upper Devonian. Data from Knoll et al. (1984).

1979, Knoll et al. 1984). After an initial burst of diversity increase, generic richness plateaus in the Middle and Late Devonian; species level compilations suggest that diversity at that taxonomic level may even drop in the Late Devonian (figure 1; Niklas et al. 1983). Microfossil genera exhibit a generally similar, but not identical pattern of diversification (Knoll et al. 1984).

What is not evident in this figure is the sharp Late Devonian diversity drop that is clearly seen in plots of marine invertebrate diversity (Raup and Sepkoski 1982). In addition

to long term diversity declines associated with changes in
biogeographic conditions that commenced in the Givetian, marine
invertebrates apparently suffered catastrophic mass extinctions
at the Frasnian/Famennian boundary. McLaren (1983) has chroni-
cled the massive and rapid deterioration of shallow marine
benthic communities that occurred at this boundary. He notes
that within any given stratigraphic section the changes are
always abrupt; there is never any transitional fauna. The synchroneity and duration of the event can be bracketed to within
a single conodont zone, thought to be approximately 500,000
years long. On the basis of these data, McLaren (1983) has
suggested that an asteroid impact, similar to that documented
at the end of the Cretaceous Period, was the most likely agent
of catastrophic extinction. At present, there is nothing in
the plant fossil record to suggest comparable levels of extinction at the same stratigraphic horizon. Indeed, a single
palynological zone transgresses the Frasnian/Famennian boundary
in Europe and North America (Banks 1980a). The question of
whether a bolide impact can decimate animal life without causing major extinctions in the contemporary terrestrial flora is
deferred until discussion of the Cretaceous/Tertiary boundary,
but my prejudices on the issue should be clear from my opening
arguments.

    Total diversity compilations such as those depicted in
figure 6 do not provide information on taxonomic turnover or
floral changes within Devonian tracheophytes. In fact, the
Devonian Period witnessed several major changes in the nature
of terrestrial communities. McLaren (1983) has lamented the
difficulty of quantifying the biotic changes associated with
massive changes in marine invertebrate faunas, correctly pointing out that what one often wants to obtain is some idea of the
ecological importance (he suggests biomass) of taxa prior to
and following an "event". The required information must come

from what I will call stratigraphic/bedding plane studies conducted in the field.

I have attempted to illustrate, qualitatively, the nature of floral changes in the Devonian and earliest Carboniferous periods (figure 7).

Although conventionally viewed as clades, the groups diagrammed in the figure represent levels of architectural

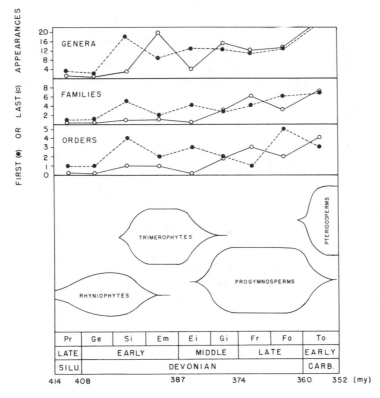

FIGURE 7. Schematic diagram illustrating the diversification, ecological dominance and subsequent extinction of successive plant groups in the Devonian and Early Carboniferous periods. Bubbles are meant to convey qualitative, not strictly quantitative, information. Also shown are first and last appearances per stage for tracheophyte genera, families, and orders.

organization and may not be monophyletic. Hence, they may
better be considered as structural grades. A large body of
literature on Devonian plant assemblages can be consulted to
document the changes cartooned in figure 7; recent papers by
Chaloner and Sheerin (1979), Banks (1980a), and Edwards (1980),
and a monograph by Gensel and Andrews (1984) are particularly
valuable.

The earliest vascular plants were simple dichotomizing
photosynthetic axes referred to the Rhyniopsida. These
appeared in the Silurian Period and diversified during the
Early Devonian. Along with the zosterophyllophytes and their
descendants the lycopods (not considered in detail here), the
rhyniophytes were the dominant vascular plants of the early
Early Devonian.

During the Siegenian, some group (or groups) of rhyniophytes gave rise to a new level of structural organization,
reflected in the Trimerophytopsida. Trimerophytes expanded
rapidly to become dominant floral elements of many environments, and concomitantly the architectural grade represented by
the rhyniophytes dwindled in importance and eventually disappeared.

The trimerophytes ultimately suffered a similar fate.
During the Middle Devonian, they gave rise to several new and
architecturally sophisticated groups of plants. Of particular
importance were the progymnosperms and several plants with an
unusual anatomical structure often grouped together as the Cladoxylopsida. These groups also expanded rapidly and came to
dominate the same environments in which the trimerophytes had
earlier thrived. Like the rhyniophytes, the trimerophytes
became insignificant ecologically and soon became extinct. The
progymnosperms diversified structurally and expanded to become
the dominant elements of Late Devonian lowland floodplain

forests, but they, too, ultimately suffered a rapid demise with
the radiation of pteridospermous gymnosperms.

The general pattern for early floodplain communities,
then, is one of sequential replacement of one dominant group by
another. It seems clear that the extinction of each group followed the initial radiation and rise to ecological prominence
of the succeeding group, and this, in turn, suggests that familial and ordinal extinctions are a consequence of competitive
displacement. If a hypothesis of competition is to be sustained, it must be defensible on the basis of functional biology (Raup 1978).

Vascular anatomy provides a good focus for functional comparisons of Devonian plants because water transport is crucial
to plant function and because xylem is often well preserved in
fossils. Sherwin Carlquist (1975) has established a framework
for the functional analysis of vascular systems. Figure 8A
illustrates the cross-sectional anatomy of Rhynia gwynne-
vaughanii, a putatively typical rhyniophyte preserved in sili-
cified peat of the Rhynie Chert, Scotland. This plant, like
all rhyniophytes, consisted of slender, naked photosynthetic
axes arising from a horizontal rhizome anchored to the ground
by small rhizoids. The vascular system of R. gwynne-vaughanii
was quite limited and structurally simple; in the figure, the
entire portion of the stem occupied by xylem consists of the
small dark patch in the center of the axis. Viewed in longitu-
dinal section, the tracheids are seen to be short, thin and
thickened in an annular pattern (Kidston and Lang 1917, Banks
1980b). Functional analysis of this system indicates that the
vascular system of R. gwynne-vaughanii and other rhyniophytes
was mechanically weak and conductively inefficient.

A picture of trimerophyte anatomy is provided by petrified
axes of Psilophyton dawsonii preserved in Emsian concretions
from New Brunswick (Banks et al. 1975). Not only were

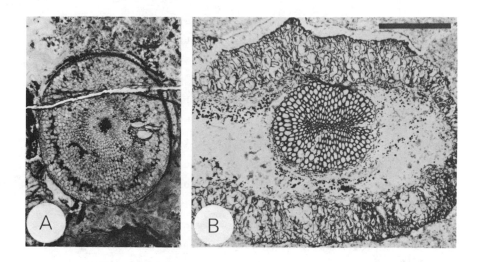

FIGURE 8. Cross sections of anatomically preserved axes of (A)
Rhynia (thought   to   be   a   typical   rhyniophyte)   and   (B)
Psilophyton, a well-known trimerophyte. (The bar in B equals 1
mm for A and 0.5 mm for B). Photographs courtesy of Harlan P.
Banks.

trimerophytes significantly larger plants than rhyniophytes,
but, as illustrated in figure 8B, a much larger proportion of
their volume was devoted to xylem (Banks 1980b). Tracheids
were larger and contained scalariform pits strengthened by a
network of trabecular struts (Hartman and Banks 1980). In
short, the trimerophyte vascular system was mechanically
stronger and a better conductor of water than that of rhyniophytes. Thus, trimerophytes were able to outcompete rhyniophytes at least in part because they were able to grow
taller (shading out the smaller plants) and photosynthesize
more actively. Thus, analysis of vascular systems provides
strong support for the hypothesis of competitive displacement.
It should be noted that xylem patterns reflect more general
changes in whole-shoot morphology that effected shading, light
gathering optima, and both vegetative reproduction and spore

production (cf. Niklas 1982). Considerations of overall shoot morphology further strengthen the competition hypothesis.

A similar set of arguments can be advanced to explain the replacement of the trimerophytes by the progymnosperms and cladoxylopsid pteridophytes. Both groups have proportionally more xylem than their antecedents, and they have primary xylem distributed in a mechanically stronger pattern. Progymnosperms evolved vascular cambia capable of producing secondary xylem, or wood, and evolved mechanically and conductively superior circular bordered pits on tracheids (Carlquist 1975, Beck 1970, see figure 9). Indeed, progymnosperms did more than that. In addition to secondary xylem, they evolved new branching patterns, true roots, laminar photosynthetic organs (leaves), and heterospory. By the Late Devonian, progymnosperms apparently dominated all but the wettest areas of lowland floodplains. The ecological success of a relatively small number of progymnosperm species and genera may explain why diversity compilations at these taxonomic levels show no late Devonian increase in spite of the opportunities for diversity increase offered by storying in plant communities.

The final floral turnover under consideration, the replacement of progymnosperms by pteridosperms, is also a case of competitive displacement, but the functional reasons for pteridosperm success have more to do with reproductive biology than vascular anatomy. Pteridosperms (descended from some line or lines within the progymnosperm complex) possessed the seed habit with all its advantages for the establishment and early growth of young sporophytes--the stage of life during which much of the competitive interaction among woody plants takes place. From the beginning of the Carboniferous onward, seed plants have dominated most non-swampy terrestrial environments.

The morphological and anatomical arguments outlined in the preceding paragraphs could be developed at much greater length.

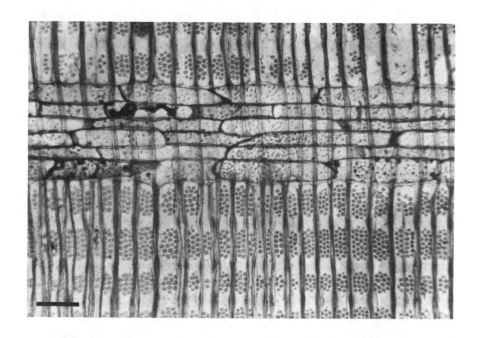

FIGURE 9. Radial section through secondary xylem of
Callixylon, a widely distributed progymnosperm stem. Note
highly organized xylem and clustered circular bordered pits.
(The bar in the lower left corner of the figure equals 100 um).
From Beck (1970), courtesy of C. B. Beck and with permission of
Cambridge University Press.

The summary point is that both stratigraphic/bedding plane analyses of fossil assemblages and functional studies of the
plants in question strongly support the hypothesis that competition was the factor of overriding importance in shaping
patterns of evolution in the early vascular plant flora. This
is striking because it stands in marked contrast to the evolutionary history of animals. Few convincing cases of competitive displacement have been documented in the metazoan fossil
record (Raup 1982, Benton 1983). Mass extinctions tend to pre-
cede faunal radiations, suggesting that, in animals, it is
often the decimation of a biota that allows radiation to occur.

Although the competition hypothesis fits observed evolutionary patterns well, it is prudent to consider other possible
influences on Devonian plant evolution. Predation, pathogens,
mutualism, climatic change, mass extinction, and chance all
constitute potentially potent forces in the shaping of the fossil record. As mentioned above, there is simply no evidence
for mass extinctions among Devonian plants; neither is there
strong evidence for climatic changes that correlate well with
observed floral patterns. Coevolution with animals probably
occurred during the Devonian Period (Kevan et al. 1975), and it
is possible that predation by ground dwelling arthropods contributed to the trend toward increasing plant stature through
time. Nonetheless, the major morphological and anatomical
changes that characterize Devonian plant evolution relate
directly to increased water transport efficiency, photosynthetic light gathering and gain (in terms of H_2O lost per unit
of CO_2 fixed), and reproductive capacity--all features that are
likely to be most important in competitive interactions among
tracheophytes.

PERMIAN AND TRIASSIC VASCULAR PLANTS: EXTINCTION ASSOCIATED
WITH CLIMATIC AND BIOGEOGRAPHIC CHANGE

The well known mass extinction of marine invertebrates at
the end of the Permian Period has been documented in considerable quantitative detail. Figure 10 shows diversity and
extinction patterns for Permian and Triassic marine invertebrate families (Sepkoski 1983, and unpublished data). Family
diversity plunged over 50% from the Middle Permian to its earliest Triassic low point, and estimates of extinction at the
species level run as high as 96% (Raup 1979).

As illustrated in figure 11, vascular plant family diversity (shown with tetrapod vertebrate patterns for comparison)
underwent a comparable percentage decline during the same

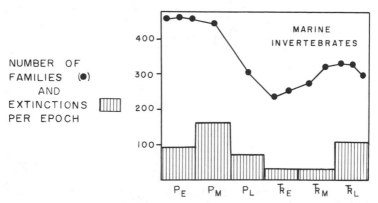

FIGURE 10. Permian and Triassic diversity and extinctions for marine invertebrate families. Data from Sepkoski (1983, and personal communication).

approximate time interval, but the diminution began earlier and continued longer--vascular plant familial diversity reached its nadir in the Middle Triassic. Once again, it is important to consider the effects of sampling. Incomplete sampling across an interval punctuated by a catastrophic mass extinction will tend to smear last appearances out over an interval whose length is correlated with the degree of sampling incompleteness (Signor and Lipps 1982). Therefore, one can ask, "If the vascular plant record were as well sampled as that of marine invertebrates, would its Permo-Triassic diversity pattern converge on that of shelly animals?" I suggest that the answer is "no", and that justification for this conclusion can be found in stratigraphic/bedding plane analyses of Permian and Triassic plant assemblages.

    As mentioned earlier, paleobotanists have long recognized the major differences between floras characteristic of the late Paleozoic (the Paleophytic floras of Gothan and Weyland 1954) and those found in Mesozoic deposits (the Mesophytic flora). Paleophytic floras of mesic equatorial regions (North America, Europe, China) are typically dominated by broad leaved

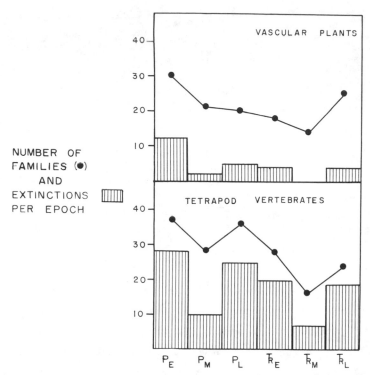

FIGURE 11. Permian and Triassic diversity and extinctions for vascular plant families, shown with figures for tetrapod vertebrates for comparison. Vertebrate data from Olson (1982).

pteridosperms with significant admixtures of cordaites, pecopterid ferns, and other pteridophytes. The contemporary vegetation in higher latitudes contained abundant glossopterid pteridosperms (Gondwana) or diverse cordaite species (Angara). Mesophytic floras, in contrast, consisted globally of conifers, cycads, cycadeoids, ginkgophytes, and distinctly different pteridophytes and pteridosperms.

Within any one geographic area, the floristic transition from Paleophytic to Mesophytic-type communities appears to have been rapid. Indeed, in incomplete sections the change often appears abrupt. However, wherever fossiliferous sequences are complete enough, demonstrably Paleophytic and Mesophytic

assemblages are separated by intermediate floras that contain
elements of both groups. In Australia, for example, typically
Mesophytic type palynofloras are often found in rocks immediately overlying those containing characteristic Permian pollen
and spores; however, in the Bowen Basin, Queensland, Foster
(1979, 1982) has described an intermediate palynoflora that
records a floral transition in latest Middle to Late Permian
times. In comparable fashion, Australian macrofloras dominated
by Glossopteris and Dicroidium species are separated in the
Sydney Basin by a distinctive intermediate assemblage characterized by "Thinnfeldia" callipteroides (Retallack 1977).

Other continents exhibit similar patterns of change (figure 12 and references cited in the figure caption). Of primary
importance is the observation that the floral transitions took
place at different times in different areas over a period of
nearly 25 million years.

The diachronous nature of the Permian floral transition
invites comparison with similarly impressive botanical changes
that have taken place during the past 25 million years. In
Australia, Neogene fossil assemblages record a dramatic expansion of sclerophyllous, arid-adapted taxa at the expense of
those found in the ecologically diverse subtropical to temperate rainforest and other woodland communities that covered
the continent at the beginning of this interval (Truswell and
Harris 1982, Sluiter and Kershaw 1982). The changing dominance
of Australian floras reflects climatic changes related, in
part, to Australia´s northward drift and the concomitant opening of the Southern Ocean.

Floras of the Indian subcontinent also underwent major
changes, particularly during the Miocene Epoch (Axelrod 1974).
The collision of India with Asia permitted families with
southeast Asian affinities such as the Dipterocarpaceae and
woody legumes to establish themselves on the subcontinent.

Climatic change related to the northward movement of India and
tectonic uplift in the early Neogene further contributed to
vegetational change.

Neogene floras of the extratropical Northern Hemisphere
are generally less diverse than Paleogene floras of the same
areas and show a much greater proportional representation by
herbaceous species (Leopold 1969, Friis 1975). Of particular
note are the spread of grasslands in the continental interiors
of North America and Eurasia and the changing nature of North

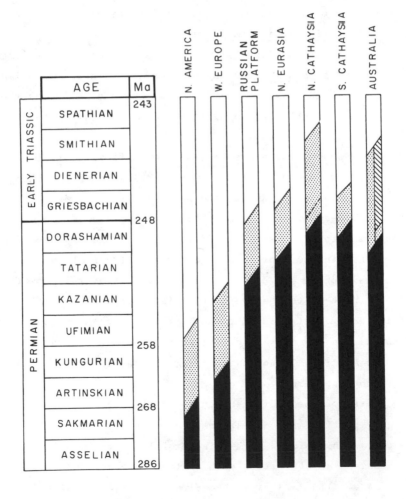

American Cordilleran and Pacific Coast floras (Wolfe 1981,
Axelrod 1958). Marked floral change also characterizes the
late Neogene of East Africa and the Mediterranean (Traverse
1982), and in Antarctica, the vascular flora was lost completely in the Oligocene or Miocene (Truswell 1982).

    In all the regions cited above, floral changes were a
consequence of tectonic activity (both horizontal and vertical)
and, in part related, climatic change (Traverse 1982). The
Permian was similarly a time of changing continental configurations, regional orogenesis, and significant changes in oceanic
circulation and world climate (Ziegler et al. 1981), and it is
reasonable to ascribe the floral changes of this period to
these factors, just as is done for Neogene alterations in the
earth´s vegetational cover.

    Conifers evolved in Late Carboniferous (Westphalian)
times, presumably in relatively dry upland habitats. The group
is not well represented in lowland floodplain assemblages of
the period. As the lowland regions of North America, Europe,

FIGURE 12.   Diagram illustrating the timing of major floral
transitions during the Permian and early Triassic periods. For
each geographic area, black indicates a typically Paleophytic
flora, white indicates a typically Mesophytic flora, and
stippled areas indicate a transitional flora. The subdivision
of the Australian transitional period indicates that while
macrofloras (left) indicate that Dicroidium species did not
expand regionally until the late Early Triassic, microfloras
record a brief transitional period followed by a distinctive
latest Permian to Early Triassic palynoflora. The dashed line
in the N. Cathaysian (China) transitional flora also indicates
differences   between   transition   times   resolvable   by
paleobotanical and palynological means. Time scale modified
from Olson (1982) and Foster (1982), with absolute dates from
Harland et al. (1983). Sources of data include Read and Mamay
(1964), North America; Frederiksen (1972), N. America and W.
Europe; Meyen (1973), W. Europe, Russian Platform, N. Eurasia;
Radczenko et al. (1973), N. Eurasia; Yao and Ouyang (1980),
Cathaysia (China); and Foster (1979, 1982) and Retallack
(1977), Australia.

and, later, China became drier in the Permian, conifers
expanded into these areas, while previously dominant pteridosperms and pteridophytes declined precipitously (Frederiksen
1972). Once again, functional analysis of vegetative remains
provides an explanation for the evident replacement pattern.
The broad leaves and vascular anatomy (large, mechanically weak
tracheids; Carlquist 1975) of late Paleozoic pteridosperms were
well suited for photosynthesis in mesic environments, but the
vascular anatomy and small, scale-like or needle-like leaves of
conifers are far better adapted for more arid environments.
Thus, conifers replaced pteridosperms, many of which became
extinct.

In terms of family losses, even more important were the
extinctions of many Paleozoic fern, lycopsid, and sphenopsid
groups. Again, the vascular anatomies of these groups suggest
a requirement for wet conditions with readily available groundwater, but equally significant, sexual reproduction in these
free-sporing plant groups requires that the sperm swim for some
distance through the environment to reach the egg. In the
absence of available surficial groundwater, completion of the
life cycle is impossible.

Actually, climate related extinctions of higher taxa began
in late Pennsylvanian times with the disappearance of arborescent lycopsids (Lepidodendron and Lepidophoios) from coal swamp
communities of North America and Europe at the Westphalian/
Stephanian boundary (Phillips et al. 1974). Phillips and colleagues have documented this event through paleoecological analyses of a stratigraphically ordered series of coal ball floras
and associate palynofloras. A complementary perspective is
provided in figure 13, assembled from data published by Braman
and Hills (1980). The figure shows first and last appearances
per million years for megaspores through the Carboniferous
Period. Megaspore producing plants (which included

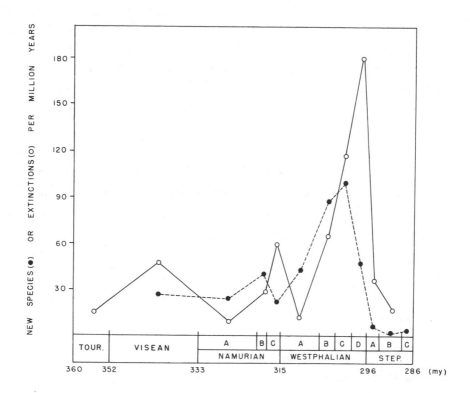

FIGURE 13. First (solid circles) and last (open circles)
appearances of megaspore species per Ma for the Carboniferous
Period, based on data compiled by Braman and Hills (1980).
Note in particular the peak in megaspore extinctions at the end
of the Westphalian. Megaspore producing plants include
calamitalean sphenopsids and noeggerathiopsids, but arborescent
lycopsids were probably the predominant megaspore producing
taxa.

noeggerathiopsids and calamites, as well as arborescent lycopsids) diversified markedly during the Westphalian, reaching a
peak in species richness in Westphalian C times. The severity
of the terminal Westphalian extinctions is clearly seen in the
figure; after this time megaspore diversity remained low until
the end of the era. DiMichele et al. (1984) have correlated
the arborescent lycopsid extinctions and other changes in

Paleozoic coal swamp floras to shifting climates, especially
moisture conditions.

In Gondwana, changing temperature regimes may have contributed to the extinction of the glossopterid pteridosperms. It
is not clear that these deciduous, cold-temperature adapted
plants had many avenues of migration open to them when climatic
conditions became warmer and more equable. Shifting geographic
patterns did provide migration routes for early corystosperm
pteridosperms (Dicroidium and relatives), which appear to have
immigrated from the Northern Hemisphere and which became dominant elements of Gondwanan Triassic floras.

To summarize, the earth´s vascular plant flora underwent a
major transition during the Permian and early Triassic periods.
The changes were diachronous, occurring over an interval of
some 25 million years, although in any individual area, the
period of transition was much shorter. Total familial diversity dropped by 50% from the Early Permian to the Middle Triassic, a consequence of conifer expansion at the expense of
Paleozoic pteridosperms and major extinctions of low latitude
pteridophyte families adapted to wet, equable climates. On the
other hand, no evidence suggests that plant biomass or species
numbers underwent a comparable Permo-Triassic decay. Most
paleobotanists who have studied the question have concluded
that the Permian/Triassic boundary was not an interval of
catastrophic change in the earth´s terrestrial flora. In many
regions, the boundary was passed rather quietly (e.g., Meyen
1973, Foster 1982).

Progressive changes in climate and continental configurations appear to have been the major forces behind Late Paleozoic botanical changes, and these same factors have often been
implicated in the late Permian mass extinctions of marine
invertebrates. Changing climate and geography may well have
been important to both vascular plants and marine animals, but

if so, the responses of the two groups were quite different.
Either the extraordinary terminal Permian extinctions of marine
invertebrates represent a threshold response to accumulated
changes, or some additional factor (e.g., regression, bolide
impact) must be considered in their explanation.

LATE CRETACEOUS EXTINCTIONS: OF ASTEROIDS AND ANGIOSPERMS
        Any study of extinction patterns must inevitably include
some discussion of the Cretaceous-Tertiary boundary; however,
before examining boundary events per se it is necessary to look
at the evolutionary context in which they took place. As figures 1 to 3 indicate, the radiation of the angiosperms constituted the most spectacular diversification in the history of
vascular plants. The three figures record only modest concomitant declines in non-angiosperm diversity, at least initially,
but these compilations drastically understate the effects of
flowering plant evolution on the preexisting flora.
        Early Cretaceous lowland floras consisted of conifers,
cycads and cycadeoids, ginkgophytes, ferns, and Mesozoic pteridosperms, the same elements that had dominated floras for the
preceding 100 million years. The taxonomic and morphological
diversification of dicotyledonous angiosperms began in the Barremian (125-119 Ma) (Hickey and Doyle 1977, Hughes 1977). Initially, flowering plants achieved ecological dominance only in
local, unstable environments, but by Cenomanian times (98-91
Ma), angiosperms had established dominance over a much broader
suite of low to middle latitude environments (Hughes 1977). As
a consequence of this expansion, populations of many gymnosperms were reduced, and by the end of the Cenomanian, the previously prominent Caytoniales, Czekanowskiales, and Bennetti-
tales (cycadeoids) had disappeared from floras below 40° paleolatitude, as had the conifers that produced the important Mesozoic pollen genera Eucommiidites and Classopollis (Hughes

1977). Cycads and ginkgos, although not disappearing completely, declined in species diversity and ecological range.
In higher latitudes, these gymnosperms survived longer, but by
the end of the period, they had disappeared from equator to
pole (Krassilov 1975, 1978).

The sequential environmental and geographic replacement
pattern of Mesozoic gymnosperms that accompanied the radiation
of flowering plants once again suggests an important role for
competition in vascular plant extinctions, and once again comparative studies of functional biology provide justification
for this view. Because of the conspicuous success of angiosperms in most modern environments, a sizable body of literature
on the adaptive advantages of angiospermy has arisen. Much of
this literature is concerned with reproductive biology (e.g.
Regal 1977, Mulcahy 1979, Tiffney 1981) and indeed such
features as double fertilization, a protective carpel, and a
relatively rapid reproductive cycle provide strong arguments
for angiosperm success. However, much of the ecological success of flowering plants may also be relatable to features of
the vegetative sporophyte (Carlquist 1975, Tiffney 1981). A
detailed review of the relevant literature is beyond the scope
of this paper. Suffice it to state that angiosperms as a group
display remarkable morphological variability, perhaps attributable to a freedom from developmental constraints made possible
by the progenetic origin of the group (Doyle 1978, Tiffney
1981). Structural (vessels, leaf and flower morphology) and
physiological (C_4 carbon fixation, CAM, a wide variety of chem-
ical defenses) innovations have allowed flowering plants to
adapt in very specific ways to both physical and biological
components of local environments.

This extraordinary radiation of angiosperms must be taken
into consideration in paleobotanical evaluations of the
Cretaceous-Tertiary boundary. Based on pollen records, Muller

(1981) determined that rates of appearance of modern angiosperm
families and orders reached their peak in the latest Cretaceous
(Maastrichtian). Inevitably, turnover and extinctions must
have accompanied early angiosperm diversification, regardless
of any effects that extrinsic perturbations may have had.

Climate, too, must be considered in the evaluations of
Cretaceous and early Tertiary fossil assemblages. Isotopic
evidence indicates that climate fluctuated throughout the
interval in question (Savin 1977), and it is clear from paleobotanical studies that vegetation responded to these changes on
a local and regional scale (e.g. Smiley 1972).

Having stated all this, what can one say about the boundary itself? Leo Hickey (1981) has scrutinized paleobotanical
changes across the boundary, carefully examining the records of
thirty-three localities from various areas of the globe that
contain both Maastrichtian (latest Cretaceous) and Early Paleocene plant fossils. Severity of extinction in each area was
gauged by determining the percentage of Maastrichtian species
that are not found in overlying Paleocene rocks (figure 14).
Hickey concluded that extinction was severe in high northern
latitudes, particularly in the so-called Aquilapollenites
biogeographic province of western North America, eastern
Siberia and boreal regions, but that levels of extinction in
other areas were moderate at best.

As Hickey (1981) explicitly recognized, his figures
overestimate the severity of boundary extinctions because
species that disappeared at any point during the Maastrichtian
are treated as boundary casualties. It is not at all clear
that all or even most extinctions occurred catastrophically in
the last moment of the Cretaceous Period. Jarsen (in Russell
and Rice 1982), in fact, has stated that boundary extinctions
in the Aquilapollenites province of western North America were

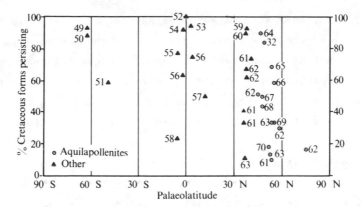

FIGURE 14. Vascular plant extinction across the Cretaceous-Tertiary boundary plotted as a function of paleolatitude. Localities from the Aquilapollenites biogeographic province are distinguished from other localities. From Hickey (1981), reprinted by permission from Nature 292:529-531; copyright 1981 MacMillan Journals Limited.

much less severe than the 70-80% maximum figures given by Hickey.

The conclusion that extinction severity increases to the north also requires examination. This may be true, but it is difficult to justify on the basis of published figures; an alternative conclusion is that extinction levels were variable in the 30 to 60° N paleolatitudinal belt and that we do not have enough data on other areas for meaningful comparison.

Reverse rarefaction techniques (Raup 1979) provide an alternative means of estimating extinction severity. Among angiosperms, family losses at the boundary must have been minimal. A 5 to 10% loss is a generous estimate; the true extinction value may well have been lower. As shown in figure 15, this level of family extinctions would be expected to result in generic losses of up to 10 or 20%; permissible levels of species extinction run as high as 35% for a 5% reduction in families and 60% for a 10% family loss. As noted, these figures are maximum permissible levels of extinction for

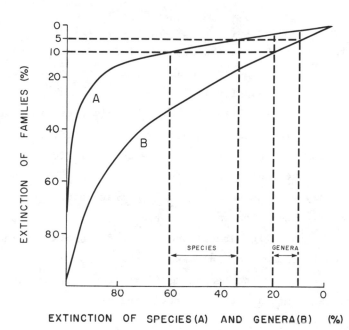

FIGURE 15. Rarefaction curve based on taxon size frequencies for 9273 species of living non-angiosperm tracheophytes. As in Raup (1979), the axes are labelled in a manner that facilitates determination of extinction intensities. Assuming that extinctions are random with respect to higher taxa, the taxonomic rarefaction curve for species within families (A) can be used to estimate levels of species extinction corresponding to a 5 to 10% loss of families at the Cretaceous/Tertiary boundary. Curve B allows similar extinction estimates to be made for genera. As noted in the text, these values represent maximum estimates of species and generic extinction; actual percent losses may well have been smaller.

angiosperms. That is, they place a ceiling on extinction estimates, but may well overestimate actual losses by a sizable amount. For example, if extinctions among angiosperm families actually totalled 3% (5 extinctions among a flora of 150 families), then estimated species and genera would be approximately 17% and 5%, respectively. These data suggest that global losses of angiosperm species at or near the Cretaceous/Tertiary

boundary were moderate. (The taxonomic distributions used to
generate figure 15 were the distributions of species and genera
within families of modern non-angiosperm tracheophytes; see
Raup, 1979 for discussion.)

In general, I believe the paleobotanical record supports
Hickey's (1981) conclusion that the major determinants of
floral change in the late Cretaceous and early Tertiary were
climate and the radiation of flowering plants. The long term
evolutionary effects of Cretaceous-Tertiary boundary events
seem to have been minor and, for the most part, indirect--for
example, Dilcher (in Russell and Rice 1982) has suggested that
a previously documented increase in the abundance of wind pol-
linated species at the beginning of the Tertiary may reflect
boundary extinctions of pollinating insects.

Does this mean that plants didn't "notice" the catastrophe
at the end of the Cretaceous or, to extrapolate further, that
nothing untoward happened at the Cretaceous-Tertiary boundary?
The latter appears increasingly unlikely. The geochemical evidence for an asteroid impact at the boundary has become very
strong (W. Alvarez et al. 1982, L. W. Alvarez 1983) and evidence for a massive and rapid disruption of marine plankton
communities is persuasive. There is even some evidence that
the impact did affect terrestrial vegetation in ecological time
if not in evolutionarily significant ways.

In the Raton Basin of northeastern New Mexico, Orth et al.
(1981) have sampled boundary beds on a centimeter by centimeter
scale. A sharp iridium anomaly in this sequence coincides with
an equally sharp perturbation in palynofloral assemblages (figure 16). Samples immediately above the anomaly contain little
woody angiosperm pollen, but abundant fern spores. Over a
short stratigraphic interval, estimated to represent 10^2 - 10^3
years, angiosperm pollen counts recover. Returning to my
introductory homily on mass mortality and mass extinctions, I

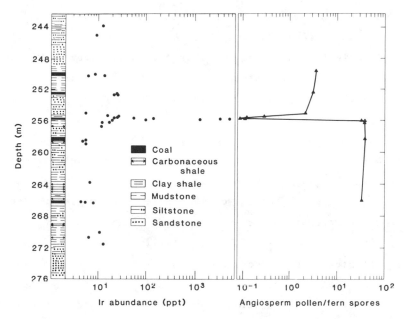

FIGURE 16. Iridium abundance and ratios of angiosperm pollen to fern spores across the Cretaceous-Tertiary boundary in the Raton Basin, New Mexico. From Orth et al. (1981), reproduced with the permission of the authors and publisher. Copyright 1981 by AAAS.

suggest that if one were to chop down all the above-ground biomass of a forest and then observe changing rains of pollen and spores over the next fifty to several hundred years, one would see a pattern very similar to that recorded at the Cretaceous-Tertiary boundary.

The Raton Basin sequence is not an isolated example of this palynological phenomenon. The same pattern has recently been found over 1000 km to the north (Orth, personal communication) and it may turn out to be a widespread feature of Cretaceous-Tertiary boundary sequences.

These limited paleobotanical data are consistent with the hypothesis that an asteroid collided with the earth to end the Cretaceous Period. Much as occurred during the Tunguska event

of 1908, but on a vastly larger scale, above ground plant cover
may have been devastated by the impact. However, because of
the biological capacity of vascular plants to endure environmental stress and regenerate from seeds and below-ground
vegetative tissues, relatively few species perished as a direct
consequence of this catastrophe.

We still have much to learn about patterns of floral
change in latest Cretaceous and early Tertiary times, especially in the tropics and high southerly paleolatitudes. However, the potential rewards of such research are great. Each
of the many scenarios for environmental crisis following
asteroid impact carries with it an implicit set of predictions
for biological consequences. Given present knowledge of vascular plant ecological tolerances and variations in such features
as dormancy and regeneration capacities, increased knowledge of
the taxonomic, ecological, and geographic patterns of botanical
change across the boundary may be extremely useful for con-
straining scenarios for the extinction of dinosaurs, calcareous
nannoplankton, and other groups.

CONCLUSION

Mass extinctions punctuate the evolutionary record of
animals, both in the marine realm (Sepkoski 1982) and on land
(Bakker 1977, Benton 1983). While the existence of mass
extinctions has been known for many years, their frequency in
geological time and, more importantly, their cardinal importance in determining large scale patterns of evolution is only
beginning to be appreciated. During episodes of mass extinction, community structures are disrupted and large percentages
of constituent species disappear. The causes of such events
are largely extrinsic to the biota, and survival may be random
or, if determinate, be related to biological tolerances that
are of little import under the ecological conditions

encountered by most organisms at most times. If this is true,
then competition, that staunchly Darwinian agency of extinction, may play a limited role in the generation of the major
patterns seen in the fossil record (Benton 1983). Predation
has been implicated in the generation of some important patterns, particularly the Mesozoic and Cenozoic radiations of
siphonate bivalves and coralline red algae, and the attendant
extinctions of non-siphonate clams and solenoporoid rhodophytes
(Stanley et al. 1983), but its importance, too, may be significantly modified by the occurrence of mass extinctions. Mass
extinctions, themselves, may be among the major generators of
large scale pattern in the paleozoological record, removing
ecologically important taxa and permitting other groups to
radiate and fill in vacated niche space (Raup 1982, McLaren
1983, Benton 1983).

As I have tried to demonstrate, vascular plants exhibit a
fundamentally different pattern of extinction and large scale
evolutionary change. There is no evidence for globally synchronous mass extinctions in the fossil record of land plants.
Indeed, it is discomfiting to realize that the twentieth century destruction of tropical rain forests (Lovejoy et al.
present volume) may result in the first true mass extinction of
vascular plant species in earth history.

Like marine invertebrates, fossil land plants document
occasional brief periods of major community reorganization.
However, in tracheophytes the causes of such events can be
demonstrably intrinsic to the biota. Extinctions of higher
taxa and restructuring of community patterns accompany the
radiation of new groups. Plant communities appear to be more
susceptible to invasion by newly evolved taxa than are those of
animals, particularly benthic marine invertebrates. Competition is affirmed as a major determinant of tracheophyte evolutionary patterns. As discussed at the beginning of this paper,

the primacy of competition over mass extinction in determining
large scale patterns of evolution in plants can be related to
fundamental attributes of vascular plant biology. (This should
not be misinterpreted as a denial of the importance of factors
other than competition in the generation of plant community
structure in an ecological time frame.)

Thus, it appears that different forces have shaped the
fossil records of vascular plants and animals. Both groups
show responses to global changes in climate; in plants, significant Permian and Triassic extinctions of pteridosperms and
pteridophyte families can be related to high latitude warming
and increasing aridity in equatorial continental environments.
Like animals, some tracheophyte extinctions, particularly at
the species level, may be non-selective and essentially random
(e.g. Raup 1981). But large scale patterns of vascular plant
evolution are definitely selective and determinate. In vascular plants, competition may actually have played the evolutionary role that biologists traditionally assumed it should.

ACKNOWLEDGMENTS
I thank H. P. Banks, C. B. Beck, L. J. Hickey, and C. J.
Orth for permission to reproduce previously published figures,
and J. J. Sepkoski, Jr., for supplying current data on the
diversity of fossil marine invertebrates. D. M. Raup kindly
performed the rarefaction calculations used to construct figure
15. I also thank a number of colleagues, especially P. Crane,
C. Foster, K. Niklas, and B. H. Tiffney for helpful discussions
and criticisms of the manuscript. E. Burkhardt skillfully
prepared the figures.

LITERATURE CITED

ALVAREZ, L. W. 1983. Experimental evidence that an asteroid
    impact led to the extinction of many species 65 million
    years ago. Proceedings of the National Academy of Sci-
    ences, USA 80:627-642.
ALVAREZ, W., L. W. ALVAREZ, F. ASARO and H. V. MICHEL. 1982.
    Current status of the impact theory for the terminal Cre-
    taceous extinction. Geological Society of America Special
    Paper 190:305-315.
AXELROD, D. I. 1958. Evolution of the Madro-Tertiary
    geoflora. Botanical Review 24:433-509.
AXELROD, D. I. 1974. Plate tectonics in relation to the his-
    tory of angiosperm vegetation in India. Birbal Sahni
    Institute of Palaeobotany Special Publication 1:5-18.
BAKKER, R. T. 1977. Tetrapod mass extinctions - a model of
    the regulation of speciation rates and immigration by
    cycles of topographic diversity. Pp. 439-468. In: Hallam,
    A., ed., Patterns of Evolution, as Illustrated by the Fos-
    sil Record. Amsterdam: Elsevier.
BANKS, H. P. 1980a. Floral assemblages in the Siluro-
    Devonian. Pp. 1-24. In: Dilcher, D. L. and T. N. Taylor,
    eds., Biostratigraphy of Fossil Plants. Stroudsburg,
    Pennsylvania: Dowden, Hutchinson, and Ross.
BANKS, H. P. 1980b. The role of Psilophyton in the evolution
    of vascular plants. Review of Palaeobotany and Palynology
    29: 165-176.
BANKS, H. P., S. LECLERCQ and F. M. HUEBER. 1975. Anatomy and
    morphology of Psilophyton dawsonii, sp. n. from the late
    Lower Devonian of Quebec (Gaspé) and Ontario, Canada.
    Palaeontographica Americana 8:75-127.
BECK, C. B. 1970. The appearance of gymnospermous structure.
    Biological Reviews 45:379-400.
BENTON, M. J. 1983. Large-scale replacements in the history
    of life. Nature 302:16-17.
BORMANN, F. H. and G. E. LIKENS. 1979. Pattern and Process in
    a Forested Ecosystem. New York: Springer-Verlag.
BRAMAN, D. R. and L. V. HILLS. 1980. The stratigraphic and
    geographic distribution of Carboniferous megaspores.
    Palynology 4:23-41.
CARLQUIST, S. 1975. Ecological Strategies of Xylem Evolution.
    Berkeley: University of California Press.
CHALONER, W. G. and A. SHEERIN. 1979. Devonian macrofloras.
    Special Papers in Palaeontology 23:145-161.
DIMICHELE, W. A., T. L. PHILLIPS and R. A. PEPPERS. 1984. The
    influence of climate and depositional environment on the
    distribution and evolution of Pennsylvanian coal swamp
    plants. In press. In: Tiffney, B. H., ed., Influences of
    Physical Environments on Vascular Plant Evolution. New
    Haven: Yale University Press.

DOYLE, J. A. 1978. Origin of angiosperms. Annual Review of
    Ecology and Systematics 9:365-392.
EDWARDS, D. 1980. Early land flora. Pp. 55-85. In: Panchen,
    A. L., ed., The Terrestrial Environment and the Origin of
    Land Vertebrates. Systematics Association Special Volume
    16. London: Academic Press.
FLESSA, K. and J. IMBRIE. 1973. Evolutionary pulsations: evi-
    dence from Phanerozoic diversity patterns. Pp. 247-285.
    In: Tarling, D. H. and S. K. Runcorn, eds., Implications
    of Continental Drift to the Earth Sciences. London:
    Academic Press.
FOSTER, C. B. 1979. Permian plant microfossils of the Blair
    Athol Coal Measures, Baralaba Coal Measures, and Basal
    Rewan Formation of Queensland. Publications, Geological
    Survey and Queensland. 372 (Palaeontological Paper 45).
FOSTER, C. B. 1982. Spore-pollen assemblages of the Bowen
    Basin, Queensland (Australia); their relationship to the
    Permian/Triassic boundary. Review of Palaeobotany and
    Palynology. 36:165-183.
FREDERIKSEN, N. O. 1972. The rise of the Mesophytic flora.
    Geoscience and Man 4: 17-28.
FRENZEL, B. 1973. Climate Fluctuations of the Ice Age. Cleve-
    land: Case Western Reserve Press.
FRIIS, E. M. 1975. Climatic implications of microcarpological
    analyses of the Miocene Fosterholt Flora, Denmark. Bul-
    letin of the Geological Society of Denmark 24:179-191.
GENSEL, P. G. and H. N. ANDREWS. 1984. Devonian Paleobotany.
    New York: Praeger.
GOLDBERG, D. E. and P. A. WERNER. 1983. Equivalence of com-
    petitors in plant communities: a null hypothesis and a
    field experimental approach. American Journal of Botany
    70:1098-1104.
GOTHAN, W. and H. WEYLAND. 1954. Lehrbuch der Palaobotanik.
    Berlin: Akademie-Verlag.
HARLAND, W. B., A. V. COX, P. G. LLEWELLYN, C. A. G. PICKTON,
    A. G. SMITH and R. WALTERS. 1982. A Geologic Time Scale.
    Cambridge: Cambridge University Press.
HARPER, J. L. 1969. The role of predation in vegetational
    diversity. Brookhaven Symposia in Biology 22:48-62.
HARRIS, G. A. 1967. Some competitive relationships between
    Agrophyron spicatum and Bromus tectorum. Ecological Mono-
    graphs 37:89-111.
HARTMAN, C. M. and H. P. BANKS. 1980. Pitting in Psilophyton
    dawsonii, an early Devonian trimerophyte. American Journal
    of Botany 67:400-412.
HICKEY, L. J. 1981. Land plant evidence compatible with gra-
    dual, not catastrophic, change at the end of the Creta-
    ceous. Nature 292:529-531.

HICKEY, L. J. and J. A. DOYLE. 1977. Early Cretaceous fossil
    evidence for angiosperm evolution. Botanical Review 43:3-
    104.
HUGHES, N. F. 1977. Palaeo-succession of earliest angiosperm
    evolution. Botanical Review 43:105-127.
HUMBOLDT, A. von. 1806. Ideen zu einer Physiognomik der
    Gewachse. Tubigen.
KEVAN, P. G., W. G. CHALONER and D. B. O. SAVILE. 1975.
    Interrelationships of early terrestrial arthropods and
    plants. Palaeontology 18:391-417.
KIDSTON, R. and W. H. LANG. 1917. On Old Red Sandstone plants
    showing structure from the Rhynie Chert bed, Aber-
    deenshire. Part 1. Rhynia gwynne-vaughanii. Transactions
    Royal Society of Edinburgh 52:643-680.
KNOLL, A. H., K. J. NIKLAS, P. G. GENSEL and B. H. TIFFNEY.
    1984. Character diversification and patterns of evolution
    in early vascular plants. Paleobiology, in press.
KNOLL, A. H., K. J. NIKLAS and B. H. TIFFNEY. 1979. Phanero-
    zoic land-plant diversity in North America. Science
    206:1400-1402.
KNOLL, A. H. and G. W. ROTHWELL. 1981. Paleobotany: Perspec-
    tives in 1980. Paleobiology 7:7-35.
KRASSILOV, V. A. 1975. Climatic changes in eastern Asia as
    indicated by fossil floras. II. Late Cretaceous and
    Danian. Palaeogeography, Palaeoclimatology, Palaeoecology
    17:157-172.
KRASSILOV, V. A. 1978. Late Cretaceous gymnosperms and the
    terminal Cretaceous event. Palaeontology 21:893-905.
LEOPOLD, E. B. 1969. Late Cenozoic palynology. Pp. 377-438.
    In: Tschudy, R. H. and R. A. Scott, eds., Aspects of
    Palynology. New York: Wiley.
LEWIN, R. 1983. Extinctions and the history of life. Science
    221:935-937.
McLAREN, D. J. 1983. Bolides and biostratigraphy. Bulletin of
    the Geological Society of America 94:313-324.
MEYEN, S. V. 1973. The Permian-Triassic boundary and its
    relation to the Paleophyte-Mesophyte floral boundary. Pp.
    662-668. In: Logan, A. and L. V. Hills, eds., The Permian
    and Triassic Systems and their Mutual Boundary. Calgary:
    Canadian Society of Petroleum Geologists.
MULCAHY, D. L. 1979. The rise of the angiosperms: a geneco-
    logical factor. Science 206:20-23.
MULLER, J. 1981. Fossil pollen records of extant angiosperms.
    Botanical Review 47(1):1-142.
NEWELL, N. 1967. Revolutions in the history of life. Geologi-
    cal Society of America Special Paper 89:63-91.
NIKLAS, K. J. 1982. Computer simulations of early land plant
    branching morphologies: canalization of patterns during
    evolution? Paleobiology 8:196-210.

NIKLAS, K. J., B. H. TIFFNEY and A. H. KNOLL. 1983. Patterns
    in vascular land plant diversification: a statistical
    analysis at the species level. Nature 303:614-616.
OLSON, E. C. 1982. Extinctions of Permian and Triassic nonma-
    rine vertebrates. Geological Society of America Special
    Paper 190:501-511.
ORTH, C. J., J. S. GILMORE, J. D. KNIGHT, C. L. PILLMORE, R. H.
    TSCHUDY and J. E. FASSETT. 1981. An iridium abundance
    anomaly at the Cretaceous-Tertiary boundary in northern
    New Mexico. Science 214:1341-1343.
PALMER, A. R. 1965. Biomere - a new kind of biostratigraphic
    unit. Journal of Paleontology 39:149-152.
PALMER, A. R. 1982. Biomere boundaries: a possible test for
    extraterrestrial perturbation of the biosphere. Geological
    Society of America Specal Paper 190:469-476.
PHILLIPS, T. L., R. A. PEPPERS, M. J. AVCIN and P. F. LAUGHNAN.
    1974. Fossil plants and coal: patterns of change in
    Pennsylvanian coal swamps of the Illinois Basin. Science
    184:1367-1369.
RAUP, D. M. 1978. Approaches to the extinction problem. Jour-
    nal of Paleontology 52:517-523.
RAUP, D. M. 1979. Size of the Permo-Triassic bottleneck and
    its evolutionary implications. Science 206:217-218.
RAUP, D. M. 1981. Extinction: bad genes or bad luck. Acta
    Geològica Hispánica 16:25-33.
RAUP, D. M. 1982. Macroevolutionary implications of large
    body impacts. Geological Society of America Abstracts with
    Programs 14(7):596.
RAUP, D. M. 1983. Evolutionary radiations and extinctions. In
    press. In: Holland, H. D. and A. Trendall, eds., Patterns
    of Change in Earth Evolution. Dahlem Konferenzen. Heidel-
    berg: Springer-Verlag.
RAUP, D. M. and J. J. SEPKOSKI, JR. 1982. Mass extinctions in
    the marine fossil record. Science 215:1501-1503.
RADCZENKO, G. P., A. A. LYUBER, M. G. MINIKH, I. Yu. NEUS-
    TRUEVA, E. K. OBONITSKAYA, V. G. OCHEV, A. G. PONOMARENKO,
    G. M. ROMANOVSKAYA, L. A. SAIDAKOVSKY and I. S. SPASSKAYA.
    1973. Floral and faunal changes in non-marine facies at
    the Permian-Triassic boundary, U.S.S.R. Pp. 655-661. In:
    Logan, A., and L. V. Hills, eds., The Permian and Triassic
    Systems and their Mutual boundary. Calgary: Canadian
    Society of Petroleum Geologists.
READ, C. B. and S. H. MAMAY. 1964. Upper Paleozoic floral
    zones and floral provinces in the United States. U. S.
    Geological Survey Professional Paper 454-K:1-35.
REGAL, P. J. 1977. Ecology and evolution of flowering plant
    dominance. Science 196:622-629.
REID, C. and E. M. REID. 1915. The Pliocene floras of Dutch-
    Prussian border. Med. Rijksopsporing v. Delfstoffen. no.
    6.

RETALLACK, G. J. 1977. Reconstructing Triassic vegetation of
    eastern Australasia: a new approach for the biostratigra-
    phy of Gondwanaland. Alcheringa 1:247-277.
RUSSELL, D. A. and G. RICE, eds. 1982. K-TEC II, Cretaceous-
    Tertiary Extinctions and Possible Terrestrial and Extra-
    Terrestrial Causes. Syllogeous 39. (National Museum of
    Natural Science, Ottawa, Canada).
SAVIN, S. 1977. The history of the earth's surface tempera-
    ture during the past 100 million years. Annual Review of
    Earth and Planet Science 5:319-355.
SEPKOSKI, J. J., JR. 1979. A kinetic model of Phanerozoic
    taxonomic diversity: II. Early Phanerozoic families and
    multiple equilibria. Paleobiology 5:222-251.
SEPKOSKI, J. J., JR. 1981. A factor analytic description of
    the Phanerozoic marine fossil record. Paleobiology 7:36-
    53.
SEPKOSKI, J. J., JR. 1982. Mass extinctions in the Phanero-
    zoic oceans: a review. Geological Society of America Spe-
    cial Paper 190:283-290.
SEPKOSKI, J. J., JR. 1983. A compendium of Fossil Marine Fam-
    ilies. Milwaukee: Milwaukee Public Museum.
SIGNOR, P. W. and J. H. LIPPS. 1982. Sampling bias, gradual
    extinction patterns and catastrophies in the fossil
    record. Geological Society of America Special Paper
    190:291-296.
SLUITER, I. R. and A. P. KERSHAW. 1982. The nature of Late
    Tertiary vegetation in Australia. Alcheringa 6:211-222.
SMILEY, C. J. 1972. Plant megafossil sequences, north slope
    Cretaceous. Geoscience and Man 4:91-100.
STANLEY, S. M., B. Van VALKENBURGH and R. S. STENECK. 1983.
    Coevolution and the fossil record. Pp. 328-349. In:
    Futuyma, J. and M. Slatkin, eds., Coevolution. Sunderland,
    Massachusetts: Sinauer Associates, Inc.
TIFFNEY, B. H. 1981. Diversity and major events in the evolu-
    tion of land plants. Pp. 193-320. In: Niklas, K. J., ed.,
    Paleobotany, Paleoecology, and Evolution, Volume 2. New
    York: Praeger.
TRAVERSE, A. 1982. Response of world vegetation to Neogene
    tectonic and climatic events. Alcheringa 6:197-209.
TRUSWELL, E. M. 1982. Antarctica: the vegetation of the past
    and its climatic implication. Australian Meteorological
    Magazine 30:169-173.
TRUSWELL, E. M. and W. K. HARRIS. 1982. The Cainozoic paleo-
    botanical record in arid Australia: fossil evidence for
    the origins of an arid-adapted flora. Pp. 67-76. In:
    Barker, W.R. and P. J. M. Greenslade, eds., Evolution of
    the Flora and Fauna of Arid Australia. Adelaide: Peacock.
VALENTINE, J. M. 1974. Temporal bias in extinctions among
    taxonomic categories. Journal of Paleontology 48:549-552.

WOLFE, J. A. 1981. Paleoclimatic significance of the Oligo-
    cene and Neogene floras of the northwestern United States.
    Pp. 79-102. Niklas, K., ed. Paleobotany, Paleoecology, and
    Evolution, Volume 2. New York: Praeger.
WOOD, C. E. 1972. Morphology and phytogeography: the classi-
    cal approach to the study of disjunctions. Annals of the
    Missouri Botanical Garden 59:107-124.
YAO, Z. Q. and S. OUYANG. 1980. On the Paleophyte-Mesophyte
    boundary. 9 pp. Nanjing: Nanjing Institute of Geology and
    Palaeontology, Academica Sinica.
ZIEGLER, A. M., R. K. BAMBACH, J. T. PARRISH, S. F. BARRETT, E.
    H. GIERLOWSKI, W. C. PARKER, A. RAYMOND and J. J. SEP-
    KOSKI, JR. 1981. Paleozoic geography and climatology.
    Pp. 231-266. In: Niklas, K. J., ed., Paleobotany,
    Paleoecology, and Evolution, Volume 2. New York: Praeger.

MARINE MASS EXTINCTIONS: A DOMINANT ROLE FOR TEMPERATURE

Steven M. Stanley

INTRODUCTION

One of the great, long-standing puzzles of paleontology has been what caused the great biotic crises that we call mass extinctions. My main purpose in this article is to evaluate possible causes of mass extinctions in the marine realm. I present evidence bearing on the relative roles of two environmental changes frequently cited as potential agents of marine mass extinctions: regression of shallow seas and worldwide temperature change. I conclude that reduction of living space due to regression has been of trivial importance, whereas temperature change has served as a prominent agent of mass extinctions. My focus on temperature change comes from the observation that certain striking patterns emerge as common elements when one examines major marine crises collectively.

PROXIMATE AND ULTIMATE FACTORS

Mass extinctions are potentially understandable at many different levels, which range from proximate to ultimate. We might, for example, establish a strong probability that loss of habitat and intensified competition were the proximate

(immediate) agents of a particular mass extinction of life on
continental shelves, and moving toward an ultimate explanation,
we might recognize that a global lowering of sealevel caused
these changes. The ultimate cause, however, might be considered to be whatever produced the drop in sea level - movements within the earth´s mantle, for example. In fact, someone
of a reductionist bent might reasonably argue that an ultimate
cause must lie at a deeper level, in an explanation of what
produced the mantle movements. The evidence that I will adduce
in this contribution relates to the importance of temperature
as a proximate agent of extinction. The ultimate causes of
temperature change remain to be considered, though I will offer
the suggestion that change in the solar "constant" and also
cooling due to increases in atmospheric CO_2 at times of marine
regression be given serious consideration as sources of biotic
crises.

LIMITING FACTORS AND MASS EXTINCTION
    It is a simple but important fact that, barring the intro-
duction of poisons, radiation, or other bizarre agents of
death, the proximate causes of extinction must be the environmental factors that normally limit the distribution and abundance of species. Extinction amounts to distribution and abundance diminished to zero, and this is readily accomplished by a
drastic change of one or more limiting factors. Arguing
against a role for such agents as poisons and radiation are
patterns of extinction that I will discuss below for several
biotic crises: complex temporal patterns of protracted extinction and geographic patterns in which tropical biotas suffered
most heavily.
    Limiting factors in the marine realm today include tem-
perature, salinity, living space, dissolved oxygen, food
resources, competitive interactions, and predation. In the

following paragraphs, I will briefly discuss the possible contribution to mass extinction of each of these limiting factors.

Temperature

Dramatic temperature changes have obviously occurred during the recent Plio-Pleistocene interval of repeated glacia-
tions. Hallam (1981a, p. 222) has argued that the Oligocene-
to-Recent interval of the Cenozoic Era, having been characterized by polar ice caps and steep latitudinal temperature gradients, should have been a time when temperature changes played
an abnormally important role in extinction. The premise here
is that during intervals like the Mesozoic, when gentle latitudinal temperature gradients have obtained, temperature has not
represented an important limiting factor in geographic distribution, and events of polar cooling have not been pronounced
enough to cause major extinctions.

On the contrary, I see earlier intervals characterized by
gentle temperature gradients as times when marine species have
been especially vulnerable to temperature-induced mass extinction because, over a large range of latitudes, species have
been adapted to a narrow range of annual temperatures. Furthermore, as I will describe below, the effects of polar cooling
have an impact in the tropics only to the degree that they are
propagated toward low latitudes, and during the latest glacial
maximum (10,000 years ago), equatorial seas experienced little
temperature change (CLIMAP project workers 1981). Possibly at
times of mass extinction latitudinal temperature gradients have
been unusually pronounced, as contended by Fischer and Arthur
(1977) in their seminal paper relating mass extinctions to
thermal patterns in the oceans. What I propose, however, is
that many ancient marine mass extinctions may have resulted
from global, as opposed to polar, cooling and that this cooling
affected tropical seas, from which there was no place for

species to migrate. We would predict that under these circumstances, low latitudes would have represented a death trap:
tropical biotas should have suffered greater losses than most
temperature biotas. Greater survival would be expected for
temperature biotas, both because of their eurythermy (great
temperature breadth) and because in most geographic regions
they should have been able to shift equatorward with the
climatic zone to which they were adapted. As I will document
below, this is precisely the geographic pattern that we observe
for most ancient mass extinctions.

Salinity

Salinity is not easily changed dramatically on a global
scale, and for this reason suggestions that a sudden salinity
increase (Fischer 1964) or decrease (Gartner and Keany 1978,
Thierstein and Berger 1970) has caused marine mass extinction
have received little support.

Living Space

Some of the great marine mass extinctions coincided partly
or entirely with intervals of global sealevel lowering that
caused widespread regression of shallow seas. This correspondence has for years fostered suggestions that mass extinction
and regression have in some way been causally connected
(Chamberlin 1898a, 1898b, 1909; Schuchert 1914, 1916, 1926;
Newell 1952, 1963, 1967). In recent years, this idea has been
expressed in a particular notion that can be called the
species-area hypothesis. According to this hypothesis, at
times of widespread sealevel regression, biotas of continental
shelves have become restricted to such small areas of sea floor
that crowding and loss of habitat space have led to widespread
extinction (Schopf 1974, Simberloff 1974, Hallam 1981a, p. 226,
Gould 1977, p. 138).

The alleged basis for the species-area hypothesis is the
relationship that biogeographers have documented empirically
for modern faunas between number of species within a fauna and
area occupied. This relationship can be described by a power
function relating number of species (S) in the fauna to geographic area occupied (A):   B = kA^z, where k and A are con-
stants (Preston 1962, MacArthur and Wilson 1963, 1967, Flessa
and Sepkoski 1978). This relationship has been established for
nonmarine faunas, for which most z-values lie between 0.15 and
0.45, with a mode of about 0.30. I will present evidence below
that the species-area effect is much too weak on the sea floor
to have caused more than a very small amount of excessive
extinction during the low stands of sealevel recorded in the
stratigraphic record.

Anoxic Events
        Intervals during which the oxygen minimum layer of the
ocean expanded to such shallow depths that it embraced shallow
seas have been cited as possible times of mass extinction by
oxygen deprivation. This idea is beset with many difficulties.
For one thing, such intervals during the Cretaceous Period, as
identified by reducing sediments in the deep sea and widespread
epicontinental black muds, sometimes did not coincide with
extinction events; the mid-Barremian to latest Albian interval
of widespread anoxic deposition (Jenkyns 1980), in fact,
represented what Fischer and Arthur (1977) termed a polytaxic
interval - one characterized by rich marine biotas. Fischer
and Arthur (1977) observed that it is times of contraction
rather than expansion of the oxygen minimum layer that seem to
coincide with intervals of mass extinction. Still another
problem with invoking anoxic events as major causes of mass
extinction is the implicit reliance on species-area effects,
which I will argue are of little significance; this reliance is

based on the idea that anoxic events have reduced the habitat-
able area of shallow seas drastically on a global scale (Hallam
1981a, p. 225).

Biotic Factors

To attribute mass extinction to a breakdown of the food
web is simply to shift the need for an explanation to a lower
trophic level, and while it is easy to imagine that nutrient
supplies for phytoplankton have varied in time and space, it is
difficult to envision any reduction to a level so low that
widespread global extinction of phytoplankton would result.
Predation seems never to have been suggested as an agent of
global extinction, presumably because it has seemed unlikely
that a new group of highly efficient predators could have
caused the decline of more than a small number of victim taxa
or that such a decline could have been as abrupt as a typical
mass extinction. Competition has been invoked as an agent of
marine mass extinction primarily through its alleged role when
species are crowded together during intervals of regression.
The arguments that follow, in derogating the species-area
effect, will by implication oppose the possibility of an important role for competition during episodes of sea floor reduction.

TESTS: DATA FROM THE CENOZOIC ERA

The rich store of biological and geographical information
provided by study of the Cenozoic stratigraphic record and by
study of the modern world afford us an excellent opportunity to
test the species-area hypothesis and the hypothesis that
climatic change is an important agent of mass extinction. In
order to exploit this opportunity, it is necessary to establish
certain premises and predictions.

One premise that I will adopt is that, if the species-area
hypothesis is valid, then every large, sustained global regression should cause mass extinction of shallow-water benthos. In
other words, if we are dealing with a fundamental ecological
rule for a particular kind of ecosystem, then response to the
rule should be universal.

It is also reasonable to predict that mass extinctions
caused by temperature change should be characterized by different patterns than mass extinctions caused by worldwide
regression. Whereas any effects of regression should have been
expressed throughout the world, mass extinction resulting from
temperature change should often have exhibited a complex geographic pattern. During the past 30 my, when polar regions
have been frigid, major episodes of cooling have emanated from
the poles, probably with little effect on equatorial sea-
surface temperatures and often with complex geographic patterns
even at high latitudes (CLIMAP project members 1981). During
earlier intervals of geological time, when latitudinal temperature gradients were weaker, we can predict that if there were
episodes of global, as opposed to polar, refrigeration, they
should have had much greater effects in the tropics, from which
there was no escape toward the equator; I will address this
point more fully below in discussing pre-Cenozoic mass extinctions.

We would also predict that temperature-related mass
extinctions should have had more complex temporal patterns.
Global temperatures are governed by many factors, and we might
expect that at certain times several factors have conspired in
an additive fashion to refrigerate the oceans of the world,
often by way of a series of pulses of cooling. Under such circumstances, critical thresholds for different taxa should have
been reached at different times.

The Species-Area Effect: Modern-Day Evidence

If the species-area effect is to be applied to ancient
shallow marine biotas, its potential power must be justified by
study of the occurrence of living species. Unfortunately,
those who have argued for the importance of this effect have
never in this way justified its application. Schopf et al.
(1977) calculated a z-value of 0.21 for a species-area power
function for 21 bryozoan faunas occupying sea floors less than
200 m deep, but found no significant species-area relationship
whatever for 20 comparably situated bivalve faunas. Wise and
Schopf (1981) nonetheless employed a z-value of 0.263 to
predict that sea level lowering of 200 m during the Pleistocene
should have reduced the global species diversity of shallow-
water benthos by 25%.

It is, in fact, impossible at the present time to plot
meaningful species-area curves for living marine benthos. In
the absence of complete sets of faunal data, Schopf et al.
(1977) used published diversities for single localities to
represent entire biogeographic provinces recognized by Ekman
(1953). Taxonomic work is also inconsistent and, in many tropical regions, far from complete. What we can do quite profitably is to examine the diversities of shallow-water faunas that
are restricted to continental shelves or equivalent regions
that are as small as or smaller than the shelf areas that
remained after major global regressions.

Of special importance here are volcanic islands, like
those of the tropical Pacific. A simple but powerful argument
against an important role for the areal effects of regression
in the mass extinction of higher taxa has to do with the coni-
cal shapes of such islands. These shapes cause the areas of
shallow sea floor surrounding the islands to expand, rather
than contract, when sea level falls (Stanley 1979, p. 299).
The second important observation about these islands is that

today they harbor enormous shallow-water marine faunas, which
include a large majority of all species-rich families of
benthos occupying warm, shallow seas (Stanley 1979, p. 299;
Jablonski 1982, in press).

A more specific empirical test of the potential of the
species-area effect can be conducted by considering diversity
data for key areas. As it turns out, these tell us that z-
values for marine benthos cannot possibly be high enough for
regressions to contribute in more than a trivial way to mass
extinction. It is important here to choose regions that are
small in size, geographically isolated, and taxonomically well
studied. I will consider the benthic Mollusca of two of these
regions - the Hawaiian archipelago, which is characterized by a
relatively large percentage of reefal and rocky surfaces, and
the Panamic-Pacific Province, which offers little reef habitat
area compared to the percentage of soft substrata.

The Hawaiian Islands lie far from other shallow-water
islands, so that they constitute a natural province (about 20%
of their species are endemic), and their Mollusca are well studied taxonomically (Kay 1979). The small area of shallow sea
floor (less than 200 m) provided by the Hawaiian Islands and
neighboring seamounts is illustrated in figure 1. This area,
which is certainly smaller than that left even within a single
biogeographic province by any major ancient regression,
nonetheless today supports a shelf-depth molluscan fauna of
nearly a thousand species!

The Panamic-Pacific Province harbors nearly 3000 species
of shelled mollusks (Keen 1971) on a very narrow shelf (figure
1). Many of the species are normal level-bottom forms, and the
high diversity obtains even in the absence of well-developed
coral reefs. This tropical province has remained isolated for
about 3.4 my, since the uplift of the Isthmus of Panama
(Keigwin 1978). Even during Quaternary high stands of

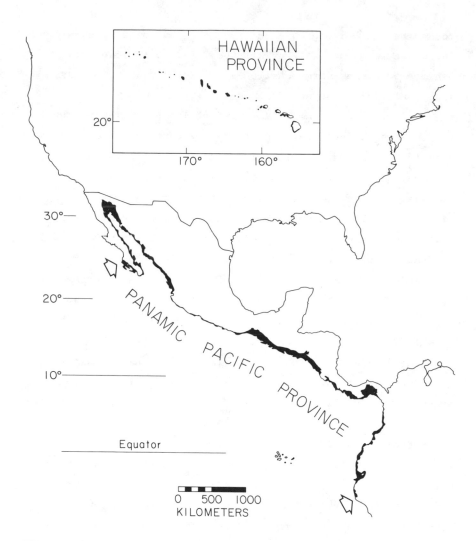

FIGURE 1. Map showing the small area occupied by two largely isolated marine biogeographic provinces of high benthic diversity. The very small tropical Hawaiian Province, superimposed on the map of North America to provide a scale for comparison, harbors nearly 1000 species living at depths less than 200 meters, and the tropical Panamic-Pacific Province, nearly 3000 such species.

sealevel, like that of today, the huge fauna here has been confined to a smaller area of shelf than has fringed continents
during major regressions of the past. The areal disparity must
have been even greater during Plio-Pleistocene glacial intervals, which dropped sea level lower than nearly all earlier
eustatic lowerings now recognized (Vail et al. 1977) and which
I will consider in the following section.

Thus, even major pre-Cenozoic regressions should have left
areas of shallow sea floor sufficiently large to support enormous biotas. These observations oppose the idea (Schopf 1979,
Wise and Schopf 1981) that regression should entirely eliminate
some biogeographic provinces by way of the species-area effect.
Only if the refugial area remaining for a provincial fauna
after a regression differed from the original habitat in some
critical variable like temperature should the regression have
decimated the fauna.

My arguments against significant area effects for regression apply whether one adopts a traditional, static approach to
area and diversity or a dynamic model that entails lag behavior
for equilibration (Carr and Kitchell 1980). My point is simply
that very small areas can support enormous faunas even if
equilibrium of one kind or another requires millions of years.

Regional Ice Age Mass Extinctions

The simultaneous episodes of cooling and regression that
the earth has experienced during the past 3 my allow us to compare the effects of these two kinds of environmental change.
We can do this by noting that, whereas regression has been a
global phenomenon during glacial episodes, refrigeration has
been restricted to certain regions. If regression has served
as an important agent of extinction for marine benthos, then we
should see its effects on a global scale. In contrast, extinction resulting from refrigeration should have been severe only

in particular areas in which cooling has occurred and from
which escape by migration has been impossible.

What pattern of mass extinction, if any, do we see with
the onset of the recent Ice Age? In contrast to the loss of
25% of all species on a global scale, as predicted by Wise and
Schopf (1981) from assumed species-area relationships, what we
find is little or no excessive extinction in some areas, but
heavy mass extinction in others. The latter represented
biogeographic traps where temperatures fell.

Among the biotically stable areas were California, the
tropical Panamic-Pacific Province, and Japan. The stability of
California and Japan is shown by Lyellian percentages for molluscan faunas of these regions. A Lyellian percentage for a
particular fauna is the percentage of species in that fauna
that survive to the present. Lyellian percentages for the
well-known Neogene faunas of California and Japan plot as
smooth bands of points that coincide for the two regions (figure 2), and this strongly suggests that the two regions experienced normal, uninterrupted rates of extinction during Pliocene
and Pleistocene time (Stanley et al. 1980). Similarly, molluscan faunas of the Panamic-Pacific Province, extending from
southern Baja California to northern Peru (figure 1), suffered
relatively little late Neogene extinction (Olsson 1961).

On the other hand, beginning about 3 my ago, or slightly
earlier, molluscan faunas fringing the Atlantic Ocean suffered
heavy extinction. The greatest losses were in the Western
Atlantic and Caribbean. The impact of this episode of excessive extinction in the Western Atlantic can be seen by comparing the Lyellian percentages of faunas in the region between
Virginia and Florida to the percentages representing California
and Japan (figure 2). Mid-Pliocene bivalve faunas of the
Western Atlantic region contain only about 20 percent living
species compared to about 70-75 percent living species in the

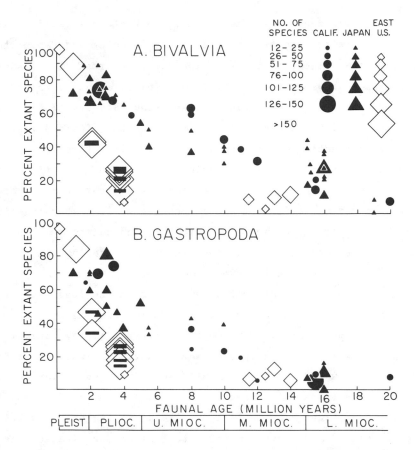

FIGURE 2. Lyellian percentages for marine bivalve faunas of
the Western Atlantic region (diamonds), contrasted with those
representing California and Japan. Data for the two Pacific
regions form a smooth, monotonic band, apparently reflecting
normal rates of extinction. Data for th Western Atlantic fall
well below this band, reflecting regional mass extinction.
(For details, see Stanley et al. 1980, and Stanley and Campbell
1981).

faunas of California and Japan. A more detailed analysis of

the data reveals that the excessive extinction in the Western

Atlantic began after about 3.5 my ago and ended before the last

Pleistocene interglacial interval; also, although continuous

stratigraphic sections are not available for study, there is

evidence from successive faunas that the Western Atlantic mass
extinction struck in two or more pulses (Stanley and Campbell
1981). A numerical analysis of the total interval of excessive
extinction shows that this crisis eliminated about 65-75 percent of the Western Atlantic bivalve fauna (Stanley 1982). The
faunas that it decimated were enormously rich (figure 3), and
the event clearly constituted a regional mass extinction.

Also suffering mass extinction at about the same time were
the large faunas of the North Sea and the Mediterranean. Here
Lyellian survivorship from mid-Pliocene time is higher than in
the Western Atlantic (about 50 percent), indicating that the
crises were less severe here than in areas bordering the
Eastern Atlantic (Stanley 1982).

Two empirical tests employing data from the fossil record
indicate that spatial effects of marine regressions during
Plio-Pleistocene glacial buildups had little, if anything, to
do with the mass extinctions of the Atlantic margins, but that
temperature was the primary agent. The first test (Stanley and
Campbell 1981) has, in effect, already been conducted in the
plotting of figure 2. In fact, figure 2 and the data for the
North Sea and Mediterranean indicate that mass extinction was a
phenomenon of the Atlantic margins, not a global event as
predicted by the species-area hypothesis; the molluscan faunas
of the narrow Pacific shelves were virtually unaffected. This
point is particularly striking for the great tropical Panamic-
Pacific Province, which as discussed above, has occupied a narrow continental shelf in isolation for about 3.4 my.

The second test entails a more detailed assessment of the
marginal Atlantic extinctions. Without knowing the distribution of temperatures and biogeographic barriers in time and
space, it is impossible to predict what geographic pattern the
regional mass extinction should have followed along the Atlantic coastline. What we can do profitably is assess the nature

of extinction within a tropical fauna, like the huge fauna of
the Pinecrest beds of central and southern Florida (figure 3).
We can recognize that such a fauna, like the modern tropical
faunas of southern Florida and the Caribbean, must have
included both purely tropical species and more eurythermal
species that ranged into temperate waters. We would then
predict that, if refrigeration caused the mass extinction, the
extant residue of this fauna should consist of species that can
tolerate cool conditions. This is precisely what we find. It
is remarkable that virtually all of the surviving Pinecrest
species range northward around the Gulf Coast to Texas or along
the Atlantic Coast to the Carolinas (Stanley, in preparation).
Thus, it is evident that a kind of thermal filter was imposed,
screening out purely tropical species. Employing a slightly
different approach, Marasti and Raffi (1980) concluded that
refrigeration was the agent of excessive late Neogene extinction in the Mediterranean; knowing something of the thermal
tolerance of Pliocene species, they observed that molluscan
taxa of tropical affinities tended preferentially to die out
with the onset of continental glaciation.

Data of the CLIMAP project members (1981), when combined
with what we know of geographic barriers to dispersal, reveal
the reason why the marginal Atlantic was the site of late Neogene mass extinction, while the marginal Pacific was not. During glacial intervals, the entire northern Atlantic gyre was
compressed, as glaciers spread southward in North America and
Europe (figure 4). In the central Caribbean, February sea surface temperatures 18,000 years ago, at the time of the last
glacial maximum, were about $4^{o}C$ lower than they are today
(CLIMAP project workers 1981). Furthermore, sea temperatures
are even cooler today than before the mass extinction, in mid-
Pliocene time, when subtropical conditions extended at least as
far north as Virginia (Stanley and Campbell 1981). It appears

FIGURE 3. The Pinecrest shell bed, at the Warren Brothers pit, Sarasota, Florida. The fauna represented here, which included more than 22 species of bivalves living sympatrically about 3.5-4 mya, was decimated by regional Plio-Pleistocene mass extinction.

that, with the onset of continental glaciation to the north
about 3 my ago, the Caribbean Sea became a trap, where temperatures repeatedly dropped markedly and from which there was little opportunity for escape. The North Atlantic also experienced severe cooling (CLIMAP project workers 1981) and the
Mediterranean became another biogeographic trap from which
southward migration was impossible, as did the North Sea, which
was a cul-de-sac terminated on the south by a land bridge
between East Anglia and France.

In contrast, although surface waters in California and
Japan have cooled somewhat during glacial maxima (CLIMAP project workers 1981), there has been no barrier in southward
migration. Tropical conditions have persisted in the Panamic-
Pacific Realm and in waters adjacent to Southeast Asia. Thus,
along the Pacific Coast of the Americas (Valentine 1961, Addicott 1966), and presumably also along the coast of Southeast
Asia, biotas have simply migrated northward and southward as
temperatures have fluctuated.

Events of the Eocene and Oligocene Epochs

What amounts to another natural experiment testing the
areal effects of regression against the affects(?) of climatic
cooling is recorded in the Eocene and Oligocene Series. Here
we can compare what happened to life during two critical intervals. One was an interval of Late Eocene and Early Oligocene
time when widespread cooling was accompanied by only a minor
drop in sea level, or none at all. The other was an interval
of later Oligocene time when there was a profound and lasting
global regression.

The cooling event near the end of the Eocene is well documented by several lines of evidence. Deep sea faunas of
ostracodes (Benson 1975) and foraminifers (Corliss 1979) reveal
that at this time the psychrosphere formed. The psychrosphere

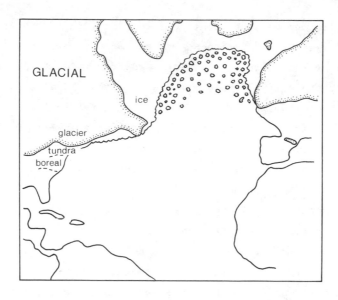

FIGURE 4. Map of the northern Atlantic region 18,000 years ago. At this time, the Gulf Stream flowed eastward toward Spain and February sea-surface temperatures in the central Caribbean were about 4 C cooler than today. (After McIntyre et al. 1976).

is the cold layer of water blanketing the deep sea and originating at the poles, where frigid water descends from the
surface. In Late Eocene and Early Oligocene time, planktonic
foraminifers suffered a global mass extinction that Cifelli
(1969) showed to have followed a striking thermal pattern. The
dominant group to emerge in the Oligocene were the globigerines, which today represent the only group of planktonic foraminifers to be concentrated in cold water masses. The extinctions of planktonic foraminifers and extinctions of warm-
adapted deep-sea foraminiferans took place not suddenly, but in
a series of steps beginning early in Late Eocene time (Aubry
1983, Corliss and Keigwin 1983, Keller 1983, Miller 1983).

     The Late Eocene extinction was more severe than commonly
realized. Although many of the taxa that disappeared were

minor ones, the total loss amounted to about 50 percent of all
marine families that have died out since the Middle Eocene
(Raup and Sepkoski, in press). In the American Pacific
Northwest, numerous molluscan taxa disappeared during a brief
interval prior to deposition of the Keasey Formation. The
Keasey is of Refugian age, and Armentrout (1983) has shown that
the formation falls within plankton zones that are Late Eocene
in age; thus, the molluscan extinction was underway before the
end of Eocene time. In documenting this extinction, Hickman
(1980, p. 9) noted that the taxa most severely affected were
apparently of warm-water affinities and described it as producing "the most pronounced changes in molluscan faunas in the
Cenozoic of the Eastern Pacific". Pomerol (1982, p. 54) attributed the simultaneous heavy extinction in the marine faunas of
Europe to sudden refrigeration. Also at latitudes in the
Southern Hemisphere, where data from the deep sea indicate
abrupt cooling (Devereaux 1967, Dorman 1966, Shackelton and
Kennett 1975) Zinsmeister (1982) found that few Eocene molluscan species of the southern circumpacific region survived into
the Oligocene Epoch.

  Terrestrial angiosperm floras offer strong corroborative
evidence that climatic cooling began before the end of the
Eocene. In Britain, for example, the transition to cold-
adapted floras began in mid-Eocene time (Collinson et al.
1981). Wolfe (1978) has shown that for living mesic angiosperm
floras the percentage of species having entire (smooth) margins
is tightly correlated with mean annual temperature, and he has
estimated that a decline in this percentage in several regions
of North America between Late Eocene and Early Oligocene time
reflected a drop in mean annual temperature of about $10^{o}C$.
Near Puget Sound, for example, paratropical rainforests were
replaced by mixed mesophyte forests. Dating of this transition
remains controversial, with neither floral assemblages nor

radiometric dating providing for accurate correlation (Turner et al. 1983). Nonetheless, there is strong evidence that cooling began long before the end of the Eocene. The Goshen assemblage is the youngest warm-adapted Eocene flora preserved in sediments that intergrade with marine strata, and Wolfe (1981) regards the Goshen as representing the interval immediately before the onset of cooling. This flora occurs in the upper part of the Fisher Formation, which interfingers with the Eugene Formation, and planktonic index fossils show the latter to be of Late Eocene age (Armentrout 1983). Furthermore, seven radiometric dates for the lower Puget Group (Turner et al. 1983) suggest an age in the vicinity of 45-41 my for a succession of fossil floras that reveal an episode of cooling (Wolfe 1981); on all recently published Cenozoic time scales, this falls within the middle or early Late Eocene, making this the likely interval for the onset of cooling.

The heavy extinction that accompanied cooling during the latter portions of the Eocene Epoch stands in marked contrast to the low level of extinction during an enormous Oligocene regression. Seismic stratigraphy (Vail et al. 1977) reveals that at the very end of Eocene time there was also a eustatic fall, but this is still regarded as only a second-order event (Peter R. Vail, personal communication 1983). In contrast, a eustatic drop during Oligocene time (lower opima zone) brought sea level to the lowest position recognized by Vail et al. (1977) in their compendium of data for the entire Phanerozoic. What actually happened to marine life during this interval? Although there seems to have been a small pulse of extinction of warm-water planktonic foraminifers, which may indicate a minor pulse of cooling (Keller 1983), there was apparently no equivalent change in the nannoplankton (Aubry 1983) or abyssal foraminifers (Miller 1983). And despite the great regression,

no excessive extinction has been reported for shallow-water
benthos.

Especially relevant here to the issue of the extinction
potential of the species-area effect are two facts: (1) Before
the great Oligocene regression, the seas had stood at a high
level for about 5 my, and (2) when they receded from the high
stand, the seas remained at a very low level for about 5 my
(figure 5).

Thus, conditions were optimal for the operation of the
species-area effect. There is no basis for any argument that
species richness had not initially equilibrated to a large area
or that the dramatic regression was too brief for equilibration
to a smaller area. If the species-area effect were ever to

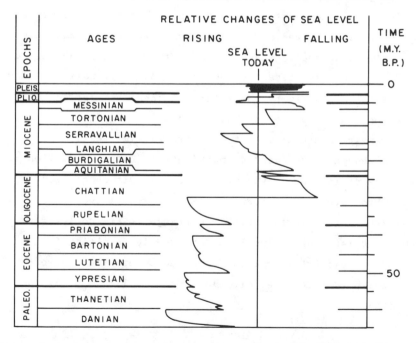

FIGURE 5. Global sea level changes estimated from seismic
stratigraphy of continental margins. The mid-Oligocene
eustatic fall may be the largest of the entire Phanerozoic.
(From Vail et al. 1977).

have devistated species of shallow water marine benthos globally, it should have done so at this time.

Suggestions, based on indirect evidence of the deep sea
record, that this later Oligocene sea level drop was less
severe than one in latest Eocene time (Olsson et al. 1980,
Angstadt et al. 1983) run counter not only to the more direct
evidence of seismic stratigraphy along continental margins, but
also ignore the more direct evidence of deposits exposed in
sections representing epicontinental and shelf seas. Loutit et
al. (1983) found evidence in an Alabama exposure of a rise n
sea level spanning the Eocene-Oligocene boundary; the same
exposure exhibits an unconformity representing the later Oligocene regression documented by Vail et al. (1977) (figure 6).
During the latter portion of the Eocene Epoch, seas occupied
large areas of Europe and Asia (figure 7). These seas were so
extensive that their presence was certainly under eustatic control, yet they survived the Eocene-Oligocene transition. They
were eliminated only by the later Oligocene regression, which
confirms the contention of Vail et al. (1977) that this regression was the dominant one of the interval in question.

Although there has been much debate about correlation and
absolute dating in the vicinity of Eocene-Oligocene boundary
(e.g. Prothero et al. 1982, Glass and Crosbie 1982), the European record reveals that both the change toward cooler floras
and the crisis for marine life (apparently resulting from an
influx of cold Arctic waters) occurred before the enormous
regression (Collinson et al. 1981, Pomerol 1982, pp. 54-56,
125-126).

EARLIER MASS EXTINCTIONS

Having argued that temperature has been an important agent
of marine extinction during the Cenozoic Era, whereas the
species-area effects of major regressions have been trivial, I

FIGURE 6. Exposure at St. Stephens quarry, in southwestern
Alabama, showing the unconformity between the Bucatunna
Formation (dark shale forming most of the quarry wall) and the
Chickasawhay Formation (light-colored limestone above).

will now review evidence suggesting that temperature change
played a prominent role in earlier mass extinctions. I will
extrapolate the preceding arguments against the efficacy of
regression to pre- Cenozoic time and pay little further attention to the areal effects of regression. There is no question
that some pre-Cenozoic mass extinctions have coincided with
eustatic lowering of seas, however, and it is reasonable to
suggest that regression has at times contributed to marine temperature changes, by mechanisms that I will consider below.

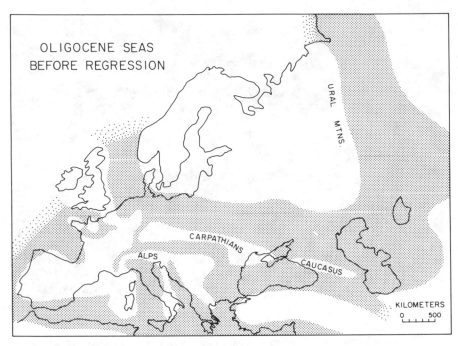

FIGURE 7. The widespread distribution of shallow seas in Europe during Oligocene time before the large regression depicted in figure 5. (Partly after Pomerol 1982).

Another important premise concerns global, as opposed to polar, cooling. Since Eocene time, climatic cooling events have emanated from the poles. This should not be taken to indicate that glacial episodes of the past could only have produced modest extionctins, like those of the Plio-Pleistocene. Some earlier glacial episodes may have resulted from global cooling associated with more general phenomena, such as a decrease in solar radiation that refrigerated the entire earth, producing extensive tropical extinctions. Other pre-Cenozoic glacial episodes may not have caused mass extinctins because, while they were occurring at high latitudes, tropical climatic zones near the equator remained unaffected. The Carboniferous

glacial episode may represent an example, having taken place at
a time of steep latitudinal temperature gradients.

In the following evaluation, I will discuss or mention all
of the Phanerozoic mass extinctions recognized in the reviews
by Raup and Sepkoski (1982) and Sepkoski (1982), but first I
will briefly consider an earlier mass extinction that preceded
the dawning of the Phanerozoic by just a few tens of millions
of years.

The Varangian Event of Latest Precambrian Time

Vidal and Knoll (1982) have documented a very late Precambrian mass extinction of the acritarchs, the dominant late Precambrian and early Paleozoic fossil phytoplankton group of
apparent eukaryotic character. Most acritarch taxa present in
Vendian time disappeared during the transition to Varangian
time, about 650 my ago, when, as Vidal and Knoll note, a major
glacial event is represented in many areas by a pair of tillite
horizons. Remarkably widespread glacial features suggest that
this glacial episode may have been the most extensive in all of
earth history (Hambrey and Harland 1981).

Fossil faunas of soft-bodied animals in many regions first
appear in rocks above the Varangian glacial deposits (Stanley
1976), and it is possible that the origin and adaptive radiation of multicellular marine animals resulted from adaptive
breakthroughs that developed in the radiation through which
acritarchs, and perhaps other algae, rebounded from the Varangian mass extinction. Possibly before the extinction,
eukaryotic evolution was stymied by ecological crowding in the
absence of efficient predation or other disturbances equivalent
to the glacial episode (Stanley 1975).

In any event, it seems likely that global cooling associated with the remarkably severe glacial episode caused the mass
extinction of acritarchs.

Terminal Events of Cambrian Biomeres

Palmer (1965) introduced the stratigraphic term "biomere" to label three successive bodies of Middle and Late Cambrian rock that record adaptive radiations of trilobites and are bounded by mass extinctions of these animals. Biomeres are best known, and perhaps best developed, in North America, where they are formed primarily of carbonate rocks with fossil faunas dominated by trilobite adaptive radiations that occurred at intervals of 5 to 7.5 my without regression of the seas; he further estimated that the mass extinction documented at the top of the Marjumiid Biomere took place during no more than 4000 to 6000 years. Th trilobites occupied warm, shallow seas, and after each mass extinction, the succeeding adaptive radiation issued from olenid trilobites. These continuously occupied deep, offshore areas of sea floor and only periodically invaded shallow habitats when these had been largely vacated by mass extinction. Thus, in part by analogy with the biogeography of modern arthropods, it has been argued that the olenids, in contrast to their descendants of shallow carbonate shelves and inland seas, were adapted to cool waters (Taylor 1977, Stitt 1977). Supporting this idea is the observation by the same authors that olenids occupied shallow-water habitats in Scandinavia, which according to the plate tectonic reconstructions of Scotese et al. (1979) lay at a higher altitude. All of these observations are consistent with the idea expressed long ago by Lochman and Duncan (1944), that it was sudden cooling events that caused the repeated mass extinctions of trilobites (Stitt 1977).

Terminal Ordovician Extinction and Glaciation

According to Sepkoski (1982, p. 285), "the Ashgillian, or terminal Ordovician, mass extinction could very well have been the second most severe extinction event of the Phanerozoic":

approximately 100 families of marine organisms disappeared during the last 5 my or less of Ordovician time. Boucot (1975)
and Sheehan (1975) noted that this extinction, like the Cambrian "biomere events", was primarily a tropical phenomenon.
Scandinavian and deep water faunas were less affected than faunas of shallow tropical seas. In addition, Skevington (1974)
noted that during Late Ordovician time, graptolite biogeographic provinces became progressively compressed toward the
equator, to the point where close to the end of the period just
a single province populated by only five or six genera
remained; Skevington pointed to cooling as the likely cause of
this temporal shift.

Strong independent support for the idea of a major cooling
event culminating at the close of the Ordovician Period comes
from evidence of glaciation. This was centered in Africa and
reached a climax at the very end of Ordovician time, when there
was a modest global regression (Berry and Boucot 1973; Sheehan
1973, 1975, 1982; Brenchley and Newall 1980). Thus, abundant
circumstantial evidence suggests a major role for cooling in
the terminal Ordovician mass extinction.

The Late Devonian Event

During a Late Devonian interval represented by rocks of
the upper portion of the Frasnian Stage and the lower portion
of the Famennian Stage, there was a mass extinction of marine
life. This event did not coincide with global regression
(House 1975a, 1975b) but, like the early Paleozoic mass
extionctions, exhibited a strong bias against shallow tropical
faunas. Evaluating all known rugose corals of Frasnian and
Famennian age, Pedder (1982) found that of 148 shallow-water
Frasnian species with some "rock forming" capacity, at most 6
species (4%) survived the biotic crisis. In contrast, 3 or 4
of 10 deep-water species (30 - 40%) survived. More generally,

Copper (1977) noted that the tropical stromatoporoid-tabulate
coral reef community, which had fluorished for tens of millions
of years, suffered almost total annihilation in the Frasnian-
Famennian event, and other tropical faunal elements also suffered heavy extinction.

In sharp contrast, the marine fauna of the Malvinokaffric
Province of South America, which was positioned adjacent to the
South Pole (figure 8), experienced little excessive extinction

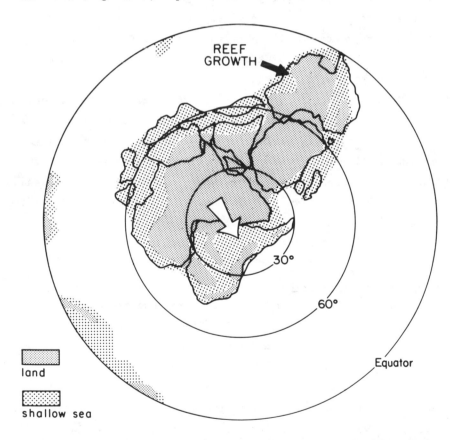

FIGURE 8. Paleogeographic map of the Southern Hemisphere late
in mid-Devonian time. Arrow points to the Malvinokaffric
Province, which lay close to the South Pole and escaped severe
extinction in the Fransnian-Fammenian crisis. (After Scotese
et al. 1979).

experienced little excessive extinction in the Frasnian-
Famennian crisis. Ninety percent of the brachiopod families
that disappeared in the crisis, for example, were not
represented in this polar province. Communities of the province are, in fact, unusual in their high diversity of infaunal
bivalves, especially deposit-feeding types; this composition
supports the paleolatitudinal evidence that the enduring Malvinokaffric fauna was adopted to cold conditions.

    Working at the species level in a detailed stratigraphic
analysis of the Frasnian-Famennian interval in New York State,
McGhee (1982) showed that mass extinction in this region was
spread over about 7 my. He also uncovered a pattern that
argues strongly in favor of a prominent role for temperature
change. While other taxa were declining, the hyalosponges
(glass sponges) diversified. In complementary fashion, the
hyalosponges subsequently declined as other taxa rediversified.
The hyalosponges are a predominantly cold-water group today and
were similarly adapted in Paleozoic time (Finks 1960).

    It is also significant that the acritarchs, which are the
dominant fossil group of pre-Famennian Paleozoic phytoplankton,
suffered greatly in the Frasnian-Famennian crisis and, in fact,
never fully recovered their high diversity thereafter (Tappan
1980). The idea that this extinction resulted from climatic
cooling is consistent with the previously cited observation
that the acritarchs also experienced mass extinction during the
late Precambrian interval of widespread glaciation.

The Problematical Permian Event

    More than half of the families of marine animals died out
in Late Permian time (Sepkoski 1982). Global sealevel lowering, though it left few shallow-water deposits of latest Permian and earliest Triassic Age, brought seas only to a level
approximating their present position (Vail et al. 1977).

Several facts suggest the possibility that climatic change was
involved in the Late Permian event, but there is no independent
evidence of an episode of cooling. Numerous authors have
observed tht the Late Permian biotic decline was not geologically instantaneous; in fact, rate of extinction of families
was almost as great near the end of Guadalupian time as in
Djulfian time (Raup and Sepkoski 1982). It is also evident
that tropical taxa, including fusulinid foraminifers, crinoids,
corals, bryozoans, and brachiopods, suffered most. Both Waterhouse (1971) and Dickens (1983) suggest that extreme warming,
rather than cooling, caused the extinction. The difficulty
with this idea is that there is no known reason why
"overheated" tropical taxa could not have migrated toward polar
regions. Climatic conditions are less well understood for Late
Permian time than for Early Permian time, when, especially at
times of continental glaciation, very steep temperature gradients extended from the south polar region to tropical equatorial regions. One hypothesis that deserves consideration is
that, in the course of Late Permian time, latitudinal temperature gradients became more gentle, perhaps without net global
cooling. Thus, tropical regions, at least briefly, may have
suffered cooling while there was warming at high latitudes.

Mesozoic Events

In addition to the famous terminal Cretaceous mass extinction, Raup and Sepkoski (1982) and Sepkoski (1982) recognized
two family-level crises for the Mesozoic Era. The first was of
Norian age (end of the Triassic), and it eliminated about 20%
of all known marine families, striking the ammonites, bivalves,
gastropods, brachiopods, and conodonts with particular force.
The second was of Tithonian age (end of the Jurassic), and it
was apparently a lesser event, which is recognized primarily
for its effect on bivalves (Hallam 1977, 1978). In addition,

Hallam (1977) has documented an Early Jurassic (Toarcian) mass
extinction that eliminated about 70% of the European species of
bivalves. In a more recent family-level analysis, Raup and
Sepkoski (in press) also recognize the terminal Jurassic event
and less pronounced peaks in rate of extinction in the
Pliensbachian, Bajocian, Callovian, Hauterivian, and
Cenomanian.

According to Hallam (1978, 1981a, 1981b), the terminal
Triassic and Jurassic crises coincided with eustatic sealevel
lowering, but the Toarcian event did not. Employing seismic
stratigraphy and global unconformiteis within cratonic strata,
Vail et al. (in press) recognize three Tithonian eustatic
drops, but a rise in sealevel across the Jurassic-Cretaceous
boundary.

For two reasons, Hallam (1969, 1971, 1977, 1981b) has
opposed the idea that temperature change played a major role in
early Mesozoic mass extinctions in the marine realm. One of
his arguments is that the Mesozoic Era, being a time of gentle
temperature gradients, should have been an interval when temperature played only a minor role in the distribution of taxa
in space and time. I disagree with this assessment. In the
first place, as I discussed above, the pre-Oligocene world may
have been one in which biotas were especially vulnerable to
refrigeration that was global in nature, rather than being centered at the poles like the cooling episodes of the past 40 my
or so; during the Mesozoic Era, stenothermal biotas occupied
broad geographic regions. In the second place, there is abun-
dart evidence that the Boreal and Tethyan realms of the Mesozoic owed their presence to latitudinal temperature gradients.
Hallam has opposed this tradition idea for Jurassic time,
believing that temperature gradients were too gentle to have
produced the boundary between the two realms within a degree or
two of latitude. Physiological analogy and homology, however,

suggest that the Boreal-Tropical transition, like nontropical-
tropical biotic transitions in modern seas, resulted from a
threshold effect. In shallow seas today, carbonate sediments
and tropical biotas give way abruptly to siliciclastic sediments and nontropical biotas of latitudes where winter temperatures seldom fall below 18°C (Hall 1964). A well-known example
is the transition in the vicinity of Palm Beach, Florida. The
existence of this physiological threshold effect means that an
abrupt biotic transition is to be expected even if temperature
gradients are relatively gentle. Certainly gradients were
steep enough during Jurassic time to be reflected in terrestrial floras (Barnard 1973). In addition, Triassic and Jurassic coral reefs in the vicinity of Europe were restricted to
the Tethys (Hallam 1981a, p. 157), and, as Fabricius (1966) has
observed, reef corals experienced major losses here at the time
of the Norian mass extinction.

Just as spatial temperature changes controlling biotic
occurrences have been overlooked by some students of Jurassic
sediments and biotas, temporal temperature changes possibly
responsible for mass extinction have gone unnoticed.
Vakhrameev (1981) has recently shown that the percentage of
pollen belonging to the extinct conifer Classopolis is a good
indicator of the climatic conditions under which a fossil flora
lived. His detailed sampling indicates that the climates of
Siberia and the central Russian platform changed from warm and
arid to temperate during the Jurassic-Cretaceous transition.

Relevant paleontological and stratigraphic data are more
readily available for the terminal Cretaceous crisis than for
the earlier Mesozoic events. At the end of the Cretaceous global sealevel was lowered only to a level approaching that of
the present (Vail et al. 1977). As for several Cenozoic and
Paleozoic mass extinctions, we can observe for the terminal
Cretaceous event temporal, and especially geographic, patterns

of extinction that suggest that temperature was an important
agent of destruction in the marine ecosystem. The tropical
Tethyan Realm was much more strongly affected than the nontropical Boreal Realm. This pattern is evident for both planktonic
and benthic life.

In the water column, the globigerines were the only sub-
group of the Globigerinacea to survive the terminal Cretaceous
crisis, possibly by way of just a single species (Smit 1982);
it should be recalled that the globigerines occupy packages of
cold water in the modern oceans and that they were also the
principal group to survive the terminal Eocene event (Cifelli
1969), for which we have independent evidence of concurrent
global cooling. The terminal occurrence or affinities (Perch-
Nielsen 1979), whereas in Denmark the dinoflagellates suffered
a relatively weak pulse of extinction.

On the sea floor, the terminal Cretaceous mass extinction
was also most pronounced in the Tethyan Realm. Here the reef-
building rudists disappeared altogether, and corals, ostreid
and trigoniid bivalves, gastropods, and larger benthic foraminifers all suffered major losses (Kauffman 1979). In Denmark,
the pulse of extinction was weaker (Rosenkrantz 1960, Kauffman
1979, Stokes 1979), as demonstrated by the lingering debate as
to whether the Danian Stage should be placed in the Paleogene
or Cretaceous System (Voigt 1981). In fact, exactly the same
kind of uncertainty has surrounded post-Maastrichtian Boreal
sediments and faunas on the western side of the Atlantic.
Here, in contrast to the heavy extinction within tropical
Tethyan faunas of the Gulf of Mexico and Caribbean, there was
little excessive extinction in the north-central United States.
The Cannonball Formation of North Dakota is of Paleocene age,
yet about 60 percent of its bivalve species are known from Cretaceous rocks several million years older (Cvancara 1966);

because of this strong similarity, the Cannonball was in the
past assigned to the Cretaceous System (Stanton 1920).

Oxygen isotopes are unreliable indicators of absolute
paleotemperatures, or even of relative temperature changes,
during intervals of 10^3 or 10^4 years. There is, however,
widespread agreement that a general cooling trend took place
after Albian time, with the Maastrichtian Stage representing
the coldest interval of the Late Cretaceous (Douglas and Savin
1975, Frakes 1979). Furthermore, terrestrial floras of Wyoming
reveal the occurrence of marked cooling across the
Maastrichtian-Paleocene boundary; leaf margin analyses (Wolfe
1978) indicate a decline in mean annual temperature of about
$10^{\circ}C$ this time in Wyoming (Hickey 1980) (figure 9). The terminal Cretaceous event caused only a modest amount of excessive
extinction in terrestrial floras, and, although, data for low-
latitude floras are meager, there is an indication in the data
now in hand of a slightly greater incidence of extinction at
high latitudes (Hickey 1981).

Not only was there a strong bias against tropical benthos
in the impact of the terminal Cretaceous extinction, there is
evidence that, during or after the crisis, nontropical taxa
spread into what had been tropical regions. Among the gastropods, which had been clearly divided into Tethyan and Boreal
provinces during the Cretaceous (Sohl 1971), a number of
Tethyan groups, like the Actaeonellidae and Nerineidae, died
out in the mass extinction; then, during Danian time, a single
biogeographic province came to occupy a vast region extending
from Greenland to northern Africa. It is a remarkable fact
that this province contained no formerly Tethyan taxa (Kollmann
1979). Accordingly, Kollmann inferred that there was "a cold
water burst at the end of the Cretaceous which killed the
exclusively tropical shallow water forms". A remarkable pattern parallelling this one has been discovered for terrestrial

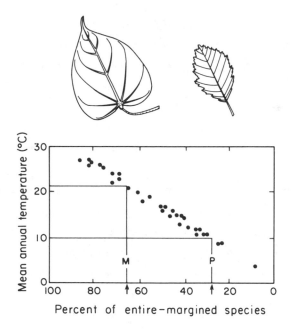

FIGURE 9. Estimates that mean annual temperature declined by
about 10% in Wyoming between late Maastrichtian time (M) and
early Paleocene time (P), as indicated by a drop in the
percentage of angiosperm leaves with entire margins (upper
left), as opposed to jagged margins (upper right).
Maastrichtian and Paleocene data are those that Hickey (1980)
interpreted according to a graph (dots) compiled by Wolfe
(1978), based on data for Recent floras of Asia.

plants (Hickey et al. 1983). Floras on Ellesmere Island, at a

very high latitude had a "Paleocene" aspect early in Campanian

time, about 15 my before similar floras appeared in Wyoming.

Thus, as suggested by Van Valen and Sloan (1977), terrestrial

biotas apparently migrated southward during a protracted

episode of coolong that spanned the Cretaceous-Paleocene boun-

dary.

There is little doubt that a number of marine taxa died

out suddenly, within a very brief interval of time, right at

what is regarded as the Maastrichtian-Paleocene boundary; this

is evident for planktonic groups (Percival and Fischer 1977,

Primoli-Silva 1977, Monechi 1979). On the other hand, several important taxa had already declined before this time. Notably, the rudist reef community suffered decimation before the end of the Maastrichtian; in sediments representing the last 1 or 2 million years of Maastrichtian time, only an impoverished rudist-coral association is found (Kauffman 1979). The inoceramid bivalves also declined drastically well before the end of the Maastrichtian. By mid-Maastrichtian time, only one inoceramid genus, Tenuipteris, remained, and near the end of the interval it was represented by only a single species (Dhondt 1983). There is also now evidence that the ammonites demise was a prolonged event. Although the Stevns Klint section in Denmark has been celebrated for its apparent documentatioin of sudden extinction of the Maastrichtian-Paleocene boundary, the Maastrichtian here terminates in a hardground (Surlyk 1979). The work of Ward and Wiedemann (1983) suggests that the section at Zumaya, Spain, is more complete. Here rich fossil deposits show that the final Maastrichtian fauna declined almost linearly from about 10 ammonite species to none, over a stratigraphic interval of about 30 meters without a change in sedimentary regime; the last ammonite is found in beds about 15 meters below the iridium layer at the top of the Maastrichtian Stage, and it appears to have died about 100,000 years before the very end of Cretaceous time.

The heavy concentration of latest Cretaceous extinction in the tropical marine realm and the evidence that this event began before the very end of the period argue against the idea that the impact of an extraterrestrial bolide was the sole cause of the biotic crisis, as suggested in the reviews by Alvarez et al. (1982) and Alvarez (1983). On the other hand, the evidence is compatible with the idea that a series of pulses of cooling, perhaps resulting from two or more ultimate causes, produced most of the excessive extinction, affecting

different taxa at different times, according to peculiarities
of temperature tolerance and geographic distribution. Possibly
a bolide impact administered the coup de grace, but even this
possibility raises the question of why in the planktonic realm
tropical phytoplankton, in particular, should have been especially vulnerable to the various lethal effects envisioned for
such an event. One possibility here might be that dinoflagel-
late species, which prevailed in nontropical seas, were able to
weather the crisis in their encysted stage, which is apparently
without counterpart in the coccolithophores and related groups.

DISCUSSION
Temperature as an Agent of Mass Extinction
     Many of the marine mass extinctions that I have described
followed a geographic pattern in which tropical taxa suffered
more than nontropical taxa, and many followed a temporal pattern in which extinction was protracted rather than instantaneous. None of the limiting factors described in the introduction to this chapter, if somehow transformed into agents of
mass extinction, would be expected to yield such patterns. It
has been suggested that marine species of high latitude are
characterized by great trophic breadth (Valentine and Moores
1970, Hallam 1977), but such adaptation has never been documented. Both suspension feeders and deposit feeders appear to
be trophic generalists at all latitudes. Stenotopy, or narrow
niche breadth, in the tropics is largely a matter of stenothermy, and it is difficult to envision the characteristic latitudinal bias of mass extinction as relating primarily to any
lethal agent other than temperature.
     To attribute heavy mass extinction at low latitudes to the
collapse of tropical food webs would only serve to transfer the
geographic bias to a lower trophic level: why should phytoplankton repeatedly suffer especially heavy extinction in the

tropics? Furthermore, there is evidence that in the terminal
Cretaceous event the extinction of consumers was not primarily
due to phytoplankton extinction. In this event, the collapse
of the tropical rudist community and the tropical ammonite
fauna before the decimation of the tropical phytoplankton suggests that the dominant pattern was not a trophic "domino
effect", in which a wave of extinction passed upward through
the food web. Instead, important groups of trophic consumers
died out before important phyto-plankton groups.

One cannot explain the tropical bias of extinction simply
by adopting a dynamic model of equilibrium like that of Carr
and Kitchell (1980), which predicts a higher incidence of
extinction where diversity is highest to begin with. In the
first place, the huge molluscan diversities that I have
described for the Hawaiian and Panamic-Pacific Provinces establish the fact that small areas in the tropics can support vast
numbers of endemic species for millions of years: whatever
species-area equation is employed for marine benthos must be
associated with extremely low z values. In the second place,
many mass extinctions totally, or almost totally, eliminated
certain tropical benthic faunas - the Late Devonian reef community, for example, and Cretaceous reef-building rudists.

We must consider the possibility that changes in the solar
"constant" have caused biotically significant episodes of temperature change in the course of earth history. One episode
for which this mechanism seems especially attractive is the
late Precambrian interval during which glaciation affected most
continents, apparently even at high latitudes (McWilliams and
McElhinny 1980), and acritarchs suffered heavy extinction.
Possibly at times, a stepwise decrease in the solar constant
over a period of 10^6 - 10^7 years has caused mass extinction by
way of pulses of cooling. We must also consider the likelihood
that two or more factors have at times conspired to yield major

climatic changes. Global regression of seas may sometimes have
played a role here. For one thing, regression may have changed
the earth´s albedo. For another, regression may indirectly
have weakened the "greenhouse effect" of carbon dioxide in the
atmosphere. Berner et al. (1983) have observed that the
equilibrium carbon dioxide level is positively correlated with
the surface area of the land, because at the land-air interface
carbon dioxide is consumed by weathering. In the model
developed by Berner et al., land area exerts a powerful control
over atmospheric carbon dioxide and, hence, global temperatures. It seems reasonable to suggest that during a major
regression, when no offsetting factors obtain, this relationship might contribute to global cooling.

CONCLUSIONS

    1. Conditions and events of the Cenozoic Era indicate
that marine regressions should have made no more than a trivial
contribution to Phanerozoic mass extinctions of marine life by
reducing the area of shallow sea floor and crowding species
together.

    2. On the other hand, many lines of evidence indicate
that temperature change has been a prominent proximal cause of
marine mass extinction.

    3. A persistent theme of mass extinctions has been the
decimation of tropical marine biotas, with less severe losses
occurring at high latitudes. This pattern characterized the
following mass extinctions, and perhaps others: Cambrian (the
"biomere events"), terminal Ordovician, Late Devonian, Permian,
terminal Cretaceous, Eocene-Oligocene, and Pliocene.

    4. It is difficult to conceive of an agent other than
temperature change that would be expected to cause mass extinction with a heavy latitudinal bias. Stenotopy in the tropics
is largely a matter of stenothermy.

5. For many mass extinctions, there is physical or biological evidence of contemporaneous climatic cooling independent of the latitudinal pattern of extinction. These mass
extinctions include the latest Precambrian (Varangian), terminal Ordovician, Late Devonian, terminal Jurassic, terminal Cretaceous, Eocene-Oligocene, and Pliocene.

6. For several crises (terminal Ordovician, Late
Devonian, terminal Permian, terminal Cretaceous, Eocene-
Oligocene, and Pliocene) there is evidence that mass extinction
occurred as a series of pulses spread over 10^6 - 10^7 years.
This temporal pattern is consistent with the idea that extinction often resulted from pulses of temperature change, with
different forms of life suffering at different times, depending
on their temperature tolerances and on the temporal and geographic pattern of cooling.

7. There is evidence that, during the terminal Ordovician
and Cretaceous mass extinctions, cold-adapted biotas of high
latitudes migrated to lower latitudes, replacing warm-adapted
biotas.

8. Major cooling events of the past 40 my, or so, may be
atypical of the Phanerozoic in general, in that they have
entailed refrigeration emanating from the poles. Earlier cooling events - even ones associated with glaciation - may, in
contrast, have resulted from global cooling, so that tropical
taxa suffered most severely because their temperature requirements could not be met by migration to lower latitudes.

ACKNOWLEDGEMENTS

The ideas expressed here were developed during the tenure
of National Science Foundation Grant EAR 8207275. I gratefully
acknowledge the following individuals for sharing information
during the preparation of this chapter: Leo Hickey, Jack Wolfe,
Peter Ward, Billie Glass, Donald Prothero, and Peter Sheehan.

LITERATURE CITED

ADDICOTT, W. O. 1966. Late Pleistocene marine paleoecology
     and zoogeography in central California. United States
     Geological Service Professional Paper 523-C. 21 pp.
ALVAREZ, L. W. 1983. Experimental evidence that an asteroid
     impact led to the extinction of many species 65 million
     years ago. Proceedings of the National Academy of
     Sciences (U.S.A.), 80:627-642.
ALVAREZ, W., L. W. ALVAREZ, F. ASARO and H. V. MICHEL. 1982.
     Current status of the impact theory for the terminal Cre-
     taceous extinction. Geological Society of America Special
     Paper 190:305-315.
ANGSTADT, D. M., J. A. AUSTIN and R. T. BUFFLER. 1983. Deep-
     sea erosional unconformity in the southeastern Gulf of
     Mexico. Geology. 11:215-218.
ARMENTROUT, J. M. 1982. Eocene-Oligocene boundary problems,
     West Coast, North America. American Association of
     Petroleum Geologists Bulletin. 67-413.
AUBRY, M. P. 1983. Late Eocene to Early Oligocene Calcareous
     nannoplankton biostratigraphy and biogeography. American
     Association of Petroleum Geologists Bulletin. 67-415.
BARNARD, P. D. 1973. Mesozoic floras. Palaeontological
     Association Special Papers in Palaeontology. 12:175-188.
BARRON, E. J., J. L. SLOAN and C. G. A. HARRISON. 1980.
     Potential significance of land-sea distribution and sur-
     face albedo variations as a climatic forcing factor; 180
     m.y. to the present. Journal of Geology. 30:17-40.
BENSON, R. H. 1975. The origin of the psychrosphere as
     recorded in changes of deep-sea ostracode assemblages.
     Lethia 8:69-83.
BERNER, R. A., A. C. LASAGA and R. M. GARRELS. 1983. The
     carbonate-silicate geochemical cycle and its effect on
     atmospheric carbon dioxide over the past 100 million
     years. American Journal of Science. 283:641-683.
BERRY, W. B. N. and A. J. BOUCOT. 1973. Glacio-eustatic con-
     trol of Late Ordovician - Early Silurian platform sedimen-
     tation and faunal changes. Geological Society of America
     Bulletin. 84:275-284.
BOUCOT, A. J. 1975. Evolution and Extinction Rate Controls.
     Amsterdam, Elsevier.
BRENCHLEY, P. J. and G. NEWALL. 1980. A facies analysis of
     Upper Ordovician regressive sequences in the Oslo region,
     Norway - a record of glacio-eustatic changes.
     Palaeogeography, Palaeoclimatology, Palaeoecology. 31:1-
     38.
CARR, T. R. and J. A. KITCHELL. 1980. Dynamics of taxonomic
     diversity. Paleobiology. 6:427-443.

CHAMBERLIN, T. C. 1898a. The ulterior basis of time divisions and the classification of geologic history. Journal of Geology. 6:449-462.

CHAMBERLIN, T. C. 1898b. A systematic source of evolution of provincial faunas. Journal of Geology. 6:597-608.

CHAMBERLIN, T. C. 1909. Diastrophism as the ultimate basis of correlation. Journal of Geology. 17:685-693.

CIFELLI, R. 1969. Radiation of the Cenozoic planktonic Foraminifera. Systematic Zoology. 18:154-168.

CLIMAP project members. 1981. Seasonal reconstructions of the earth's surface at the last glacial maximum. Geology Society of America Map and Chart Series. MC-36.

COLLINSON, M. E., K. FOWLER and M. C. BOULTER. 1981. Floristic changes indicate a cooling climate in the Eocene of southern England. Nature. 291:315-317.

COPPER, P. 1977. Paleolatitudes in the Devonian of Brazil and the Frasnian-Famennian mass extinction. Palaeogeography, Palaeoclimatology, Palaeoecology. 21:165-207.

CORLISS, B. H. 1979. Response of deep-sea benthonic Foraminifera to development of the psychrosphere near the Eocene/Oligocene boundary. Nature. 282:63-65.

CORLISS, B. H. and L. E. KEIGWIN. 1983. Eocene-Oligocene benthic Foraminifera: Implications for deep-water circulation history. American Association of Petroleum Geologists Bulletin. 67:443.

CVANCARA, A. M. 1966. Revision of the Cannonball Formation (Paleocene) of North and South Dakota. University of Michigan, Museum of Paleontology Contributions. 20:277-370.

DEVEREAUX, I. 1967. Oxygen isotope paleotemperature measurements on New Zealand Tertiary fossils. New Zealand Journal of Science. 10:988-1011.

DHONDT, A. V. 1983. Campanian and Maastrichtian inoceramids: a review. Zitteliana (Munich). 10:689-701.

DICKENS, J. M. 1983. Evolution and climate in the upper Paleozoic. Fossils and Climate Symposium, Glasgow (in press).

DORMAN, F. H. 1966. Australian Tertiary paleotemperatures. Journal of Geology. 74:49-61.

DOUGLAS, R. G. and S. M. SAVIN. 1975. Oxygen and carbon isotope analyses of Cretaceous and Tertiary microfossils from Shatsky Rise and other sites in the North Pacific Ocean. Initial Reports of the Deep Sea Drilling Project 2 (United States Government Printing Office; Washington, D. C.) 32:509-520.

EKMAN, S. 1953. Zoogeography of the Sea. 417 pp. Sidgwick and Jackson Ltd. London.

FABRICIUS, F. 1966. Beckensedimentation and Riffbildung an der Wende Trias/Jura in den Bayerisch. 143 pp. Brill, Leiden.

FINKS, R. M.   1960.   Late Paleozoic sponge faunas of the Texas
    region. American Museum of Natural History Bulletin.
    120:1-160.
FISCHER, A. G.   1964.   Brackish oceans as a cause of the
    Permo-Triassic faunal crisis. Pp. 566-574 in Nairn, A. E.
    M., ed., Problems in Palaeoclimatology. Interscience, New
    York.
FISCHER, A. G. and M. A. ARTHUR.   1977.   Secular variations in
    the pelagic realm. Society of Economic Paleontologists
    and Mineralogists Special Publications 25:19-50.
FLESSA, K. W. and J. J. SEPKOSKI.   1978.   On the relationship
    between Phanerozic diversity and changes in habitable
    area. Paleobiology. 4:359-366.
FRAKES, L. A.   1979.   Climates throughout Geologic Time.   310
    pp. Amsterdam, Elsevier.
GARTNER, S. and J. KEANY.   1978.   The terminal Cretaceous
    event: a geologic problem with an oceanographic solution.
    Geology. 6:708-712.
GLASS, B. P. and J. R. CROSBIE.   1982.   Age of Eocene/Oligocene
    boundary based on extrapolation from North American micro-
    tektite layer. Geology. 66:471-476.
GOULD, S. J.   1977.   Ever Since Darwin. 285 pp. W. W. Norton,
    New York.
HALL, C. A.   1964.   Shallow water marine climates and molluscan
    provinces. Ecology. 45:226-234.
HALLAM, A.   1969.   Faunal realms and facies in the Jurassic.
    Palaeontology. 12:1-18.
HALLAM, A.   1971.   Provinciality in Jurassic faunas in relation
    to facies and palaeogeography. Geological Journal Special
    Issue. 4:129-152.
HALLAM, A.   1977.   Jurassic bivalve biogeography.
    Paleobiology. 3:58-73.
HALLAM, A.   1978.   Eustatic cycles in the Jurassic.
    Palaeogeography, Palaeoclimatology, Palaeoecology. 23:1-
    32.
HALLAM, A.   1981a.   Facies Interpretation and the Stratigraphic
    Record. 291 pp. W. H. Freeman, San Francisco.
HALLAM, A.   1981b.   The end-Triassic bivalve extinction event.
    Palaeogeography, Palaeoclimatology, Palaeoecology. 35:1-
    44.
HAMBREY, M. J. and A. B. HARLAND.   1981.   Earth's Pre-
    Pleistocene Glacial Record. Cambridge. Cambridge Univer-
    sity Press. 1004 pp.
HICKEY, L. J.   1980.   Paleocene stratigraphy and flora of the
    Clark's Fork basin. University Michigan Paper in
    Paleontology. 24:33-49.
HICKEY, L. J.   1981.   Land plant evidence compatible with gra-
    dual, not catastrophic, change at the end of the Creta-
    ceous. Nature. 292:529-531.

HICKEY, L. J., R. M. WEST, M. R. DAWSON and D. CHOI. 1983.
    Arctic terrestrial biota: paleomagnetic evidence for age
    disparity with mid-latitude occurrences during the Late
    Cretaceous and early Tertiary. Geological Society of
    America Abstracts with Programs. 15 (North Central Sec-
    tion):249.
HICKMAN, C. S. 1980. Paleogene marine gastropods of the
    Keasey Formation of Oregon. Bulletins of American
    Paleontology. 78:1-112.
HOUSE, M. R. 1975a. Facies and time in Devonian tropical
    areas. Yorkshire Geological Society Proceedings.
    40:233-287.
HOUSE, M. R. 1975b. Faunas and time in the marine Devonian.
    Yorkshire Geological Society Proceedings. 40:459-488.
JABLONSKI, D. 1982. Marine regressions and mass extinctions:
    species-area effects are not enough. Geological Society
    of America Abstracts with Programs. 14:521.
JABLONSKI, D. (in press). Marine regressions and mass extinc-
    tions: a test using the modern biota. In J. W. Valen-
    tine, ed., Phanerozoic Diversity Patterns: Profiles in
    Macroevolution. American Association for the Advancement
    of Science and Princeton University Press.
JENKYNS, H. C. 1980. Cretaceous anoxic events: from con-
    tinents to oceans. Journal of the Geological Society of
    London. 137:171-188.
KAUFFMAN, E. G. 1979. The ecology and biogeography of the
    Cretaceous - Tertiary extinction event. Pp. 29-37. In
    Birkeland, T. and R. G. Bromley, eds., Cretaceous/Tertiary
    Boundary Events. Vol. 2. Univ. of Copenhagen.
KAY, E. A. 1979. Hawaiian Marine Shells. 653 pp. Honolulu,
    Bishop Museum Press.
KEEN, A. M. 1971. Seashells of Tropical West America. 1064
    pp. Stanford, California, Stanford University Press.
KEIGWIN, L. E. 1978. Pliocene closing of the Isthmus of
    Panama, based on biostratigraphic evidence from nearby
    Pacific Ocean and Caribbean sea cores. Geology. 6:630-
    634.
KELLER, G. 1982. Eocene-Oligocene: a time of transition.
    American Association of Petroleum Geologists Bulletin.
    67:494.
KOLLMANN, H. A. 1979. Distribution patterns and evolution of
    gastropods around the Cretaceous/Tertiary boundary. Pp.
    83-87. In Birkeland, T. and R. G. Bromley, eds.,
    Cretaceous/Tertiary Boundary Events. Vol. 2. Univ. of
    Copenhagen.
LOCHMAN, C. and D. DUNCAN. 1944. Early Upper Cambrian faunas
    of central Montana. Geological Society of America Special
    Paper. 54:1-179.

LOUTIT, T. S., G. R. BAUM and R. C. WRIGHT. 1983. Eocene-
    Oligocene Sea Level Changes as Reflected in Alabama
    Outcrop Sections. American Association of Petroleum
    Geologists Bulletin. 67:506.
MacARTHUR, R. H. and E. O. WILSON. 1963. An equilibrium
    theory of insular zoogeography. Evolution. 17:373-387.
MacARTHUR, R. H. and E. O. WILSON. 1967. Island Biogeography.
    Princeton University Press Monographs in Population Biol-
    ogy. 1, 203 pp.
MARASTI, R. and S. RAFFI. 1980. Extinction of polysyringian
    bivalves in the Mediterranean Pliocene. University degli
    Studi, Parma. Volume Dedicato a Sergio Venzo, pp. 107-
    115.
McGHEE, G. R. 1982. The Frasnian-Famennian extinction event:
    a preliminary analysis of Appalachian marine ecosystems.
    Geological Society of America Special Paper. 190:491-500.
McINTYRE, A., N. G. KIPP, A. W. H. BÉ, J. V. GARDNER, W. PRELL
    and W. F. RUDDIMAN. 1976. Glacial North Atlantic 10,000
    years ago: a CLIMAP reconstruction. Geological Society
    of America Memoir. 45:43-76.
McWILLIAMS, M. O. and M. W. McELHINNY. 1980. Late Precambrian
    paleomagnetism of Australia: the Adelaide Geosyncline.
    Journal of Geology. 88:1-26.
MILLER, K. G.. 1983. Paleogene bathymetry and oceanography of
    deep-sea benthic Foraminifera from the Atlantic Ocean.
    American Association of Petroleum Geologists Bulletin.
    67:515-516.
MONECHI, S. 1979. Variations in nannofossil assemblage at the
    Cretaceous/Tertiary boundary in the Bottaccione section
    (Gubbio, Italy). Pp. 164-169. In Birkeland, T. and R. G.
    Bromley, eds. Cretaceous/Tertiary Boundary Events. Vol.
    2. University of Copenhagen.
NESS, G. E. 1983. Comment on "Oligocene calibration of the
    magnetic polarity time scale". Geology. 11:429-431.
NEWELL, N. D. 1952. Periodicity in invertebrate evolution.
    Journal of Paleontology. 26:371-385.
NEWELL, N. D. 1963. Paleontological gaps and geochronology.
    Journal of Paleontology. 36:592-610.
NEWELL, N. D. 1967. Revolutions in the history of life.
    Scientific American. 208:76-92.
OLSSON, A. A. 1961. Mollusks of the Tropical Eastern Pacific
    Region, Panamic-Pacific Pelecypoda. 547 pp. Ithaca, New
    York, Paleontological Research Institute.
OLSSON, R. K., K. G. MILLER and T. E. UNGRADY. 1980. Late
    Oligocene transgression of middle Atlantic coastal plain.
    Geology. 8:549-554.
PALMER, A. R. 1965. Biomere--a new kind of biostratigraphic
    unit. Journal of Paleontology. 39:149-153.
PALMER, A. R. 1979. Biomere boundaries re-examined.
    Alcheringa. 3:33-41.

PEDDER, A. E. H. 1982. The rugose coral record across the
    Frasnian/Famennian boundary. Geological Society of
    America Special Paper. 190:485-489.
PERCH-NIELSEN, K. 1979. Calcareous nannofossil zonation at
    the Cretaceous/Tertiary boundary in Denmark. Pp. 115-135.
    In Birkeland, T. and R. G. Bromley, eds.
    Cretaceous/Tertiary Boundary Events. Vol. 1. University
    of Copenhagen.
PERCIVAL, S. F. and A. G. FISCHER. 1977. Changes in calcare-
    ous nannoplankton in the Cretaceous. Tertiary biotic
    crisis at Zumaya, Spain. Evolutionary Theory. 2:1-35.
POMEROL, C. 1982. The Cenozoic Era: Tertiary and Quaternary.
    Chichester, Ellis Horwood Limited.
PRESTON, F. W. 1962. The canonical distribution of commonness
    and rarity. Part I. Ecology. 43:185-215; Part II.
    43:410-432.
PRIMOLI-SILVA, I. 1977. Biostratigraphy. In Arthur, M. A. et
    al. Geological Society of America Bulletin. 88:371-374.
PROTHERO, D. R., C. R. DENHAM and H. G. FARMER. 1982. Oligo-
    cene calibration of the magnetic polarity time scale.
    Geology. 10:650-653.
RAUP, D. M. and SEPKOSKI, J. J., JR. 1982. Mass extinctions
    in the marine fossil record. Science. 215:1501-1503.
RAUP, D. M. and SEPKOSKI, J. J., JR. (in press) Periodicity
    of extinctions in the geologic past. Proceedings of the
    National Academy of Sciences. (U.S.A.).
ROSENKRANTZ, A. 1960. Danian Mollusca from Denmark. Report
    International Geological Congress. 21 (Copenhagen).
    Sess. Norden Pt. V. The Cretaceous-Tertiary Boundary:
    193-198.
SCHOPF, T. J. M. 1974. Permo-Triassic extinctions: relation
    to sea-floor spreading. Journal of Geology. 82:129-143.
SCHOFP, T. J. M. 1979. The role of biogeographic provinces in
    regulating marine faunal diversity through geologic time.
    Pp. 449-457. In: Historical Biogeography, Plate
    Tectonics, and the Changing Environment. Gray, J. and A.
    J. Boucot, eds. Corvalis, Oregon, Oregon State Univ.
    Press.
SCHOFP, T. J. M., J. B. FISHER and C. A. F. SMITH. 1977. Is
    the marine latitudinal diversity gradient merely another
    example of the species area curve? Pp. 365-386. In:
    Battaglia, B. and J. A. Beardmore, eds., Marine Organisms:
    Genetics, Ecology, and Evolution. New York, Plenum Press.
SCHUCHERT, C. 1914. The delimitation of the geologic periods
    illustrated by the paleogeography of North America. 12th
    International Geological Congress, Canada. Compte Rendu,
    pp. 555-591.
SCHUCHERT, C. 1916. Correlation and chronology in geology on
    the basis of paleogeography. Geological Society of
    America Bulletin. 27:491-514.

SCHUCHERT, C. 1926. Stille's analysis and synthesis of the
    mountain structures of the earth. American Journal of
    Science, Ser. 51. 12:277-292.
SCOTESE, C. F., R. K. BAMBACH, C. BARTON, R. Van der VOO and A.
    M. ZIEGLER. 1979. Paleozoic base maps. Journal of
    Geology. 87:217-277.
SEPKOSKI, J. J., JR. 1982. Mass extinctions in the Phanero-
    zoic oceans. A review. Geological Society of America
    Special Paper. 190:283-289.
SHACKELTON, N. J. and J. P. KENNETT. 1975. Paleotemperature
    history of the Cenozoic and the initiation of Antarctic
    glaciation: oxygen and carbon isotope analyses in DSDP
    Sites 277, 279, and 281. Initial Reports of the Deep Sea
    Drilling Project (U. S. Govt. Printing Office, Washington,
    D. C.) 29:743-755.
SHEEHAN, P. M. 1973. The relation of Late Ordovician glacia-
    tion to the Ordovician-Silurian changeover in North Ameri-
    can brachiopod faunas. Lethaia. 6:147-154.
SHEEHAN, P. M. 1975. Brachiopod synecology in a time of
    crisis (Late Ordovician - Early Silurian). Paleobiology
    1:205-212.
SHEEHAN, P. M. 1982. Brachiopod macroevolution at the
    Ordovician-Silurian boundary. Third North American
    Paleontological Convention Proceedings. 2:477-481.
SIMBERLOFF, D. 1974. Permo-Triassic extinction: effects of
    area on biotic equilibrium. Journal of Geology. 82:267-
    274.
SKEVINGTON, D. 1974. Controls influencing the composition and
    distribution of Ordovician graptolite faunal provinces.
    Palaeontological Association Special Paper in
    Palaeontology. 13:59-73.
SMIT, J. 1982. Extinction and evolution of planktonic Foram-
    inifera after a major impact at the Cretaceous/Tertiary
    boundary. Geological Society of America Memoir.
    190:329-352.
SOHL, N. F. 1971. North American Cretaceous biotic provinces
    delineated by gastropods. Proceedings of the North
    American Convention, Sept. 1969. Part I: 1610-1638.
STANLEY, S. M. 1975. Ideas on the timing of metazoan diver-
    sification. Paleobiology. 2:2009-219.
STANLEY, S. M. 1976. Fossil data and the Precambrian-Cambrian
    evolutionary transition. American Journal of Science.
    276:56-76.
STANLEY, S. M. 1979. Macroevolution: Pattern and Process.
    332 pp. San Francisco, W. H. Freeman.
STANLEY, S. M. 1982. Species selection involving alternative
    character states: an approach to macroevolutionary
    analysis. Third North American Paleontological Convention
    (Montreal) Proceedings. 2:505-510.

STANLEY, S. M. (in preparation) Regional cooling and the
    Plio-Pleistocene mass extinction of Western Atlantic
    Mollusca.
STANLEY, S. M., W. O. ADDICOTT and K. CHINZEI. 1980. Lyellian
    curves in paleontology: possibilities and limitations.
    Geology. 8:422-426.
STANLEY, S. M. and L. D. CAMPBELL. 1981. Neogene mass extinc-
    tion of Western Atlantic molluscs. Nature. 293:457-459.
STANTON, T. W. 1920. The fauna of the Cannonball marine
    member of the Lance Formation. United States Geological
    Survey Professional Paper. 128-a:1-60.
STITT, J. H. 1977. Late Cambrian and earliest Ordovician tri-
    lobites, Wichita Mountains Area, Oklahoma. Oklahoma
    Geological Survey Bulletin. 124:1-79.
STOKES, R. B. 1979. Analysis of the ranges of spatangoid
    echinoid genera and their bearing on the
    Cretaceous/Tertiary boundary. Pp. 78-82, In Birkeland, T.
    and R. G. Bromley, eds. Cretaceous-Tertiary Boundary
    Events. Vol. I. Univ. of Copenhagen.
SURLYK, F. 1979. Guide to Stevens Klint. Pp. 164-170. In
    Birkeland, T. and R. G. Bromley, eds. Cretaceous/Tertiary
    Boundary Events, Vol. I. Univ. of Copenhagen.
TAPPAN, H. 1980. The paleobiology of plant protists. San
    Francisco, W. H. Freeman.
TAYLOR, M. E. 1977. Late Cambrian of Western North America:
    trilobite biofacies, environmental significance, and bios-
    tratigraphic implications. Pp. 397-425 in Kauffman, E. G.
    and J. E. Hazel, eds. In Concepts and Methods of
    Biostratigraphy. Stroudsburg, Pennsylvania, Dowden,
    Hutchinson, and Ross.
THIERSTEIN, H. R. and W. H. BERGER. 1978. Injection events in
    ocean history. Nature. 276:461-466.
TURNER, D. L., U. A. FRIZELL, D. M., TRIPLEHORN, and C. W.
    NAESER. 1983. Radiometric dating of ash partings in coal
    of the Eocene Puget Group, Washington: Implications for
    paleobotanical stages. Geology. 11:527-531.
VAIL, P. R., J. HARDENBOL and R. G. TODD. (in press) Jurassic
    unconformities, chronostratigraphy and sea-level changes
    from seismic stratigraphy and biostratigraphy. American
    Association of Petroleum Geologists Memoir.
VAIL, P. R., R. M. MITCHUM and S. THOMPSON. 1977. Global
    cycles of relative changes of sea level. American
    Association of Petroleum Geologists Memoir. 26:83-97.
VAKHRAMEEV, V. A. 1981. Pollen Classopolis: Indicator of
    Jurassic and Cretaceous climates. The Palaeobotanist.
    28-29:301-307.
VALENTINE, J. W. 1961. Paleoecologic molluscan geography of
    the California Pleistocene. University of California
    Publications in Geological Science. 34:309-442.

VALENTINE, J. W. and E. M. MOORES. 1970. Plate-tectonic regu-
     lation of faunal diversity and sea level: a model.
     Nature. 228:657-659.
VAN VALEN, L. and R. E. SLOAN. 1977. Ecology and the extinc-
     tion of the dinosaurs. Evolutionary Theory. 2:37-64.
VIDAL, G. and A. H. KNOLL. 1982. Radiations and extinctions
     of plankton in the late Proterozoic and early Cambrian.
     Nature. 297:57-60.
VOIGT, E. 1981. Critical remarks on the discussion concerning
     the Cretaceous-Tertiary boundary. Newsletters on
     Stratigraphy. 10:92-114.
WARD, P. D. and J. WIEDEMANN. 1983. The Maastrichtian ammon-
     ite succession of Zumaya, Spain. In Birkeland, T., ed.
     Abstracts, Symposium on Cretaceous Stage Boundaries.
     Copenhagen, University of Copenhagen.
WATERHOUSE, J. B. 1971. The Permian-Triassic boundary in New
     Zealand and New Caledonia and its relationship to world
     climatic changes and extinction of Permian life. Canadian
     Society of Petroleum Geologists. 2:445-464.
WISE, K. P. and T. J. M. SCHOPF. 1981. Was marine faunal
     diversity in the Pleistocene affected by changes in sea
     level? Paleobiology. 7:394-399.
WOLFE, J. A. 1978. A paleobotanical interpretation of Terti-
     ary climates in the Northern Hemisphere. American
     Scientist. 66:694-703.
WOLFE, J. A. 1981. A chronologic framework for Cenozoic
     Megafossil Floras of northwestern North America and its
     relation to marine geochronology. Geological Society of
     America Special Paper. 184:39-47.
ZINSMEISTER, W. J. 1982. Late Cretaceous - early Tertiary
     molluscan biogeography of the southern circum-Pacific.
     Journal of Paleontology. 56:84-102.

EXTINCTION IN HOMINID EVOLUTION

Alan Walker

INTRODUCTION

For a number of years there was a debate over the fate of
the robust species of Australopithecus. The single species
hypothesis, espoused by Brace (1967) and Wolpoff (1971), survived as late as 1976, when decisive evidence of two contemporaneous species of hominid was found (Leakey and Walker
1976). It became clear then that in East Africa at least, Homo
erectus and Australopithecus robustus (or A. boisei for those
who prefer it) were contemporaneous from at least 1.6 my to
about 1 my. Since H. erectus survived in both Africa and Asia,
and since that species is believed to be the one immediately
antecedent to our own, A. robustus must have become extinct.
Before leaving the single species hypothesis, it is instructive
to look at its premises.

As most clearly spelled out, the single species hypothesis
depends on the assumption that the primary hominid adaptation
is a dependence upon culture. Most basic hominid adaptations,
such as bipedal locomotion, reduced canine teeth, delayed physical maturity and increasingly complex behaviors and central
nervous system, were explained by this assumption. Tool use,

as one part of culture, enabled the early hominids to expand
into open country environments. Coupling this idea with Gauss'
(1950) competitive exclusion hypothesis led to the view that
there could never be more than one species of hominid at any
one time, because the dependence upon culture would make one
very broad niche such that competition would be inevitable and
no new species could possibly become established. The single
species hypothesis is false, but its falsification came from
new empirical evidence. Nevertheless, I do feel that competition has been a very important factor in human evolution. But
it was competition within the guild (Root 1967) of large carnivores, which at least our own ancestors joined, rather than
between hominid species.

HOMINID PHYLOGENY

I shall deal here only with the East African fossil
record. There are important hominid fossils in South Africa,
but despite some progress they have not yet been reliably dated
and that makes it difficult to include them in this account.
Figure 1 is a simplified phylogeny. Prior to about 2 million
years ago, hominids are represented in the East African record
as species of Australopithecus. Fossils from Laetoli and Hadar
have been placed in A. afarensis (Johanson, White and Coppens
1978, Johanson and White 1979) though not without opposition
(Tobias 1980). It has also been suggested that among the
material from Hadar, which is about three-quarters of a million
years later than the Laetoli hominids, there may be more than
one species represented (Leakey and Walker 1980). This issue
is not important here.

Out of this or these ancestral species of Australopithecus
arose two new species a little before 2 million years ago. One
of these is characterized by hypertrophy of the premolars and
molars, but not of the anterior teeth, and by gorilla-sized

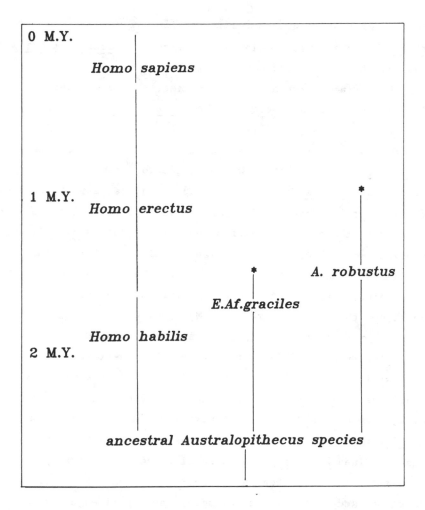

FIGURE 1. Simplified phylogeny of hominids. Asterisks mark extinctions. Note that the existence of a separate lineage of gracile hominids is disputed.

cranial capacities - the robust Australopithecus. In East Africa this species has been seen sometimes as both the same as and as distinct from the South African robust Australopithecus and has been given either the name A. boisei or A. robustus. There are good points to be made on both sides of this minor taxonomic question, but since there only seems to be one species present in either area, I shall call them both $\underline{A}$. robustus - the first-named species of robust Australopithecus. The robust species persisted until about 1 million years ago.

Appearing at roughly the same time, and very plausibly derived from a less specialized Australopithecus than $\underline{A}$. robustus, is Homo (or Australopithecus) habilis. I prefer to reserve the generic name Homo for those species, H. erectus and H. sapiens, about which no worker seems to disagree. In the case of H. habilis, even the type specimen has been the subject of argument (Robinson 1965, LeGros Clark 1967). While everyone accepts that a distinct species that can be called habilis was present around 2 million years ago, a telling point is that their hypodigms are often not the same. This seems to be a case in which we do not have enough evidence to answer all the questions that might be raised. My view, which of course uses my hypodigm, is that the species is a large-brained Australopithecus and further that it is large-brained only because it is large in body size. Since I am in a minority, I shall use H. habilis here, for the sake of clarity. In any case, I am not in disagreement with the others who feel that H. habilis is a perfectly good intermediate species between some small-brained Australopithecus species and H. erectus. The robust species persisted until about 1 million years ago. I have included in my simple phylogeny another lineage which I have called East African gracile Australopithecus. My evidence for this extra species includes some very well preserved fossils, including crania, but since I have not been able to convince my skeptics, I obviously do not have enough evidence to settle the issue. If I am right, there was a third species, approaching in characteristics the ancestral Australopithecus condition, which persisted until about 1.5 million years ago.

Homo erectus appears in East Africa about 1.6 million years ago. It survived, relatively unchanged except in size,

for more than a million years. It also was the first hominid
to leave Africa. No Australopithecus fossils have yet been
found outside of Africa, despite some claims (Robinson 1978).

H. sapiens appears late in the fossil record, probably no
earlier than about 200,000 years ago. Anatomically-modern
humans appeared quite suddenly about 40,000 years ago.
Strange-looking archaic H. sapiens, the Neandertals, are
present in Europe and the Near East from about 130,000 years
ago to about 35,000 years ago. There have been great debates
in the past about the fate of the Neandertals. How they became
extinct was once a big issue in paleoanthropology. It seems
that this issue is not now of great concern, and instead people
are fashionably disposed to look at this for evidence of one
type of evolutionary mode or another. The climate of three
years ago can be summarized by the following quotation.

"Do any paleoanthropologists believe that no European
Neandertal populations contributed genetically to the later
populations living in the same area? Do any suggest that all
Neandertal populations gave rise to later populations? When
the positions are stated in this extreme way, the answer to
both questions is really ´no´." Wolpoff (1980) p. 289.

That, then, is a brief and simplified narrative of the
human evolutionary story. In order to understand the extinction of the robust Australopithecus, I wish to look at some
broader aspects of hominid evolutionary biology. Among these
are the following: rates of evolution, for one rapidly-
evolving species might have affected other members of the community; whether one can tell if two extinct species were sympatric or not; what the trophic levels of the hominids were,
because the archaeological record alone tells us that at least
one hominid species changed its level; and since that species
became more carnivorous, what was the status of the other large
carnivores at the same time?

RATES OF EVOLUTION

   In order to look at the first aspect, that of rates of
evolution within the presumed hominid lineages, I have chosen
to use a method of shape analysis that has its virtues but,
like any method, its own problems. It is quite common today
for morphologists to use multivariate methods, where several
measurements are taken and analyzed statistically to give estimates of difference of one sort or another. In some cases the
reader is asked at the end of the statistical manipulation to
examine a set of curves to see which are the closest (Oxnard
1975). This seems to me to be presenting the reader with a
substitute shape choice. I would rather make a choice between
the shapes of, say, skulls (which I know something about) than
between a set of sine-cosine curves from -Pi to +Pi on a mul-
tidimensional display of a canonical analysis based upon the
same skulls.

   I have applied the method used here to only two major
skull profiles. Any conclusions must be taken in that light.
However, since I suspect these two profiles make up a great
deal of our perception of a cranium, and since many fossil
specimens are missing the facial skeleton, the method probably
has some utility. Casts of fossil hominids were positioned
with their midlines either parallel to or normal to a standard
plane. A vertical sheet of paper was placed a set distance
behind this plane and a slide projector placed some 50 feet in
front of the specimen so that its light rays were as nearly
parallel as possible. Tracings were taken of the shadows
thrown on the paper. These tracings were then digitized using
a Hewlett-Packard 9874A digitizer controlled by a 9845B mini-
computer. Because of accuracy and speed of recording, only 20
points along the profiles were recorded for this study. For
the sagittal profiles, the most forward and most backward pro-
jections of the calvaria were used as the reference points. An

imaginary line between these two points was taken as the ordinate and the measured points along the profile recorded as cartesian coordinates. The distance between the minimum and maximum values on the ordinate was standardized, i.e., all calvarial lengths were made equal. A curve was then fitted through these points using a cubic spline-fit function (Greville 1969). After this, 200 cartesian coordinates were calculated which fitted the spline-fit curve in even increments along the ordinate. For the coronal profiles, the same procedure was followed, but the sagittal plane was the ordinate, the minimum value of x being the vertex of the profile and the maximum the tip of the mastoid process. Thus sagittal profiles began and ended with zero y values, but coronal ones only began with them. A sample of 20 modern H. sapiens was used. It included 12 from a fairly recent archeological site in Iran, one North American and one South American Indian and the rest from dissecting room cadavers.

At this point it is necessary to deal with the question of homology. It is true that the maximum forward projection of the calvaria may not represent the "same" part of the skull in all individuals, although the tightness of the plots for the rather disparate H. sapiens sample suggests that this is not a major problem. I did check, on a series of 40 recent Kikuyu skulls, whether the more usual homologous points (nasion, bregma, lambda and opisthocranion) would give more accurate or more useful information. In the Kikuyu sample the sagittal arc lengths on the three major calvarial bones between these homologous points were not significantly correlated with each other. This means that in an individual skull, the length of one of the cranial vault bones does not predict the length of each of the other two. The length of any one of the bones was significantly correlated with the total (i.e., summed arc length) from nasion to opisthocranion, but the standard errors of the regression were very large (see table 1). Simply put, I think this demonstrates that as far as the structural capability of the brain-case is concerned, it does not matter whether the frontal makes up more than its usual share or not as long as the needed volume is achieved. It would appear, then, than the use of these standard landmarks, which are homologous in terms of ossification centers, is likely to be equally misleading.

The shape analysis data were used in three ways. First, a purely visual representation was made by plotting mean or individual curves over each other or plotting envelopes within which all profiles of one species fell (figs. 2 and 3). This shows, for example, that the profiles of the best-known H. habilis cranium (Kenya National Museum ER 1470) are extremely close to the Australopithecus mean curves (fig. 4). One

TABLE 1. Correlation matrix for least-squares regression analysis of Kikuyu crania (correlation coefficients and signifcance levels).

	Nasion-Bregma	Bregma Lambda	Lambda-Opistho	Total Arc L
Nasion-Bregma	--	.3954 (n.s.)	.1820 (n.s.)	.6228 (p<.001)
Bregma-Lambda		--	.1317 (n.s.)	.7490 (p<.001)
Lambda-Opisthocranion			--	.6499 (p<.001)
Total Arc Length (Nasion-Opisthocranion)				--

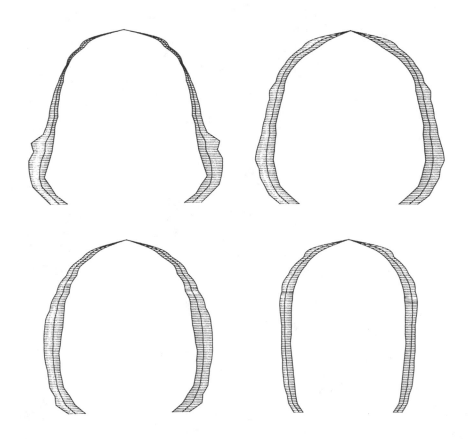

FIGURE 2. Coronal shape plots showing envelope enclosing
maximum and minimum points and mean profiles. Upper left
Australopithecus; Upper right H. erectus; Lower left
Neanderthals; Lower right H. sapiens (20 modern crania). All
to same vertex-mastoid length.

cranium, which I consider to be an East African gracile (Kenya
National Museum ER 1813), is extremely close to the
Australopithecus and much farther from the H. erectus mean
curves. This at least confirms my own prejudice. Of more
relevant interest here is that the H. erectus specimens from
East Lake Turkana fall within the shape envelope for the later
members of the species, indicating that in these two profiles
at least there was over a million years of stasis (fig. 4). Of

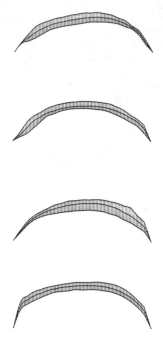

FIGURE 3. Sagittal shape plots showing envelope enclosing maximum and minimum points. Anterior to the left. From top downwards: Australopithecus; H. erectus; Neanderthals; H. sapiens.

great surprise to me was the comparison between the H. erectus and Neandertal means. (The H. erectus sample included crania from Olduvai, Koobi Fora, Java and China, but not Solo, and the Neandertal sample included crania from Spy, Neander, La Chapelle-aux-Saints, Shanidar, Amud, Monte Circeo and Saldahna). These were much more like each other than either was to H. sapiens. It appears that in these profiles, Neandertals, like H. habilis, were large versions of an antecedent species.

The second way the shape data were used was to take all the y values in a comparison, and to calculate the difference between them for each interpolated value of x. It did not matter whether a negative or positive difference was found; either was recorded as percent difference of the maximum value

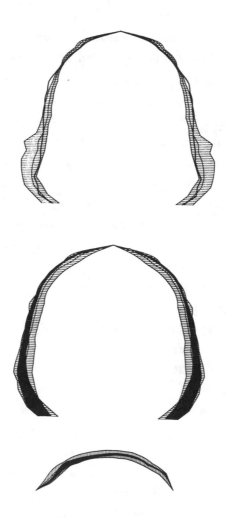

FIGURE 4. Top: Coronal envelope for Australopithecus with
coronal profile of H. habilis (KNM-ER 1470) superimposed in
heavy line. Middle: Coronal envelope for late H. erectus with
envelope for 2 early (Koobi Fora) H. erectus superimposed in
black. Bottom: Sagittal envelope for late H. erectus with
envelope for 2 early (Koobi Fora) H. erectus superimposed in
black.

of x. These differences for the 200 interpolated points were
then treated as a univariate data set and mean differences and
standard deviations calculated. This gives an "average"

difference value between two curves. I do not think that too
much reliability should be placed on the exact numbers given
here, because there are a number of problems with this "average" value that I can think of and there are probably many more
that others can think of. Two of them are these. Both curves
to be compared must start and finish at the same point and
because of the standardization for size, differences are going
to be minimized at the beginning and the end of the profile.
Secondly, two curves of the same "shape" may give a large
difference value because the major features of the shape are
out of phase. In the case of the first problem, I can think of
correction factors, but they are complicated. In the case of
the second I do not feel that it confuses the picture of these
rather simple profiles.

The third way in which the data were used was to determine
where differences were between two profiles (figs. 5 and 6).
This seems most useful in terms of the evaluating the evolution
of cranial shape. If the percent differences are plotted
against their interpolated x values, a difference profile can
be seen. For example, a difference profile which has fairly
even values across the plot shows that the two profiles examined are similar in shape, but one is elevated in height relative to the other. Difference profiles with a series of peaks
and valleys have some regions where they are more and others
where they are less different. Examination of these places on
the original profiles shows which anatomical regions are
responsible for the difference.

The following summary of the rate of evolution in hominids
can be made, bearing in mind that it is only based on the two
major cranial profiles. From the ancestral, rather generalized
Australopithecus species there arose a short-lived large
species, H. habilis. This seems to be a good intermediate both
in size and shape between the ancestral form and H. erectus.

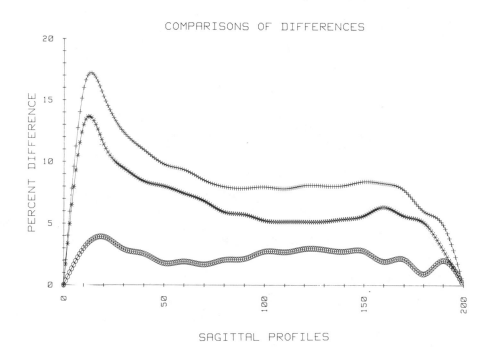

FIGURE 5. Difference profiles based on mean sagittal profiles
for: H. sapiens versus H. erectus (+ - +); H. sapiens versus
Neanderthals (* - *) and Neanderthals versus H. erectus (O -
O). Glabella is at x=0. The two difference profiles which
involve H. sapiens are very similar, showing that Neanderthals
are different from H. sapiens in the same way as H. erectus but
to a lesser degree. Note especially the brow-ridge
differences. The low levels of difference between Neanderthals
and H. erectus can be seen, with minor differences in the brow
and occipital regions.

H. erectus evolved relatively quickly and then survived relatively unchanged for over a million years. Archaic H. sapiens
appear to be what H. habilis was to its ancestor, i.e. a large
version with little shape change. Anatomically-modern humans
appeared with great suddenness about 40,000 years ago, in much
the same rapid way as H. erectus. It is tempting to think that
these two examples show a pattern, where morphologically "new"
species arise after a major size change, but we need more examples before this can be established. For hominid evolution,

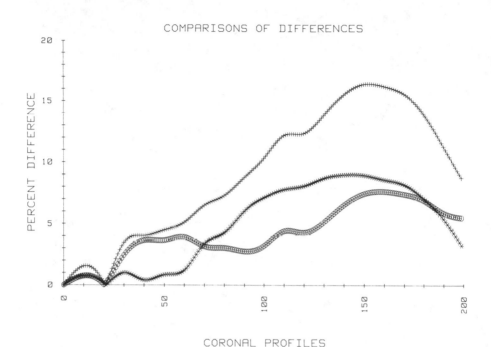

COMPARISONS OF DIFFERENCES

CORONAL PROFILES

FIGURE 6. Difference profiles based on mean coronal profiles. The cranial vertex is at x=0 and the tip of the mastoid process at x=200. Note again the similarity between the two profiles which involve H. sapiens. Greatest differences are seen at the supramastoid regions.

there is another, very important factor which has to be considered. This is that cultural changes were occurring concomitant with the morphological evolution. The appearance of H. habilis coincides almost exactly with the appearance of the earliest record of stone tools, at least in the East Lake Turkana and Omo stratigraphic record (Clark, 1976). The stone industries associated with H. erectus, or from strata laid down when that species was already in East Africa, are more advanced, and are known as Acheulian (Leakey M.D. 1971). In the Olduvai sequence the Acheulian occurs first, immediately above the Lemuta Member of Bed II, which is dated at about 1.6 million years (Hay 1976). At Koobi Fora, the earliest H.

erectus is also dated to about 1.6 million years (Walker et al.
1982). Also present with the Acheulian are many remains of
animals and it is clear that there was a qualitatively different use of animals by upper Bed II times from that which
took place before (Leakey M.D. 1971). Several workers on the
early archaeological sites have now begun to test whether H.
habilis was an active or an occasional hunter or just a
scavenger (Potts 1982, Shipman 1983). The results are not yet
conclusive, but all indications are at present that this
species, which was the first with a stone tool culture, was
mainly a scavenger on animal carcasses left by other predators.
It must be recognized that no large mammal can be only a
scavenger - an alternative food resource is needed (Schaller
and Lowther 1969). Houston (1979) has pointed out that large
mammals are not able to maintain a diet based solely on
scavenging and that all scavenging mammals retain the ability
to kill prey. He showed, however, that many scavenging birds,
particularly vultures, have been able to abandon predation for
clear energetic reasons. In Africa griffon vultures are
thereby the major carnivores, eating over two-thirds of the
available ungulate flesh (Houston 1979). It is most likely,
therefore, that H. habilis had other food sources than
scavenged meat, but what these were will be very difficult to
determine. Later H. erectus, with its different tool kit
appears to have been an efficient predator, an attribute which
some human societies still have today.

SYMPATRY OF SPECIES
     Before considering the other carnivores with which these
early hominids would have been forced to interact, at least
indirectly, I want to make a cautionary note about presumed
sympatry of species. Both fossil carnivores and hominids are
rare in the record. This is for a variety of complex reasons,

one of which is that higher trophic level guilds (Root 1967)
must, for energy transfer reasons, be comprised of much less
biomass than lower ones (Odum 1971). Thus large carnivores
always occur in smaller numbers than the herbivores upon which
they feed. Given this rarity in the record, it is extremely
difficult to show that certain species were sympatric even
though their ranges overlap in geological time. Taphonomic
problems aside, there is a small exercise in paleoecology that
makes this point. It is well known that primary plant productivity is closely correlated with rainfall (Whittaker 1970).
When it comes to mammals that depend upon plants, it might be
expected that their biomass would also be proportional to rainfall, but this is not the case entirely. Using data from Bourliere (1963), the large mammal biomass of several African areas
can be plotted against rainfall (fig. 7). It can be seen that
from desert areas, with little primary plant productivity and
very little large herbivore biomass, to wetter areas, there is
a general trend towards increasing mammalian herbivore biomass.
But when plant productivity is at its highest, the mammalian
herbivore biomas is not (fig. 8). This is because with the
highest rainfall in tropical equatorial forest, much of the
plant biomass is in the form of wood and mammals use this
resource very little. For example, in the Gabon rain forest,
most of the large mammal herbivore biomass is made up of higher
primates. The highest mammalian herbivore biomass is found in
very wet grasslands of the sort present in the Parc Nationale
Albert in Zaire. If we now consider mammalian herbivore
species richness, a different picture emerges. Instead of the
greatest richness coinciding, as one might expect, with the
greatest biomass, the peak is at a lower rainfall level. In
fact it is represented in these data by Nairobi National Park.
The reason for this is, probably, that the wet grasslands of
Zaire are low in numbers of plant species and such homogeneity

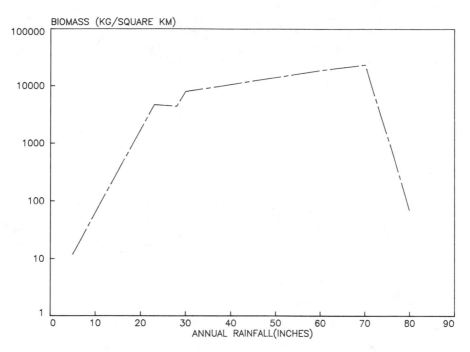

FIGURE 7. Large mammal biomass changes with rainfall (data from Bourliere 1963). Note the general trend towards increased herbivore biomass with higher rainfall. The much lower biomass with the highest rainfall (Ghana) is because plant biomass is mainly in the form of wood, a resource not used much by mammals.

of plant life does not afford much niche partitioning. In the drier, more varied and more seasonal habitat of Nairobi National Park, many more discrete feeding niches are available (fig. 9).

How can we apply this information to the fossil record? We can see that even if East Africa were very much wetter in the past, the large herbivore biomass would not necessarily be higher than it is today, for the point would be reached where forest formation would make it difficult for large herbivores

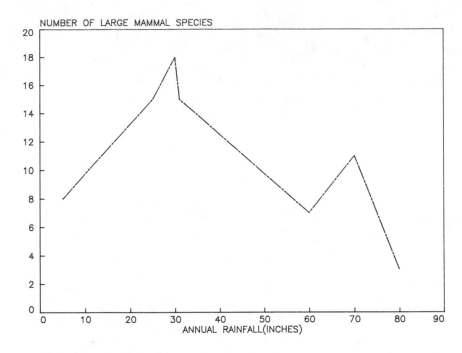

FIGURE 8. African large mammal species richness changes with rainfall. Note that the greatest number of large herbivore species does not coincide with the biomass peak in fig. 7.

to feed in great numbers. Secondly, it seems unlikely that the species richness in the past would have been much greater than the greatest encountered today. Bourliere's data are mostly from virgin areas or from game parks, and although domestic stock are found in some of them, I have included them in the large herbivore numbers. It might easily have been somewhat higher, but not two or three times. The fossil record with which I am most familiar is that from the Plio-Pleistocene of East Lake Turkana. Here the level of stratigraphic resolution, stratigraphic disputes aside, within which fossils can be collected across this vast area is what has been called a

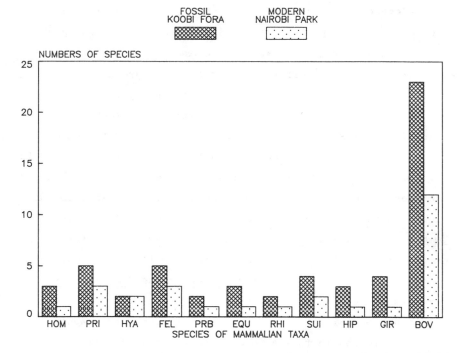

FIGURE 9. Numbers of species of large mammals in Nairobi National Park and one collection unit at Koobi Fora. Abbreviations: HOM-hominids; PRI-cercopithecoid primates; HYA-hyenas; FEL-felids; PRB-proboscideans; EQU-equids; RHI-rhinoceroses; SUI-suids; HIP-hippopotamids; GIR-giraffids; BOV-bovids.

collection unit (Harris 1978). Simply, these are thicknesses of strata that are preceded by a recognizable marker tuff, the base of which marks the beginning of the unit. These units represent several hundred thousand years. Further division of these units by, for example, sediment thickness, seems unwise, since channel and overbank deposits are often intercalated with lacustrine or deltaic sediments and there have been several major and undoubtedly many minor periods of non-deposition or erosion. Thus stratigraphic columns within a collection unit

may be composed of rocks with low or high sedimentation rates
and actually have parts of the sedimentary record missing.
When we compare the numbers of large mammal species from just
one collection unit (Harris 1978) with those present in our
richest modern example, we see that the fossil sample contains
between two and three times as many taxa as the recent one. I
think that the simplest explanation, that there were between
two and three times as many species living in one area then, is
unlikely to be correct for the reasons given above. I think it
much more likely that the sample represents an integration of
mammalian faunas from successive habitats which themselves
"migrated" back and forth over the area where sedimentation was
occurring. If I am right about this, then it is extremely difficult to say that, for example, H. erectus and A. robustus
were sympatric, at least in the sense that they might have seen
each other occasionally. Everything said about the record of
large carnivores in this area must be taken with this caution
in mind.

EVOLUTION OF THE AFRICAN LARGE CARNIVORE GUILD
        It is clear, both from the archeological record and
present day societies, that humans entered the guild of large
carnivores. Ewer (1967) noted that the fossil record showed
changes through time in the composition of the guild and suggested not only that some species were eliminated by competition with others but also that early man might have taken a
direct or indirect role in carnivore extinctions. Klein (1977)
concluded on the basis of frequencies of carnivore and prey
taxa in South Africa:

        "These data indicate that sometime between the early
        Pliocene and the mid-Pleistocene there was a substan-
        tial reduction in the diversity of carnivorous
        species and, if anything, an increase of potential

prey species. It seems likely that the decrease in
carnivore taxa was at least in part due to the
arrival and subsequent evolutionary success of meat-
eating hominids." (Klein 1977: p. 116)

Following them I contend that the species composition of
the large carnivore guild (fig. 10) in East Africa during and
after the period when hominids entered the guild should show
signs of hominid involvement. Others have advocated the use of
behaviors of large carnivores as models with which to elucidate
early human behavior (e.g. Schaller and Lowther 1969, Eaton
1978), but here I am more concerned with the paleoecological
consequences of the entry by an essentially non-carnivorous
species into the guild of large carnivores. Changes might be
expected in the hominid lineage as well as in guild composition.

Million Years B.P.		2	1.5	1	.5	0
Stalking Hunters	4	5	5	3 *	3 *	
Running Hunters	1	2	2	2	2	
Scavengers	1	3 *	2	2	2	

* — includes 1 Hominid

FIGURE 10. The Large Carnivore Guild in East Africa through
geological time (from many sources).

Million Years B.P.	2	1.5	1.0	.5	0
Hyaena hyaena					
Crocuta crocuta					
Euryboas sp.		*			
Homotherium sp.			*		
Megantereon sp.		*			
Dinofelis lineage			*		
Panthera leo					
Panthera pardus					
Panthera crassidens		? *			
Acinonyx lineage					
Lycaon lineage					
Homo habilis					
Homo erectus					

FIGURE 11. Ranges in geological time for large carnivores in East Africa. Asterisks mark extinctions. Panthera crassidens is a disputed taxon in East Africa (from many sources).

Figure 11 gives the ranges in geological time for large mammalian carnivores in East Africa. For a useful summary for the whole of Africa see Brain (1981) based on original research by Ewer (1955, 1956a, 1956b, 1967, 1973), Hendey (1974a, 1974b, 1981) and Hemmer (1965). For East Africa see Howell and Petter (1976), Leakey M. G. (1976) and Savage (1978). For mainly taphonomic reasons, the fossil record of large carnivores from the Plio-Pleistocene is better in South Africa than East Africa. Much of our knowledge of their morphology comes from studies of South African fossils. The early work of Broom (e.g. 1939) was built upon by Ewer (1955, 1956a, 1956b, 1967,

1973) whose works are of seminal importance. The research in
South Africa is now being continued with major contributions by
Hendey (1974a, 1974b, 1981). Given that the fossil record for
these animals is poor, and given the limitations imposed upon
us by being unable to date many sites using present radiometric
and paleomagnetic dating methods, the following picture seems
to emerge.

Several species of stalking hunters were present before
two million years ago. These were three monospecific genera of
sabretooths (Homotherium, Megantereon and Dinofelis). The
first two of these are machairodontines while Dinofelis is a
true feline. All three, however, possessed very elongated
upper canines from which their common name is derived. The two
machairodonts were of different size. Homotherium was about
the size of a lion, with long carnassial teeth and relatively
slender limb bones. Megantereon was about the size of a leopard, with slender upper canines and short, massive forelimbs
and weak hindlimbs. The false sabretooth, Dinofelis (see Hemmer 1965 for taxonomy and phylogeny), was a leopard-sized cat
which was heavily built and short-tailed. It had evolved in
parallel both the cranial and postcranial characteristics of
the machairodontines (Hendey 1974a). A poorly-known species of
large (leopard-lion sized) cat, Panthera crassidens, has some
cranial and post-cranial features reminiscent of the cheetah,
but all authorities seem uncertain about the assignment of
material to this taxon (there are no associated cranial and
postcranial fossils) and its phylogenetic affinities. There
was also one species of cursorial hunter, the running hyena
(Euryboas). This "hunting hyena" is well known from Europe.
It seems to have been (Kurtén 1968) a fast cursor, for it had
long, slender limb bones like the cheetah and teeth not as specialized for bone-crushing as in more typical hyenas. The
ancestry of the modern striped hyena (Hyaena hyaena) can be

traced back as far as 5 million years ago in South Africa (Hendey 1974a) and was established in East Africa in virtually its
modern form by at least three million years ago (Howell and
Petter 1976). Modern striped hyenas are medium-sized, mainly
solitary animals. They are very omnivorous, taking fruit,
invertebrates and small vertebrates as well as large mammal
carrion (Kruuk 1972). They are also the lowest in rank in
interference competition in the modern African large carnivore
guild (Eaton 1979).

An extra stalking hunter, the leopard (Panthera pardus)
and an extra running hunter, the cheetah (Acinonyx jubatus)
appeared during the period from about 2 to 1.6 million years
ago. The leopard, which now has a very wide geographic range,
is a medium-sized, powerfully built stalking hunter. It is
usually nocturnal. Its diet consists mainly of small to
medium-sized ungulates and, in East Africa, it avoids losing
its prey to others by carrying it up trees. The diurnal
cheetah is the fastest terrestrial mammal. It has a number of
postcranial specializations which give it the ability to run
down small to medium-sized ungulates. It does not ambush its
prey or stalk to within leaping distance, but instead begins
its runs from a distance of some 100 m or so. It eats its prey
rapidly and is easily displaced from its kill by other predators. The scavenging hyaena was joined by the spotted hyena
(Crocuta crocuta). This powerful medium-sized carnivore is, in
some circumstances, a very successful predator, but in others
mainly a scavenger (Kruuk 1972). Group composition varies
greatly according to circumstances. It has a peculiar loping
locomotion which it can maintain for great distances when running down prey and jaws and digestive system which enable it to
eat practically every part of a carcass, including the bones.
Most importantly, Homo habilis appeared at this time. A possi-
bles explanation for the increase in scavenging species is that

there was more meat available for scavenging. This can only be
accounted for by an increase in herbivore biomass, which in
turn can only be accounted for by wetter conditions. Both pollen analysis (Bonnefille in Potts 1982) and oxygen isotope
analysis (Cerling et al. 1977) of the sediments at Olduvai show
that early Bed I conditions (about 1.9 million years ago) were
twice as wet as they are today. This would mean at least a
doubling of today's large herbivore biomass which on the
Serengeti Plains stands at 4000 kg/sq km.

At about 1.6 million years ago, there were still 5 stalking hunters in this guild of large predators, but some species
had changed. The lion (Panthera leo) made its appearance.
This is the largest living cat and is capable of taking any
prey weighing less than about 1000 kg (Schaller 1972). Lions
are powerful, mainly nocturnal hunters which stalk their prey
and hunt singly or cooperatively. They are the highest ranking
guild member, not counting humans. Homo erectus had joined
this group, for surely it was a stalking species of hunter, as
men are today. Megantereon and possibly P. crassidens had
become extinct. What I call the East African gracile
Australopithecus became extinct at this time. Also, although
two cursorial hunters were present at this time, there was a
change, in that the running hyena became extinct and the hunting dog (Lycaon) had appeared. Hendey (1973) notes that the
last local running hyena and the earliest South African hunting
dog occur at the Swartkrans site (roughly 1.5 million years old
(White and Harris 1977). The African hunting dog (Lycaon
pictus) is a small-sized animal in this guild. It is, however,
social and almost invariably hunts in packs. Its prey is small
to medium-sized ungulates although scavenging, as with all predators, is common. They do not stalk their prey, but instead
run it down over a long distance, often choosing weak, young or
sick animals (Schaller 1972). The same two scavenging hyenas

were present then and still are today. Hay (1976) reports that
about 1.7 million years go at Olduvai a drier environment (as
judged from the sediments) replaced the former moist one and
that this was climatically and not tectonically controlled.
About one million years ago, or a little before, the only
stalking hunters left were the lion, leopard and H. erectus.
The same two modern running hunters and the same two modern
scavengers were present. The large carnivore guild was, by a
million years ago, completely modern both in composition and
numbers. At the same time as the modern large carnivore guild
became established, the robust Australopithecus became extinct
together with the archaic carnivores.

It appears from this brief overview that periods of hominid speciation and times of extinction are roughly coupled
either with periods of climatic change and the appearance and
disappearance of large carnivore species or both. As Hendey
(1981) has said: "The evolution of specialized carnivores such
as the lion, leopard, cheetah, spotted hyena, and hunting dog
can be ascribed ultimately to the changing environment of the
late Tertiary..." (p. 80). Here I am not concerned with ultimate causes, but only with those that might account for the
extinction of the robust Australopithecus. It is also probably
true that there were associated changes in the composition of
the large herbivore guild and these probably for complex reasons. Following our own presumed lineage first, it seems that
selection acted only to increase body size of some ancestral
Australopithecus and that the newly-formed species began to
scavenge using stone tools at a time when large herbivore
biomass and therefore carcass availability was high. The next
dry period of any major duration saw the advent of a morphologically different hominid (H. erectus) that was, by the evidence
available, a hunting species. Whether or not this was a major
part of early human activity is impossible to say. However,

joining initially the scavengers and later the stalking hunters
would have profound effects on the behavior of the early hominids. Interference competition between members of any large
carnivore guild is high (Eaton 1979). Direct competition for
carcasses results in deaths of carnivores out of proportion to
their numbers. This is seen in carnivores being over-
represented in the bones in other carnivore lairs (Brain 1981).
It has also led, for instance, to the cheetah's unique way of
life. This hunter is the fastest and is highly adapted to
bolting down meat and leaving the scene of the kill. Cheetahs
always fare badly in interactions with other carnivores
(Schaller 1972). It has recently been suggested that H.
habilis had a cheetah-like way of life and that they used stone
tools to remove parts from scavenged carcasses (Potts 1982).
Shipman (1983) has shown that the distribution of hominid cut-
marks from Bed I, Olduvai cannot be distinguished from that of
carnivore tooth marks from the same beds, but both the carnivore and early hominid mark distributions are significantly
different from cut-marks in a Neolithic butchery site. She
also showed that the same was true when the distributions of
marks near joints was analyzed. It seems that these early hominids were not disarticulating carcasses. Recently Shipman
(pers. comm.) has shown that there are overlapping marks from
the oldest levels at Olduvai. Some of these are carnivore
tooth-marks over hominid cuts, indicating carnivores scavenging
from hominids, but the reverse have also been found, showing
that hominids cut bones that had first been chewed by carnivores.

Potts' suggestion that H. habilis may have been cheetah-
like really keeps the analogy to one major aspect of cheetah
behavior, that of processing food quickly. The cheetah is
ranked very low in the modern carnivore guild, almost always
losing its prey to other guild members in interference

competition. Eating quickly and retiring from the carcass is
its main defense against food loss. Eaton (1979), following up
a point made earlier by Schaller and Lowther (1969), tested
whether body size is a good predictor of interspecific rank in
interference competition in carnivores. He found that grouping
behavior severely distorted the predicted ranking based on body
size. Species which always, or under certain circumstances,
formed groups were able to displace individually larger animals
from a kill by outnumbering them. Individual early hominids
would have been ranked lowest in interference competition when
they joined this guild. Either increasing body size or grouping behavior, or both, would have enhanced their ranking. The
hominid fossil record appears to show that body size was
increased at this time (Day et al. 1976). Presence or absence
of grouping behavior is something that appears impossible to
test directly from the fossil record. For large carnivores,
there are several suggested reasons why grouping is advanta-
geous. Schaller and Lowther (1969) listed the following: 1)
it increases hunting success rate, 2) it enables the killing of
larger prey and thereby increases the food resource base, 3)
single animals often have too much food to deal with at a kill
and much gets lost, but a group could totally consume the kill,
4) division of labor is possible between different members (or
sexes or ages) thereby increasing reproductive success, and 5)
it allows increase in rank in competitive interactions. While
all these advantages appear to be real, none of them might have
been the adaptive reason for the origins of grouping behavior.
MacDonald (1983) has recently argued that there are ecological
circumstances of food dispersion in which benefits of grouping
may not be the same as those which come from social grouping,
such as those listed above. He argues that the dispersion of
food resources can itself create situations in which groups of
one species will form and that the many different types of

social groupings and their observed variability in carnivores
are a consequence of interspecific variation in benefits of
group living subsequent to the basic one caused by resource
dispersion. It is likely, since most higher primates have some
sort of grouping behavior, that early hominids would already be
in groups before they entered the large carnivore guild. It is
not as likely, however, that the advantages conferred upon the
ancestral non-carnivorous species by its grouping habits would
carry over once a major change in guild was under way. The
dispersion of resources would be expected to change dramatically and it is probable that the type of grouping would too.

The evidence of butchery sites of large herbivores and of
very large animals (Deinotherium, Hippopotamus) (Leakey M.D.
1971) as well as the size and complexity of Acheulian tools
suggests that H. erectus was an efficient hunter. If so, then
H. erectus must have come into direct or indirect competition
with several large hunting carnivores and have had to deal with
the scavenging animals, particularly the spotted hyena. We
have one tantalizing example suggesting that they did. The
earliest H. erectus at Koobi Fora is the most complete skeleton
known for this species. It is also, however, diseased. It has
been suggested that this was a case of hypervitaminosis A
(Walker et al. 1982). Poisonous doses of vitamin A cannot
easily be obtained from plants, but can result easily from ing-
esting the livers of carnivores. Walker et al. speculated that
this was a result of hominid-carnivore interference competition
over a carcass causing the carnivore's death and subsequent
consumption. This may or may not be true, of course, since in
paleopathology only those presently-known diseases that evoked
the same symptoms in the past are capable of diagnosis.

EXTINCTIONS

If hominids had entered this large carnivore guild in a major way, i.e. relied upon hunting for a large part of their diet, then there must have also been other consequences. We have seen that, for energetic reasons, there cannot be a large biomass of large carnivores. Estimates vary, but they are on the order of 1% of large herbivore biomass (Schaller 1972). Therefore, in moving from the herbivorous to the higher carnivorous trophic level, the population of the species in question must be reduced, if the species is a large one. (This reasoning does not follow for blow-fly larvae or dermestid beetles!) Even if it could altogether displace the existing large carnivores, its population density could only be as high as theirs, given some correlation for body size. For example, if humans completely replaced all the large carnivores on the Serengeti Plain, they would displace only 15 kg of carnivore per sq km (data from Schaller 1972). Thus each 45 kg carnivorous human would require 3 sq km to support himself in that habitat. At the same time, the newly-carnivorous species would now be able to extend its total range, for whereas a herbivore is limited to the plants (and water) to which its physiology is adapted, a carnivorous species is not so limited. It can take its food from various herbivores and by so soing take advantage of the many different herbivore adaptations. This is my explanation for the huge ranges seen today in many carnivore species. For example, the lion ranged all over Africa, the Near East and northern India until 1800 A.D. and the cheetah had an even larger range in historical times (Neff 1982). It is also my explanation for why H. erectus was the first hominid species to migrate from Africa and might lend support to the idea that H. habilis was not an efficient or fully committed hunter. H. erectus continued to occupy much of the Old World until fairly recent advent of H. sapiens.

Taking the robust Australopithecus species, all indications are that it was a herbivore (Walker 1981). It is
interesting that A. robustus arose during a wet period in East
Africa when we have speculated that herbivore biomass on the
plains might have been high. Robust Australopithecus persisted, however, through drier times so apparently the climatic
changes were not a direct cause of the extinction. The only
occurrence coincident with their extinction in this analysis is
the establishment of the modern large carnivore guild when the
last archaic carnivores became extinct. Dramatic direct competition between hominid species does not seem to have
occurred, since the robust Australopithecus persisted for
between a half and three-quarters of a million years after the
first appearance of the hunting Homo erectus. It may have been
that prior to the demise of the archaic carnivores that there
was a partitioning of prey species by the guild which meant
that the modern carnivores, although present, were restricted
to certain prey species or kinds of prey species. Subsequent
upon the extinction of the last archaic carnivores, their pre-
ferred prey species would then have been exposed to the hunting
strategies of the more efficient modern carnivores. This might
have been too much for the robust Australopithecus populations.
I am suggesting here, that as long as their specialized predators survived, this hominid would have been hidden as a prey
item from the modern carnivores by interference competition and
a balanced division of all prey species by the guild. Brain
(1981) in concluding his marvellous account of who were the
hunters and who the hunted in the Sterkfontein Valley caves,
hypothesized that Dinofelis might have been a specialized predator upon primates (including Australopithecus robustus). His
hypothesis, after his enormous amount of evidence had been
carefully considered, still remained in his own word "persuasive". It is unwise, given our present inadequate

knowledge, to speculate exactly what caused this extinction, but perhaps some of the broader paleoecological aspects discussed here will help establish testable hypotheses.

LITERATURE CITED

BOURLIERE, F. 1963. In: F. C. Howell and F. Bourliere. African Ecology and Human Evolution. New York: Wenner-Gren, pp. 43-54.

BRACE, C. L. 1967. The Stages of Human Evolution. Engelwood Cliffs: Prentice Hall.

BRAIN, C. K. 1981. The Hunters or the Hunted? Chicago: University of Chicago Press.

BROOM, R. 1939. A preliminary account of the Pleistocene carnivores of the Transvaal caves. Annals of the Transvaal Museum 19:331-338.

CERLING, T. R., R. HAY, and J. O'NEIL. 1977. Isotopic evidence for dramatic climatic changes in East Africa during the Pleistocene. Nature 267:137.

CLARK, J. D. 1976. In: G.L. Isaac and E. R. McCOWN. Human Origins. Menlo Park: Benjamin, pp. 1-53.

CLARK, W. E. LeGROS. 1967. Man-ape or Ape-men? New York: Holt, Rinehart and Winston.

DAY, M. H., R. E. F. LEAKEY, A. C. WALKER and B. A. WOOD. 1976. New hominids from East Turkana, Kenya. American Journal of Physical Anthropology 45:369-436.

EATON, R. L. 1978. The evolution of trophy hunting. Carnivore 1:110-121.

EATON, R. L. 1979. Interference competition among carnivores: a model for the evolution of social behavior. Carnivore 2:9-16.

EWER, R. F. 1955. Hyaenidae, other than Lycyaena, of Swartkrans and Sterkfontein. Proceedings of the Zoological Society of London 124:815-837.

EWER, R. F. 1956a. The fossil carnivores of the Transvaal caves: Felinae. Proceedings of the Zoological Society of London 126:83-95.

EWER, R. F. 1956b. The fossil carnivores of the Transvaal caves: Canidae. Proceedings of the Zoological Society of London 126:97-119.

EWER, R. F. 1967. In: W. W. Bishop and J. D. Clark. Background to Evolution in Africa. Chicago: University of Chicago Press, pp. 109-123.

EWER, R. F. 1973. The Carnivores. London: Weidenfeld and Nicolson.

GAUSS, G. F. 1950. The struggle for existence. Baltimore: Williams and Wilkins.

GREVILLE, T. N. E. 1969. Theory and Applications of Spline
    Functions. New York: Academic Press.
HARRIS, J. M. 1978. In: M. G. Leakey and R. E. Leakey.
    Koobi Fora Research Project (1). Oxford: Clarendon
    Press, pp. 32-63.
HAY, R. L. 1976. Geology of the Olduvai Gorge. Berkeley:
    University of California Press.
HEMMER, H. 1965. Zur Nomenklatur und Verbreitung des Genus
    Dinofelis Zdansky, 1924. Palaeontologica Africana 9:75-
    89.
HENDEY, Q. B. 1973. The Transvaal Museum´s collection of fos-
    sil carnivores. Bulletin of the Transvaal Museum 14:7.
HENDEY, Q. B. 1974a. The Late Cenozoic Carnivora of the
    south-western Cape Province. Annals of the South African
    Museum 63:1-369.
HENDEY, Q. B. 1974b. New fossil carnivores from the Swart-
    krans australopithecine site. Annals of the South African
    Museum 69:215-247.
HENDEY, Q. B. 1981. Palaeoecology of the Late Tertiary fossil
    occurrences in ´E´ Quarry, Langebaanweg, South Africa, and
    a reinterpretation of their geological context. Annals of
    the South African Museum 84:1-104.
HOUSTON, D. C. 1979. In: A. R. E. Sinclair and M. Norton-
    Griffiths. Serengeti. Chicago: University of Chicago
    Press, pp. 263-286.
HOWELL, F. C. and G. PETTER. 1976. Carnivora from Omo Group
    Formations, Southern Ethiopia. In: Y. Coppens, F. C.
    Howell, G. LI. Isaac and R. E. F. Leakey. Earliest Man
    and Environments in the Lake Rudolf Basin. Chicago:
    University of Chicago Press, pp. 314-331.
JOHANSON, D. C., T. D. WHITE and Y. COPPENS. 1978. A new
    species of the genus Australopithecus (Primates: Homini-
    dae) from the Pliocene of eastern Africa. Kirtlandia
    28:1-14.
JOHANSON, D. C. and T. D. WHITE. 1979. A systematic assess-
    ment of early African hominids. Science 202:321-330.
KLEIN, R. G. 1977. The ecology of early man in Southern
    Africa. Science 197: 115-126.
KRUUK, H. 1972. The spotted hyena. Chicago: University of
    Chicago Press.
KURTÉN, B. 1968. Pleistocene mammals of Europe. London:
    Weidenfeld and Nicolson.
LEAKEY, M. D. 1971. Olduvai Gorge - excavations in Beds I and
    II (1960-1963). Cambridge: Cambridge University Press.
LEAKEY, M. G. 1976. In: Y. Coppens, F. C. Howell, G. LI.
    Isaac and R. E. F. Leakey. Earliest Man and Environments
    in the Lake Rudolf Basin. Chicago: University of Chicago
    Press, pp. 302-313.

LEAKEY, R. E. F. and A. C. WALKER. 1976. Australopithecus, Homo erectus and the single-species hypothesis. Nature 261:572-574.

LEAKEY, R. E. G. and A. C. WALKER. 1980. On the status of Australopithecus afarensis. Science 207:1103.

MACDONALD, D. W. 1983. The ecology of carnivore social behavior. Nature 301:379-384.

NEFF, N. A. 1982. The big cats. New York: Abram.

ODUM, E. P. 1971. Fundamentals of Ecology. Philadelphia: W. B. Saunders.

OXNARD, C. E. 1975. Uniqueness and Diversity in Human Evolution. Chicago: University of Chicago Press.

POTTS, R. B. 1982. Lower Pleistocene Site Formation and Hominid Activities at Olduvai Gorge, Tanzania. Ph.D. Thesis, Harvard University.

ROBINSON, J. T. 1965. Homo "habilis" and the australopithecines. Nature 205: 121-124.

ROBINSON, J. T. 1978. Early Hominid Posture and Locomotion. Chicago: University of Chicago.

ROOT, R. B. 1967. The niche exploitation pattern of the blue-gray gnatcatcher. Ecological monographs 37:317.

SAVAGE, R. G. 1978. In: V. J. Maglio and H. B. S. Cooke. Evolution of African Mammals. Cambridge: Harvard University Press, pp. xx.

SCHALLER, G. 1972. The Serengeti Lion. Chicago: University of Chicago Press.

SCHALLER, G. and G. R. LOWTHER. 1969. The relevance of carnivore behavior to the study of early hominids. Southwestern Journal of Anthropology 25:307-341.

SHIPMAN, P. 1983. In: J. Clutton-Brock and C. Grigson. Animals and Archeology (I): Hunters and Their Prey. London: British Archeological Reports, pp. 31-51.

TOBIAS, P. V. T. 1980. Australopithecus afarensis and A. africanus - critique and an alternative hypothesis. Palaeontologica Africana 23:1-17.

WALKER, A. 1981. Dietary hypotheses and human evolution. Phil. Trans. Roy. Soc. Lond. (B) 292:57-64.

WALKER, A., M. R. ZIMMERMAN, and R. E. F. LEAKEY. 1982. A possible case of hypervitaminosis A in Homo erectus. Nature 296:248-250.

WHITE, T. D. and J. M. HARRIS. 1977. Suid evolution and correlation of African hominid localities. Science 198:13-21.

WHITTAKER, R. H. 1970. Communities and Ecosystems. London: Collier-MacMillan.

WOLPOFF, M. H. 1971. Competitive exclusion among lower Pleistocene hominids. Man 6:601-614.

WOLPOFF, M. H. 1980. Paleoanthropology. New York: Knopf.

CATASTROPHIC EXTINCTIONS AND LATE PLEISTOCENE BLITZKRIEG:

TWO RADIOCARBON TESTS

Paul S. Martin

Faunal extinctions at the end of the Pleistocene are both
highly dramatic and relatively insignificant. They are
dramatic in that hundreds of species of mammals and birds
disappeared; and insignificant compared with earlier mass
extinctions at the end of the Permian and the Cretaceous which
involved considerably more species of organisms and higher
taxa. Nevertheless, the geologically late Pleistocene extinctions are intriguing because they especially involve a group of
large animals taxonomically closest to man himself, the mammals. Radiocarbon dating makes it possible to test for synchroneity of extinction, an event not regarded seriously by
most paleontologists until recently. Current developments in
the geology and ecology of the late Pleistocene extinctions are
found in Martin and Klein (in press).

THE PATTERN OF PLEISTOCENE EXTINCTION

The pattern of loss displays distinctive features: 1) on
the continents mass extinction of the late Pleistocene is limited to the large mammals; 2) beyond the continents on oceanic

islands, land vertebrates of all sizes and in some cases land
snails and other invertebrates were lost in excessive numbers;
3) when dating information is available it appears that continental losses preceded those of the oceanic islands; 4) continents with a long history of human evolution, i.e., Africa
and Asia, suffered a less precipitous extinction of "megafauna"
than land masses reached relatively late by Homo sapiens, i.e.,
the Americas, Australia, and Madagascar; and 5) while archaeological evidence linking prehistoric societies and the extinct
fauna of America is sparse, the first unmistakable evidence of
hunting cultures coincides with the time of maximum extinction
(Martin 1967). Finally, the late Pleistocene extinctions were
diachronous. Australian megamarsupials disappeared many
thousands of years before American mastodonts and ground sloths
while these in turn vanished long before Malagasy giant lemurs.
If dinosaurs were destroyed throughout the globe within a few
years or less, as modeled by the asteroid impact theory
(Alvarez et al. 1980), we can show by radiocarbon dating that
the loss of the late Pleistocene megafauna was much more gradual, at least between different continents.

The pattern I have mentioned strongly suggests a series of
human impacts. Outside the Afro-Asian heartland the initial
arrival of Paleolithic people on large land masses would be
felt by large mammals much more than small mammals. On smaller
oceanic islands other side effects of human colonization such
as introduction of alien fauna, fire, and land clearing would
obliterate endemic species of all sizes. The chronology of
extinction is in close alignment with the prehistoric dispersal
of Homo sapiens. Land masses where humans originated were less
affected by late Pleistocene extinction than those of human
invasion, as one would predict under a gradual as opposed to a
sudden destabilization of prey by prehistoric hunters.
Finally, the archaeological inventory of kill sites yielding

extinct megafauna is sparse or negligible in lands of invasion
such as America, Australia, and Madagascar. This is a key
prediction of the blitzkrieg model, a consequence of a swift
and successful colonization.

The popular view that climatic change was an undeniable
agent of many biotic transformations during the ice age including at least in part, the late Pleistocene extinctions, has
been the main alternative model (Martin and Wright 1967). The
debate between different schools continues (Martin and Klein in
press). A direct test of the blitzkrieg model appears to lie
in the chronology of extinction. If catastrophic human impact,
possibly magnified by a "fifth column" of trophically doomed
large carnivores (Janzen 1983), triggered sudden losses, the
extinctions must be precipitous. If the American extinctions
happened gradually, blitzkrieg can be eliminated and, in the
absence of many cultural associations with extinct fauna, so
can any significant human impact, i.e., overkill.

First it is necessary to reexamine the assertation that
dramatic change in the late Pleistocene of North America was
limited to large mammals. Following Martin (1967) 100 lbs of
adult body weight (44 kg) was taken as the boundary between
"large" and "small" terrestrial mammals and all living and
extinct mammals tabulated by Kurtén and Anderson (1980) were
divided accordingly.

Small mammals north of Mexico include all North American
members of the following four orders: the marsupials, bats,
insectivores, and lagomorphs plus all rodents with the exception of the giant beavers (Procastoroides and Castoroides) and
the capybaras (Hydrochoeridae). The small carnivores include
the mustelids, the procyonids, the canid genera Cuon, Urocyon
and Vulpes, and all species of Canis except C. lupus, C. dirus,
C. rufus, and C. armbusteri. Other large canid genera include
Protocyon and Borophagus. Among the living or extinct felids

all are small except <u>Meganteron</u>, <u>Smilodon</u>, <u>Ischrysosmilus</u>,
<u>Homotherium</u>, <u>Dinofelis</u>, <u>Panthera</u>, <u>Acionyx</u>, and the mountain
lion, <u>Felis</u> <u>concolor</u>.

Orders of the large mammals north of Mexico include the
edentates (except the armadillo, <u>Dasypus</u> <u>novemcinctus</u>), proboscideans, sirenians, odd-toed ungulates, and most of the even-
toed ungulates. The artiodactyls that are smaller than 100 lbs
include living peccaries (<u>Tayassu</u>) and the smaller extinct
pronghorn, <u>Ceratomeryx</u>, <u>Capromeryx</u> and perhaps <u>Stockoceros</u>.
Species within only three genera, <u>Dasypus</u>, <u>Canis</u>, and <u>Felis</u>,
incorporate fossil or living species both larger and smaller
than 100 lbs. A late Pleistocene or Wisconsin (=Wisconsinan)
fauna of seven families, 37 genera, and 78 species disappeared
in North America (see tables 1 and 2). Of these all but four
genera were larger than 100 lbs. The only genus from the late
Pleistocene to suffer extinction that would appear neither to
have been highly desirable prey for early hunters nor a carnivore or scavenger trophically dependent on the megafauna is
the spotted skunk relative, <u>Brachypotoma</u>. Most of the genera
and most of the wide ranging species of mammals that disappeared from North America were large and thus would have been
an attractive size for hunters.

Kurtén and Anderson's (1980) detailed review of North
American Pleistocene mammals makes it possible to examine
Pleistocene appearances (originations) as well as disappearances (extinctions) and to examine the standing diversity (taxonomic richness) during the last three million years. Data
displaying history of faunal change are plotted for nine chronological division of the Plio-Pleistocene, four of Blancan
age, 3.0-1.8 mya, three of Irvingtonian age, 1.8-0.7 mya, and
three of Rancholabrean age, 0.7-0.0 mya (figures 1 and 2). As

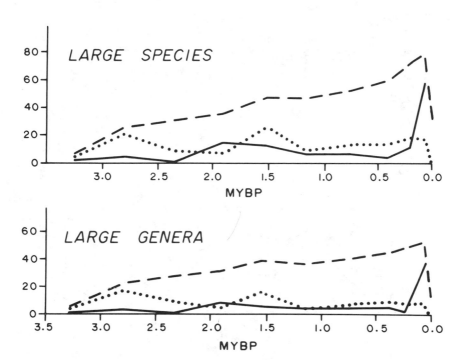

FIGURE 1. Extinction (solid line), origination (dotted line) and standing diversity (dashed line) for large (>100 lbs) mammals of the Plio-Pleistocene; data points plotted from table 1 and derived from Kurtén and Anderson (1980)

Kurtén and Anderson mention, and as one would expect, origina-tions and extinctions occur continually. The question is whether any important departures from "baseline" extinctions (Raup and Sepkoski 1982) are seen. The outstanding event since the Miocene occurred near the end of the Rancholabrean when 37 genera of large mammals vanished from North America, (figure 1, tables 1 and 2). The total of all other large mammal extinc-tions in the previous 3.0 million years is only 20 genera. Even the small mammals, which maintain a higher standing diver-sity at all times (compare figures 1 and 2) do not lose more than 11 genera within a sampling interval (table 1). At the end of the Pleistocene the large mammals were reduced from 51

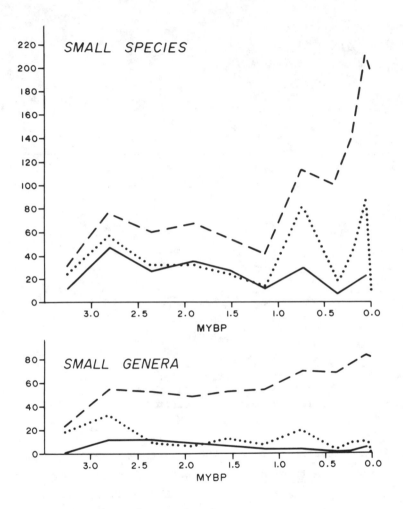

FIGURE 2. Extinction (solid line), origination (dotted line) and standing diversity (dashed line) for small (<100 lbs) mammals of the Plio-Pleistocene; data ponts plotted from table 1 and derived from Kurtén and Anderson (1980).

to 16 genera, fewer than North America had supported at least since the very early Blancan (table 1).

My emphasis on the extinction of large mammals at the end of the Pleistocene does not discount earlier and more severe episodes of mammalian extinction (Savage and Russell 1983) such

as the loss of 60 genera of late Hemphillian land mammals near
the Miocene/Pliocene boundary five million years ago (Webb
1969, in press). The Miocene losses differ in a very important
way from those of the late Pleistocene. Unlike the latter
roughly half of the late Miocene (Hemphillian) genera that
became extinct were small, i.e., under 100 lbs (Martin in
press). In addition, there were important extinctions of large
and small mammals within the late Pliocene and early Pleistocene, long before any possible human intrusion. Thirty genera
of small mammals became extinct in the Blancan (see table 1).

     The Pliocene and early Pleistocene ice age climates may
have severely trimmed Tertiary biotas. For example, excessive
Neogene extinction related to lethal decline of temperatures in
the Plio-Pleistocene is evident among marine molluscs on certain coasts, especially the western Atlantic (Stanley and Campbell 1981). It is worth repeating that the late Pleistocene
loss of land mammals was unaccompanied by any marine extinctions. Mass mammalian extinctions within the last 10 million
years may very well accompany climatic changes in the manner
that Webb (in press) and others have proposed. The same solution could easily be applied to the late Pleistocene if the
losses entailed excessive numbers of small as well as the large
mammals, and if marine life was also affected.

     The use of the genus in extinction analysis may be biased
(see Graham and Lundelius in press). Since many large genera
of Pleistocene mammals were monotypic, extinction of half the
species would mean extinction of half the genera. Within poly-
typic genera, as in the case of many small mammals, the same
number of species extinctions would less often yield extinctions of genera. Kurtén and Anderson (1980, p. 358) also urge
the analysis of extinction of species in preference to genera,
an approach now possible for the Pliocene and Pleistocene, due
to their review and to the work of others.

TABLE 1. Pliocene and Pleistocene mammals of North America. Numbers of originations, extinctions and total fauna (standing diversity) for various divisions of the Pliocene and Pleistocene are plotted from Kurtén and Anderson (1980): E = early; M = middle; L = late; I = Illinoian; S = Sangamon; W = Wisconsin; R = Recent. Small-large size separation set at 100 lbs. (44 kg).

| | Blancan | | | | Irvingtonian | | | Rancholabrean | | | | |
	1	2	3	4	E	M	L	I	S	W	R	Total
SPECIES												
Originations:												
small	24	57	31	31	23	13	81	17	42	86	7	412
large	4	20	9	6	25	8	12	12	17	16	1	130
Total	28	77	40	37	48	21	93	29	59	102	8	542
Extinctions:												
small	11	46	26	36	25	10	29	5	12	21	–	221
large	1	4	0	14	12	5	5	3	10	57	–	111
Total	12	50	26	50	37	15	34	8	22	78	–	332
Standing Diversity:												
small	30	76	61	66	54	40	112	100	139	211	197	
large	5	24	30	36	46	45	51	58	72	79	22	
Total	35	100	91	102	100	85	163	158	211	290	220	
GENERA												
Originations:												
small	18	32	9	6	12	7	19	2	8	9	2	129
large	4	16	8	3	14	2	5	7	5	6	0	71
Total	22	48	17	8	26	9	24	9	12	15	1	197
Extinctions:												
small	–	11	11	8	6	3	3	1	1	4	–	48
large	–	2	0	7	4	2	2	2	1	33	–	53
Total	–	13	11	15	10	5	5	3	2	37	–	101
Standing Diversity:												
small	23	55	53	48	52	53	69	68	75	83	81	
large	5	21	27	30	37	35	38	43	46	51	16	
Total	28	76	80	77	88	87	106	110	119	132	95	

Dividing the Wisconsin species in Kurtén and Anderson's
Appendix into those above or below 100 lbs yields 57 species
extinctions of large mammals and 21 of small mammals (table 2).
Discounting genera, critics of blitzkrieg have seized on the
small mammal species extinctions as discordant with human
impacts as a cause of the extinction (Graham and Lundelius in
press).

However, compared with earlier chronological divisions
(table 1) the loss of Wisconsin age small mammals is not
unusual; it is exceeded by the record of species extinctions in
the Blancan 2, 3, 4, and in the Early and Late Irvington.
Small mammal standing diversity during the Wisconsin was 211
species, ten times the number of extinctions. Small animal
originations in the Wisconsin exceeded the extinctions by 65
species. Finally, none of the extinct small mammals were common or wide-ranging and none can be viewed as hallmarks of the
late Pleistocene, animals whose remains might be expected when-
ever a Pleistocene fauna is analyzed, such as bones of mammoth,
mastodon, extinct horse and camel.

The standing diversity of species of large mammals rose
steadily from 51 in the late Irvingtonian to 58 in the Illinoian, 72 in the Sangamon, 79 in the Wisconsin and dropped by
70% to 22 species in the Recent. For large mammals the loss
was catastrophic. There were fewer large mammals in North
American in the Recent than in any of the earlier division of
the Plio-Pleistocene since the poorly known Blancan 1 (table 1,
figure 1). Whether extinctions are better gauged by the disappearance of species or of genera is irrelevant. Both taxonomic
levels display the same result, a massive loss of large mammals
and a sharp drop in their standing diversity very late in the
Pleistocene (figures 1 and 2, table 1).

Could the late Pleistocene extinctions be the inevitable
outcome of excessive earlier originations with late Pleistocene

TABLE 2. Wisconsin age small and large mammal extinctions. Extinct genera = †; extinct species = *; the vampire genus Desmodus and the dohle, Cuon, the cheeta, Acionyx, the spectacled bear, Tremartos, the capabara, Hydrochoerus, the horses, Equus, the tapir, Tapirus, the antelope, Saiga, and the yak, Bos, withdrew from North America at the end of the Pleistocene and may be viewed continentally as generic extinctions.

Small (<100 lbs)

CHIROPTERA
  Phyllostomatidae
    *Desmodus stocki
  Vespertilionidae
    *Myotis rectidentis
    *M. magnamolaris
    *Plecotus tetralophodon
  Molossidae
    *Tadarida constantinei

CARNIVORA
  Mustelidae
    *Martes nobilis
    *Mustela eversmanni beringiae
    †Brachyprotoma obtusata
  Canidae
    Cuon alpinus
    *Bassariscus sonoitensis
  Felidae
    *Felis amnicola

RODENTIA
  Geomyidae
    *Thomomys orientalis
    *T. microdon
  Cricetidae
    *Peromyscus nesodytes
    *P. anyapahensis
    *P. imperfectus
    *P. cochrani
    *Synaptomys australis

LAGOMORPHA
  Leporidae
    *Sylvilagus leonensis

ARTIODACTYLA
  Antilocapridae
    †Capromeryx minor
    †C. mexicana

Large (>100 lbs)

ENDENTATA
  Dasypodidae
    †Holmesina septentrionalis
    *Dasypus bellus
  Glyptodontidae
    †Glyptotherium floridanum
    †G. mexicanum
  Megalonychidae
    †Megalonyx jeffersonii
  Megatheriidae
    †Eremotherium rusconii
    †Nothrotheriops shastensis
  Mylodontidae
    †Glossotherium harlani

PERISSODACTYLA
  Equidae
    *Equus hemionus
    *E. tau
    *E. giganteus group
    *E. occidentalis
    *E. complicatus
    *E. fraternus
    *E. scotti
    *E. niobrarensis
    *E. conversidens
    *E. lambei
  Tapiridae
    *Tapirus californicus
    *T. copei
    *T. veroensis

CARNIVORA
  Felidae
    †Smilodon fatalis
    †Homotherium serum
    *Panthera leo atrox
    *Acionyx trumani
  Canidae
    *Canis dirus
  Ursidae
    *Tremarctos floridanus
    †Arctodus pristinus

ARTIODACTYLA
  Tayassuidae
    †Mylohyus nasutus
    †Platygonus compressus
  Camelidae
    †Camelops huerfanensis
    †C. hesternus
    †Hemiauchenia macrocephala
    †Palaeolama mirifica
  Cervidae
    †Navajoceros fricki
    †Sangamona fugitiva
    *Alces latifrons
    †Cervalces scotti
  Antilocapridae
    †Tetrameryx shuleri
    †Stockoceros corklingi
    †S. onusrosagris
  Bovidae
    Saiga tatarica
    *Oreamnos harringtoni
    †Euceratherium colinum
    †Symbos cavifrons
    †Bootherium bombifrons
    *Bison priscus
    *B. latifrons
    *Bos grunniens

RODENTIA
  Castoridae
    †Castoroides ohioensis
  Hydrochoeridae
    *Hydrochoerus holmesi
    †Neochoerus pinckneyi

PROBOSCIDEA
  Mammutidae
    †Mammut americanum
    †Cuvieronius sp.
    †Mammuthus jeffersoni
    †M. primigenius

extinctions restoring an equilibrium according to the
MacArthur-Wilson theory (1967) proposed for islands? Gingerich
(in press) explores such a solution and the division of mammals
into large and small groups as shown in figures 1 and 2 and
table 1 offers a test. Since the late Pleistocene extinctions
involve mainly large mammals and the Pliocene-early Pleistocene
originations involve mainly small mammals one must postulate a
long enduring trophic interaction between unrelated animals of
dissimilar size, ending in sudden collapse of the large herbivores. Such a lingering outcome appears ecologically implau-
sible.

       If competition is discounted, climatic change, human
impact, or a combination of these factors may be the main
causes for the events of the late Pleistocene. I believe that
the large extinct mammals were not hunted in the Holocene
because they were already extinct. With rare exceptions
(Frison et al. 1978) Folsom, Hell Gap, Agate Basin, Midland and
younger hunting cultures typically reveal only bison and other
extant species (Stafford 1981, Haynes 1982). By extensive
radiocarbon dating Haynes (1970, in press) dated repeatedly the
stratigraphic contacts between extinct and extant megafauna in
southwestern alluvial sections, and found them to be sudden at
about 11,000 yr BP (figure 3).

TESTING BLITZKRIEG
       Refutations may in turn be falsified, and if archaeologi-
cal evidence emerges that clearly links cultures either before
or after Clovis with the extinct large mammals a model of gradual extinction could be resurrected. At least some Holocene
records of extinct megafauna must be rejected as it appears
that prehistoric people sometimes collected Pleistocene fossils
including mammoth teeth (Wyman 1973, DiPeso et al. 1974, p.
448). Those large mammals commonly found in archaeological

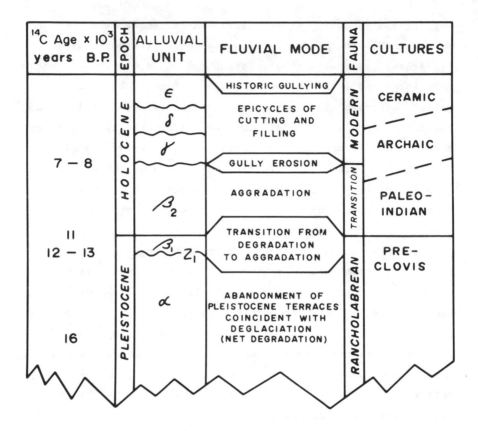

FIGURE 3. Lithostratigraphic, faunal and cultural changes of the last 16,000 years, from Haynes, ms. when available, in primary context in dated sedimentary sections extinct megafauna is known only below unit B_2. The "pre-Clovis" culture is hypothetical.

sites of Holocene age are bison, deer, caribou, mountain sheep, elk, moose, antelope, and other species that survived into modern times. The older record is ambiguous and if prehistoric people were actually in America prior to 12,000 yr BP their foraging activities are ill-defined. Only the mammoth hunters of the 9th millennium BC are well known, stratigraphically if not culturally (Haynes 1982).

Thus, if overkill is to explain the chronosequence, a
model of sudden human impact (blitzkrieg) appears the only
theoretical solution. Ethnographic and other objections have
been raised against the concept of sudden overkill. Webster
(1981, p. 594) concludes that, "It is, fortunately, a
hypothesis susceptible to refutation, and I expect that it will
soon be rejected, at least in its present form..." A direct
refutation can be attempted by radiocarbon dating. The
blitzkrieg model (Mosimann and Martin 1975) entails a sudden
severe impact by the new invaders proceeding in a "bow wave"
from Alaska to Patagonia at an average rate of 160 km per
decade. Local extinctions will follow swiftly and will be
younger to the south. Accordingly, radiocarbon dating of the
extinct fauna should yield refutations of the "blitzkrieg"
model specifically and of catastrophic extinction in general.

Certain limitations of the radiocarbon technique that
might affect interpretations are considered. Radiocarbon calibration of C^{14} samples from wood of known ages indicate that
the uncertainty exceeds "counting" statistics by approximately
115 years for samples older than 6000 years (Klein et al.
1982). Tree ring samples exceeding 8000 years are not yet
available, thus direct calibration of North American Pleistocene extinctions is not possible. The cosmic ray bombardment
"... reaching the earth and producing C^{14} has probably remained
constant to within +10% over the past 50,000 years or more..."
(Klein et al. 1982). For older samples they propose that "an
uncertainty of 1000 years, or the measurement uncertainty
quoted by the laboratory, whichever is larger, would constitute
a reasonable estimate of the uncertainty for the calendric age
of the sample." An International Study Group (1982) suggests
that unexplained experimental variability could be corrected by
multiplying by two or three the quoted errors derived from the
counting procedure.

Thus a single uncontaminated carbon sample from an extinct Pleistocene animal may be burdened by an uncertainty of 1000 years due to potential vagaries in cosmic ray flux. With repeated or replicate sampling the error may be narrowed.

In dating Clovis mammoth sites Haynes (1970, 1982) has sampled charcoal from fire pits or hearths constructed by the early hunters. The association of archaeological charcoal with cultural events, i.e., either hunting or butchering or process- ing of mammoth remains, can be clearly defined. In Southwestern sites such as Lehner (21 dates), Murray Springs (10 dates), and five other Clovis mammoth sites (9 dates), the associations center on the 9th millennium B.C. or 11,000 yr BP with little scatter (Haynes 1970, 1983). The thousand year uncertainty is narrowed when multiple dates on one site are available. Unlike bison hunting which can be studied in High Plains sites for thousands of years the Clovis-mammoth associa- tion was brief.

Supposed earlier associations of artifacts with mammoth remains, as at the Selby and Dutton sites (Stanford 1979), have not as yet yielded convincing evidence (Haynes 1982). This is not to say that the widely entertained concept of a pre-Clovis occupation of America is easily refuted. In fact it may not be vulnerable to disproof.

On the other hand "blitzkrieg" and a late entry of man into America can be disproved by the discover of a single archaeological deposit older than 12,000 BP. Such a site should not be trivial. It should be comparable in quantity of cultural material to Sungir (Bader 1978), Tabun (Jelinek 1982), or at least to Fraser Cave, Tasmania (Kiernan et al. 1983). Thousands of Old World Paleolithic sites yielding abundant stone and bone tools, radiocarbon dated human burials and rich grave or ceremonial artifacts are found in popular volumes on Old World archaeology (Jelinek 1975, Klein 1973). In Australia

discoveries of recent decades have yielded an impressive record
of dozens of archaeological sites predating 12,000 years (Jones
1979). Nothing as substantial has been found in America.

Those who embrace the theory of pre-Clovis or pre-Llano
cultures in America may regard the theory as a major obstacle
to an endorsement of a blitzkrieg by the Clovis culture (MacNeish 1976, Morlan and Cinq-Mars 1982, Carlson 1982). However,
the failure to prove claims has long haunted and continues to
haunt pre-Clovis archaeology. Assumed discoveries of pre-
12,000 year old sites in the New World crumble when reviewed
closely (e.g., Dincauze 1981 on Meadowcroft, West 1983a on Old
Crow, Taylor and Payen 1979 on Calico Hills, and Taylor et al.
1983 on Sunnyvale). Few would deny the value of the search for
early sites. Nevertheless if a pre-Clovis occupation of America cannot easily be disproved, it is important that the
claimed sites be rigorously scrutinized and that replication be
demanded. Meanwhile the theory of a pre-Clovis occupation,
however popular, will not alter the lack of ample associations
between man and extinct megafauna in the New World, until after
12,000 yr BP. The narrow time frame within which mammoth and
mammoth hunters are definitely known to coexist means that one
may ask blunt questions about the theory of a pre-Clovis occupation. What causes pre-Clovis claims to proliferate while
replications of pre-Clovis claims founder? "A chain of weak
evidence does not gain strength by being made longer" (West
1983b).

Besides the discovery of an incontestable pre-Clovis
archaeology there are other means of disproving American
blitzkrieg. To seek disproof is necessary because the true
cause of geological extinction can never be properly known,
given the limits of the fossil record and the vast array of
possible causes. "Our failure to be explicit about particular
instances of extinction is not because such an event is

esoteric and inexplicable in detail but, quite to the contrary,
because there are so many possible detailed explanations that
we cannot choose among them" (Simpson 1953, p. 303). According
to Karl Popper (Schilpp 1974) the operational method to be followed is to place a premium on those hypotheses or models which
offer maximum vulnerability to refutation. Thus, an extinction
hypothesis which survives despite its refutability is more useful than one more resistant to tests, whatever its other attributes. The asteroid impact model of late Cretaceous extinctions is an example. There are a variety of untestable explanations for the disappearance of dinosaurs at the end of the
Cretaceous. The asteroid model requires anomalous geochemical
conditions, that is, excessive iridium and other platinum
metals of extraterrestrial origin must reside in the boundary
layer between the Cretaceous and the Tertiary. Refutation can
occur if excessive platinum metals are found in strata elsewhere, unaccompanied by mass extinction. An enthusiastic
search for evidence pro or con is underway, establishing the
value of the asteroid model.

In the case of the American blitzkrieg Haynes' man-mammoth
associations at 11,000 yr BP cannot themselves be used as a
chronological test without risk of circularity, since the 11th
millennium was already incorporated in establishing the "clock
time" for the North American extinctions (Martin 1973). When
the radiocarbon dates on extinct animals other than mammoth,
and on mammoth outside Clovis sites are assembled from the
pages of Radiocarbon "as is", they include a variety of ages
extending from 20,000 years ago well into the Holocene (Martin
1958; Hester 1960, 1967; Webb 1969; Kurtén and Anderson 1980).
If accepted "as is", the radiocarbon dates display a gradual or
stepwise decline with different genera dropping out at different times over thousands of years (see figure 4, curve "A").

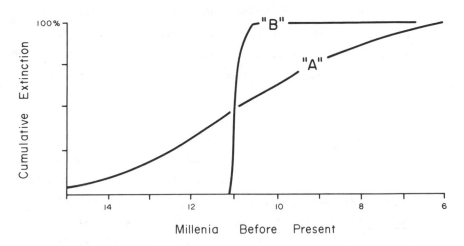

FIGURE 4.   Theoretical curves for decline of the Pleistocene
megafauna.   Curve   "A"   approximates   the North American
extinction chronology of Hester (1967), i.e., a gradual loss of
genera   over   eight   thousand years at least; curve "B"
approximates the extinction record of selected populations of
megafauna from the southwestern part of the United States (see
text). Depending on how events are modelled, either curve or
any intermediate   solution   could   be shown to correspond with
climatic changes at the end of the last ice age.   If
catastrophic   overkill by Clovis hunters caused megafaunal
extinctions,   curve   "B"   uniquely   defines   the   predicted
chronology for the Southwest.

On such grounds the blitzkrieg model has been refuted, for
example by Alford (1974).

        However, when radiocarbon dates from depositional environ-

ments more favorable to the protection and preservation of

unaltered bone collagen, keratin, or dung are selected, the

pattern changes. When more stringent criteria for sample qual-

ity are applied to radiocarbon dates published in Radiocarbon

and the worst of the "as is" results are pared away, the time

of extinction shrinks from the mid to the very early Holocene,

approximately 10,000 yr BP (Meltzer and Mead 1982, see figure

5). Thus the possibility of a sudden loss of at least the more readily dated extinct species is reopened. Two tests are now offered for dating megafaunal extinctions in two parts of North America, one on ground sloth dung and the other on amino acids from sabertooth bone.

SHASTA GROUND SLOTHS IN THE SOUTHWEST

The best known organic remains ideally suited to radiocarbon dating of extinction are found in the arid southwest. A few favored dry caves yield dung of the Shasta ground sloth (Nothrotheriops shastensis) and other extinct species. Ground sloth dung from upper levels in Rampart Cave in the western Grand Canyon yielded nitrogen/carbon ratios comparable to modern cow and burro dung from the region (Clark et al. 1974). The distribution of caves containing Shasta ground sloth dung and other fossil sites are shown in figure 6. The Shasta ground sloth, the smallest of the North American extinct ground sloths outside the West Indies, was no larger than a black bear, and about one meter high at the shoulders. Its fecal remains are larger in size and coarser in texture than those of other native or introduced herbivores in the region (Spaulding and Martin 1979). Dietary studies of ground sloths at Rampart Cave (Hansen 1978) reveal that the animal ate globe mallow and Mormon tea (Ephedra). Dung was deposited more rapidly in the last 2000 years of the Rampart Cave record than during earlier periods (Long and Martin 1974). In the Southwest the animal ranged from 300 m elevation at Gypsum Cave, Nevada, to 2000 m in the Guadalupe Mountains of West Texas and even higher in the Sandia Mountains of New Mexico.

To date a total of 41 dung samples and one sample of sloth body tissue have been dated. The results are listed in table 3 and the youngest 37 samples are plotted in figure 7. As in the case of Meltzer and Mead's 1982 plot of premium radiocarbon

dates on all extinct megafauna, there is a peak around 11,000
yr BP, truncating sharply afterward. The low frequency of samples older than 13,000 years reflects increasing diagenetic
vulnerability of dung in older deposits and less interest on
the part of field collectors concerning age of older portions
of thick deposits. Only exceptionally is dung preserved from
full glacial time (>18,000 yr BP). Surface samples from the
best deposit, Rampart Cave, were taken to determine as closely
as possible when deposition ended (Long and Martin 1974).

If all 42 dates are accepted "as is" the record can be
interpreted as a population rapidly declining around 11,000
years ago, yet lingering to 8500 yr BP as evidenced by sample
C-222 from Gypsum Cave, Nevada. With increased sampling a
growing number of young dates would be expected and extinction
could accordingly be projected forward even later than 8500 yr
BP. Such a record with a model of gradual extinction and was
adopted by Martin et al. (1961).

However, C-222 (along with C-221, 10,455 yr BP) is a solid
carbon sample, dated by a technique prone to laboratory contam-
ination that has been superceded by better methods (Long and
Martin 1974). Survival of the Shasta ground sloth to 8500 yr BP
(or later) is unsupported by the exclusively older dates
obtained since 1961. C-222 could be resurrected only if it
were to be replicated in some future study.

Another date of great interest is Y-1163 A on body tissue
of a Shasta ground sloth from Aden Crater, New Mexico. The
result, 9840 + 160 yr BP, was not run on a solid carbon sample
and would not be suspect if it were not associated with Y-1163B
dung supposedly from the same animal and dated at 11,080 yr BP.
Further analysis is needed to resolve this discrepancy.

Finally, L-473 A, 10,000 yr BP was obtained on both humic
and non-humic fractions. Dick Shutler collected the sample in
the 1950´s from the top of a trampled layer of dung at Rampart

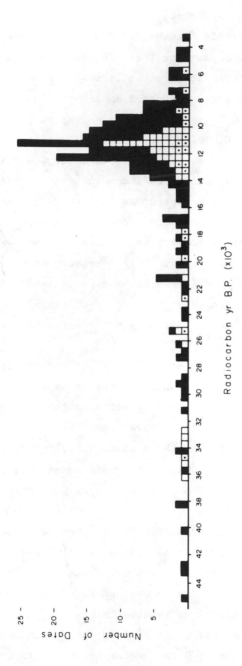

FIGURE 5. Distribution of 232 ^{14}C dates from 150 sites in North America. Solid squares = not critical test; squares with dots = bone "collagen" of uncertain purity; open squares = dates meeting highest standards of sample association and sample quality (after Meltzer and Mead 1982).

Cave. The profile was resampled by Long and Martin (1974). L-473 A has been tabulated as a last occurrence for the Shasta ground sloth by Kurtén and Anderson (1980) following Martin (1967). It was rejected by Long and Martin (1974) when they failed to replicate it in their sample of the Shutler profile. Rather than a single bolus, loose, trampled material was dated and sloth dung may have been mixed with packrat fecal pellets and debris, accounting for the result.

If these exceptions are excluded, all of the youngest radiocarbon dates on ground sloth dung except A-2174 and I-442 either fall within one standard deviation of 10,750 yr BP or within two standard deviations of 11,000 yr BP. All fall within two standard deviations of 10,750 yr BP. Unless the "young" samples, C-222, Y-1163 A, and L-473 A, can be rejuvinated, and barring any future discovery of a population of animals that managed to survive in some natural refuge to a much later time, I conclude that the Shasta ground sloths became extinct around 11,000 years ago. According to the blitzkrieg model the only North American ground sloths that should have survived much later were those of West Indies. Their extinction chronology is, however, yet to be determined. As in the case of claimed pre-Clovis archaeological sites, single radiocarbon dates indicating a Holocene survival of extinct megafauna cannot easily be disproved. For this reason alone, dates indicating the late survival of megafauna should be examined closely and if possible rerun with great care.

Under a climatic model, megafaunal extinction is not usually envisioned as happening within only 1000 years. If climatic or nutritional stresses were a contributing factor during North American deglaciation one might expect the ground sloths of increasingly arid regions to abandon the lower and drier portions of their range several thousand years before their extinction at higher elevations. Until their extinction

SHASTA GROUND SLOTHS

● Dung Caves
○ Late Pleistocene Sites
X Early and Mid Pleistocene

FIGURE 6. Distribution map of the Shasta ground sloth, after
Gregg MacDonald. From west to east the solid dots represent
the following caves harboring dung balls attributed to the
Shasta ground sloth: Nevada, Gypsum Cave; Arizona, Rampart
and Muav Caves; Utah, Cowboy Cave; New Mexico, Aden Crater
and Shelter Cave; Texas, Williams Cave and the Upper Sloth
Caves. The youngest dung deposit in many caves was about
11,000 years old (see text).

the sloths found at Rampart Cave (535 m) and Muav Cave (400 m)
both lived in a woodland of juniper, single-leaf ash and Mohave
desert shrubs. The woodland lingered several thousands of
years after the extinction of the sloths (Phillips 1977, in
press). Shasta ground sloths from the Upper Sloth Caves in the
Guadalupe Mountains occupied a woodland of Douglas fir,
Gambel's oak and southwestern white pine, an environment decid-
edly more boreal and 1465 m higher in elevation than Rampart
Cave. The population of the Upper Sloth Caves is dated to
within two standard deviations of 11,000 yr BP (A-1583, A-
1584). The synchroneity of extinction of various Shasta ground
sloth populations from various localities is impressive and
does not support any model of gradual or sequential decline
(table 3).

Finally, it is likely that, of all the large herbivores of
the North American late Pleistocene, the ground sloths were
especially slow moving and easy to track. They should have
been particularly vulnerable to the first human invaders and
American ground sloths should have been just as vulnerable to
prehistoric hunters as New Zealand's moas and Madagascar's
giant lemurs. Lack of evidence of a population decline in
American ground sloths prior to 11,000 yr BP and lack of
archaeological sites yielding butchered ground sloth bones does
not improve the chances for a lengthy pre-Clovis occupation of
America.

SABERTOOTHS AT RANCHO LA BREA
A second test of rapid extinction may be found in criti-
cally dated bones at Rancho la Brea, in downtown Los Angeles,
California. Bones of large extinct mammals are commonly
encountered in floodplains. Carbon from such materials is
vulnerable to post depositional alteration and "... it should
not be automatically assumed that any of these preparations,

TABLE 3. Radiocarbon dates on Shasta ground sloth dung. An asterisk (*)
indicates a questionable result (see text).

Site	^{14}C Age	Lab. No.	Reference
1. Gypsum Cave, Nevada	8,527±260*	C-222	Long and Martin 1974
2. Gypsum Cave, Nevada	10,455±340*	C-221	"
3. Gypsum Cave, Nevada	11,360±260	A-1202	"
4. Gypsum Cave, Nevada	11,690±250	LJ-452	"
5. Gypsum Cave, Nevada	21,470±760	A-1611	Thompson et al. 1980
6. Gypsum Cave, Nevada	33,910±3720	A-1607	Thompson et al. 1980
7. Rampart Cave, Arizona	10,035±250*	L-473A	Long and Martin 1974
8. Rampart Cave, Arizona	10,400±275	I-442	Long and Martin 1974
9. Rampart Cave, Arizona	10,500±180	A-2174	Thompson et al. 1980
10. Rampart Cave, Arizona	10,780±200	A-1067	Long and Martin 1974
11. Rampart Cave, Arizona	11,000±140	A-1066	"
12. Rampart Cave, Arizona	11,020±200	A-1068	"
13. Rampart Cave, Arizona	11,090±190	A-1602	this paper
14. Rampart Cave, Arizona	11,140±250	A-1453	Phillips 1977
15. Rampart Cave, Arizona	11,160±130	A-1395	this paper
16. Rampart Cave, Arizona	11,370±300	A-1392	Long and Martin 1974
17. Rampart Cave, Arizona	11,480±200	A-1041	"
18. Rampart Cave, Arizona	12,050±400	L-473C	"
19. Rampart Cave, Arizona	12,440±300	A-1070	"
20. Rampart Cave, Arizona	12,470±170	A-1318	"
21. Rampart Cave, Arizona	13,140±320	A-1207	"
22. Rampart Cave, Arizona	32,560±730	A-1210	"
23. Rampart Cave, Arizona	36,200±6000	A-1043	"
24. Rampart Cave, Arizona	>40,000	A-1042	"
25. Muav Cave, Arizona	10,650±220	A-2626	this paper
26. Muav Cave, Arizona	11,060±240	A-2627	this paper
27. Muav Cave, Arizona	11,140±160	A-1212	Long and Martin 1974
28. Muav Cave, Arizona	11,290±170	A-1213	"
29. Muav Cave, Arizona	11,610±60	A-2625	this paper
30. Muav Cave, Arizona	11,810±70	A-2628	this paper
31. Aden Crater, New Mexico	9,840±160*	Y-1163A	Long and Martin 1974
32. Aden Crater, New Mexico	11,080±200	Y-1163B	"
33. Shelter Cave, New Mexico	11,330±370	A-1878	Thompson et al. 1980
34. Shelter Cave, New Mexico	12,330±190	A-1879	"
35. Shelter Cave, New Mexico	12,430±250	A-1880	"
36. Williams Cave, Texas	11,410±320	A-1589	Spaulding and Martin 1979
37. Williams Cave, Texas	11,930±170	A-1588	"
38. Williams Cave, Texas	12,100±210	A-1563	"
39. Guadalupe Mts., Texas	10,750±140	A-1583	"
40. Guadalupe Mts., Texas	10,780±180	A-1584	"
41. Guadalupe Mts., Texas	11,060±180	A-1585	"
42. Guadalupe Mts., Texas	11,590±230	A-1519	"

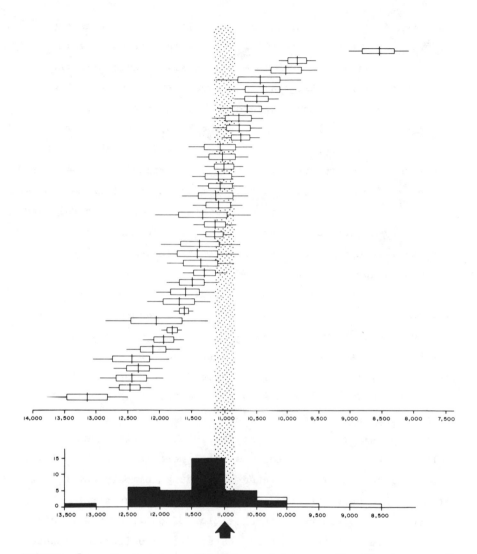

FIGURE 7. Youngest radiocarbon dates on the Shasta ground sloth dung plotted from values shown in table 3. The arrow and shaded panel indicates approximate time of activity of Clovis mammoth hunters in the North American Southwest.

especially in Pleistocene age bones, will contain only ... collagen-derived organics" (Taylor 1980, p. 969). At Rancho la Brea petroliferous residues impregnated and preserved the

collagen in the bones of extinct mammals. The residues can be
removed by ether; carbon from isotopically pure amino acids was
recovered by the method of Ho et al. (1969). Even with favorable preservation a large sample of between 75 gm and 300 gm of
cleaned bone powder is needed for preparation of amino acids
(Marcus and Berger in press). It should be emphasized that
this method is a refinement of radiocarbon dating that is unrelated to the controversial amino acid racemization dating technique. Radiocarbon dates on bone carbonate fractions and on
bone apatite were considered unreliable and were not considered
further by Marcus and Berger (in press). The advantage of dating the tar-impregnated bone is that higher than usual yields
of amino acids could be obtained.

Results of 56 amino acid bone dates are shown in table 4
and plotted in figure 8. The dates were obtained from specimens collected at varying depths in a series of pits, most of
which were excavated before 1915. The most common elements
dated were limb bones of the sabertooth, Smilodon. While
Marcus and Berger (in press) do not comment on the possibility
of multiple dates on different bones, the distribution of
specimens between pits and from layers within pits makes it
unlikely that any individual was dated more than once. Unlike
the specimens of extinct ground sloth dung commonly obtained at
or near the top of the deposit in a deliberate effort to obtain
the youngest, yielding a concentration of dates around 11,000
yr BP, Smilodon dates are distributed fairly uniformly between
38,000 years and 11,130 ± 275 yr BP (see figure 8).

The latter, QC-413 on Smilodon femur, is concordant with
the dung dates on extinction of Shasta ground sloths. It is
also not significantly different from the youngest Rancho la
Brea date on Equus, 10,940 ± 540 and the youngest Bison
antiquus, 12,275 ± 775 (table 4). The three average 11,200 ±
230 yr BP. If this is the youngest date for the Rancho la Brea

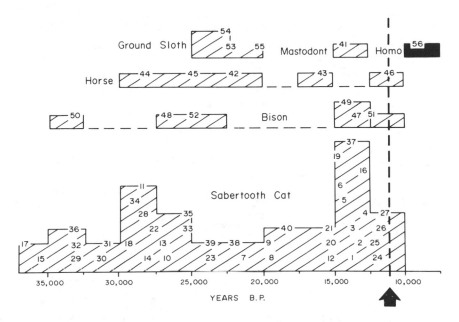

FIGURE 8. Radiocarbon dates on amino acid residues from bones of Rancho la Brea megafauna. Numbers refer to C^{14} dates of samples in table 4 in their chronological position. The arrow and heavy line indicates approximate time of activity of Clovis mammoth hunters in the North American Southwest.

extinct fauna, "Then these three individuals died more than 10,800 years ago (95 percent confidence level)... the best estimate of the date for extinction of the Pleistocene fauna in the vicinity of Rancho la Brea is thus somewhat later than 11,000 yr BP." (Marcus and Berger in press). While Bison survived in other parts of North America, its range diminished appreciably. Along with other megafauna the genus left southern California permanently at the end of the last Ice Age.

As a top carnivore, Smilodon should have been an especially sensitive indicator of gradual extinction. If large herbivore fanuas were slowly declining for thousands of years prior to 11,00 yr BP, Smilodon might be expected to have disappeared first or even to have suffered size reduction as Kurtén

TABLE 4. Bone amino acid radiocarbon dates from Rancho la Brea; for discussion and references see Marcus and Berger (in press).

Depth	Age	Average Error	Dated Material	Radiocarbon Lab. No.
SMILODON				
1. Pit 3:1'-4.5'	13,820	840	femur	QC401
2. Pit 3:6'	13,035	275	femur	QC279
3. Pit 3:6'	13,745	160	humerus	QC414
4. Pit 3:7'	12,650	160	femur	UCLA1292B
5. Pit 3:11.5'	14,400	2100	femur	UCLA1292E
6. Pit 3:12'	14,500	190	femur	UCLA1292C
7. Pit 3:22'	21,400	560	femur	UCLA1292A
8. Pit 3:26'	19,300	395	femur	UCLA1292K
9. Pit 4:4.5'-8.5'	19,800	300	femur	UCLA1292R
10. Pit 4:8'	26,700	900	femur	UCLA1292G
11. Pit 2051:16'	28,250	1030	ulna	QC438
12. Pit 4:11.5'	15,200	800	tibia	UCLA1292L
13. Pit 4:15'	26,995	4000	femur	QC386
14. Pit 4:15.5'	28,000	1400	femur	UCLA1292D
15. Pit 4:18'	35,500	2200	femur	UCLA1292S
16. Pit 4:18.5'	12,760	150	femur	
17. Pit 4:20'-22'	>36,000		femur	UCLA1292M
18. Pit 4:23.5'	29,600	1100	femur	UCLA1292O
19. Pit 13:11'	14,950	430	femur	UCLA1292F
20. Pit 13:13'	15,360	480	femur	QC339
21. Pit 13:14.5'	15,300	200	femur	UCLA1292I
22. Pit 60:8'-9'	27,900	2700	femur	QC280
23. Pit 60:9'-12'	23,700	600	femur	UCLA1292H
24. Pit 61-67:10'	12,000	125	femur	UCLA1292X
25. Pit 61-67:15'-20'	12,200	200	femur	UCLA1292Y
26. Pit 61-67:16'-18.5'	11,640	135	femur	QC302A
27. Pit 61-67:18'-20'	11,130	275	femur	QC413
28. Pit 77:9'-11'	28,200	980	femur	UCLA1292W
29. Pit 77:13'-15'	33,100	600	femur	UCLA1292U
30. Pit 77:18.5'-21'	31,300	1350	femur	UCLA1292V
31. Pit 91:6'-7'	30,800	600	sacrum	UCLA1718
32. Pit 91:7.2'-7.5'	32,600	2800	femur	UCLA1738D
33. Pit 91:8'-8.3'	25,100	1100	tibia	UCLA1738F
34. Pit 91:8.1'-8.5'	29,100	1200	femur	UCLA1738C
35. Pit 91:8.5'-8.8'	25,100	850	humerus	UCLA1738A
36. Pit 91:8.8'-9'	33,000	1750	humerus	UCLA1738B
37. Pit 2051:6.8'	13,950	1570	humerus	QC436
38. Pit 2051:11'	22,355	3400	rib	QC431
39. Pit 2051:15'	23,850	1200	femur	QC440
40. Pit 2051:16'	18,475	320	humerus	QC435
MAMMUT				
41. Pit 3:14'	14,350	175	ulna	UCLA1292T
EQUUS				
42. Pit 4:9'	22,000	1200	femur	QC412
43. Pit 10:4'-4.5'	15,700	530	femur	UCLA1292CC
44. Pit 60:9'-9.5'	>28,850		metapodial	QC365
45. Pit 60:14'	24,900	3360	tibia	QC410
46. Pit 81:caved	10,940	510	tibia	QC405
BISON				
47. Pit 4:10.5'	13,500	170	scapula	UCLA1292Q
48. Pit 4:	27,000	1600	axis	UCLS1292Z
49. Pit 13:20'-23'	14,310	920	femur	QC420
50. Pit 16:3'-6'	>32,850		metatarsal	QC277II
51. Pit 16:4.5'	12,275	775	metatarsal	QC371
52. Pit 16:12'-14'	24,400	535	metacarpal	QC278
GLOSSOTHERIUM				
53. Pit 60:12'	23,420	350	rib	QC361
54. Pit 2051:5'	22,890	500	rib	QC443
55. Pit 2051:8'	20,450	460	rib	QC390
HOMO				
56. Pit 10:6'-9'	9,000	80	femur	UCLA1292BB

(1965) claimed for its Florida disappearance. No size reduction in sabertooth is evident at Rancho la Brea (Marcus and
Berger in press). However, the evidence of a late survival of
Smilodon claimed elsewhere, at the First American Bank site in
Tennessee (Guilday 1977), causes major difficulties for the
concordance of extinction of sabertooth and ground sloth and
for the model of blitzkrieg. Thus, continued radiocarbon tests
are warranted and the alleged concordance may crumble.

Meanwhile, the extinction of members of the Ranch la Brea
megafauna dated on amino acid residues, and the extinction of
separate populations of the Shasta ground sloth dated directly
on untreated dry fecal remains, converge on the array of dates
on southwestern mammoths dated by charcoal from a series of
separate cultural associations. The approximate age of the
convergence is 11,000 yr BP. This result coincides with the
time of Clovis hunters in the region and is in accord with a
model of catastrophic extinction.

DISCUSSION AND SUMMARY

For the geologist the most useful feature of late Pleistocene extinction is its chronology. The disappearance of mammoths, mastodonts, horses, and camels, among a mammalian
megafauna of 37 genera in North America alone, took place very
late in geological time. The development of radiocarbon dating
over the past three decades has made it possible to devise
chronologies of extinction for different groups of animals in
different regions with hundreds of radio carbon dates from the
United States and Canada alone.

If all radio carbon dates on the extinct fauna are
accepted "as is" the pattern of loss between 14,00 and 6,000 yr
BP is gradual and a model of "blitzkrieg" devised to maximize
growth rate, expansion and impact of an invading population of
hunters while minimizing their total population (Mosimann and

Martin 1975) is disproved. If restrictive criteria for accept-
ing radiocarbon dates are adopted (Meltzer and Mead 1982), and
if only dates of high standards for sample quality and for sample association with extinct fauna are accepted, the evidence
for a mid-Holocene survival of extinct megafauna is not supported and an earlier catastrophic extinction as predicted by
"blitzkrieg" is not refuted.

If only premium dates on undecomposed dry Shasta ground
sloth dung are used it can be shown that ground sloth populations from for different states, Nevada, Arizona, New Mexico
and Texas, disappeared around 11,000 years ago. At Rancho la
Brea, where tar-impregnated bone yields ample well-preserved
bone collagen, purified amino acid residues show that the last
machairodonts (the sabertooth cat), bison, and horse, died more
than 10,800 years ago (95% confidence level). The convergence
of Shasta ground sloth extinction with that of sabertooth,
horse , and bison on 11,000 yr BP is noteworthy since all converge on the age of Clovis-mammoth associations uniquely dated
at this time interval by Haynes (1970, 1982). The result supports a model of catastrophic extinction. While the result
does not exclude other possible causes, no other unique or
improbable event impacting North America at the same time as
the arrival of Clovis hunters is yet recognized.

Blitzkrieg can be refuted by the discovery of an earlier
presence of man (pre-Clovis or pre-Llano) and proponents of
this popular view may reject the blitzkrieg model. Since a
pre-Clovis occupation of America is not easily refuted, the
unequivocal demonstration of sites, preferably accompanied by
site replication, must be achieved before the existence of a
pre-Clovis culture can be fully endorsed. Difficulties in ver-
ifying older sites have been encountered (West 1983b). America
is unlike Australia where dozens of sites from 12,000 to at
least 30,000 yr BP have been found recently (Jones 1979) and

continue to be found (Kiernan et al. 1983), without chronic
methodological or contextural controversy. The discrepancy
between the archaeological record of the two continents suggests that only Australia harbored man before 12,000 years ago.

Blitzkrieg was proposed to explain the scarcity of associations between extinct megafauna and prehistoric people in
America (Mosimann and Martin 1975). The model is not refuted
by the fact that not all large mammals of the Wisconsin have
yet to be found in deposits of Clovis age. Chance may explain
such an outcome. The model can be rejected if associations of
hunters and extinct animals predating 12,000 years are shown to
exist. It can be rejected if extinct animals on the continent
survived well after 11,000 years ago. It can also be rejected
if endemic ground sloths and giant rodents in the West Indies
became extinct around 11,000 years ago, long before human invasion of the West Indies.

Grayson (in press) notes that a refutation of blitzkrieg
will not refute American overkill. I view gradual overkill as
already disproved by the lack of a long fossil record between
hunters and large extinct prey in America to match the Paleolithic of Eurasia. The coexistence of extinct megafauna and
prehistoric cultures over thousands of years without kill or
processing sites would refute both blitzkrieg and overkill.
Finally, a comparison with the asteroid model of dinosaur
extinction is pertinent. Both are subject to intense public
and professional interest. In the case of the ice age
megafauna a sudden global extinction of all species for whatever reason is disproved as the late Pleistocene losses were
diachronous between continents. Many millennia separated
extinction of Australian diprotodons, American mammoths, and
Malagasy giant lemurs (figure 9). Without the technique of
radiocarbon dating, these age differences would be difficult to
demonstrate conclusively. In North America the possibility of

MAJOR EXTINCTION EVENTS

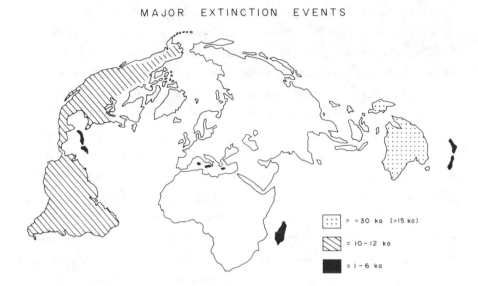

FIGURE 9. Late Pleistocene extinction of mammals and birds in different parts of the globe. Extinction in Australia preceeded that in America which preceeded that on Madagascar and other oceanic islands; ka = 1000 years.

coextinction of ground sloths, sabertooth, and mammoths, as determined by radiocarbon dates, would be impossible to prove by stratigraphy alone. Demonstrating synchroneity of extinction of dinosaurs by stratigraphic means should be even more difficult. Failure to achieve such a demonstration will not refute the asteroid or other catastrophic models.

The major anomaly in the fossil record of the late Pleistocene is the excessive loss of terrestrial megafauna (70% in America alone) unaccompanied by any mass extinction of marine life such as that occurring at the end of the Cretaceous. Just as the geochemist seeks to define certain sedimentary anomalies on the Cretaceous-Tertiary boundary as a test of the asteroid model, so the archaeologist seeks to define the Clovis anomaly of mammoth hunters as a test of the blitzkrieg model. Did Clovis progenitors enjoy a long genealogy in America or did

they suddenly sweep in from Asia 12,000 years ago? In both
late Cretaceous and late Pleistocene extinction models, short-
term events are vitally significant. Those investigating the
late Pleistocene enjoy a great advantage. They are 65 million
years closer to the monumental changes they seek to comprehend
and they can determine the absolute age of those changes to
within at least a millennium. Ironically, despite this advantage, explanations for megamammal extinction trigger as much
debate as those for dinosaur extinction.

ACKNOWLEDGMENTS

     By his overview in Quaternary Extinctions and in
correspondence Donald Grayson has stimulated my search for test
demarcations. Margaret Hardy developed the analysis of large
and small mammal extinctions shown in table 1 and figures 1 and
2. Jim I. Mead reviewed the radiocarbon dates on extinct
megafauna; Robert S. Thompson assembled radiocarbon dates on
extinct ground sloth dung; C. Vance Haynes responded to queries
about the Clovis culture and convinced me that pre-Clovis
claims are not readily refutable; Leslie F. Marcus and Ranier
Berger kindly made available their unique amino acid radiocarbon record from Rancho la Brea. Various drafts were reviewed
by D. K. Grayson, M. Hardy, C. V. Haynes, L. F. Marcus, R. S.
Thompson, R. Graham, L. G. Marshall, D. Meltzer, J. J.
Saunders, and F. H. West.

LITERATURE CITED

ALFORD, J. J. 1974. The geography of mastodon extinction.
     The Professional Geographer 26:425-429.
ALVAREZ, L. W., W. ALVAREZ, F. ASARO, and H. V. MICHEL. 1980.
     Extra-terrestrial cause for the Cretaceous-Tertiary
     extinction. Science 208:1095-1108.
BADER, O. N. 1978. Sungir, an Upper Paleolithic Site. Mos-
     cow: Nauka. (unpublished translation).

CARLSON, J. B. 1982. An argument against "overkill". Early
    Man 4:3.
CLARK, F. E., W. A. O'DEAN, and D. E. BELAU. 1974. Carbon,
    nitrogen and N^{14} content of fossil and modern dung.
    Journal of the Arizona Academy of Science. 9:95-96.
DIPESO, C. C., J. B. RINALDO and G. J. FENNER. 1974. Casas
    Grandes: A Fallen Trading Center of Gran Chichimeca. Vol.
    7, Flagstaff: Northland Press.
DINCAUZE, D. F. 1981. The Meadowcroft Papers. Quarterly
    Review of Archaeology 10:385-400.
FRISON, G. C., D. H. WALKER, S. D. WEBB, and G. M. ZEIMENS.
    1978. Paleo-Indian procurement of Camelops on the
    northwestern Plains. Quaternary Research 10:385-400.
GINGERICH, P. D. (in press). Pleistocene extinctions in the
    context of origination-extinction equilibria in Cenozoic
    mammals. In: P. S. Martin and R. G. Klein, eds.
    Quaternary Extinctions: A Prehistoric Revolution. Tuc-
    son, University of Arizona Press.
GRAHAM, R. W. and E. L. LUNDELIUS, JR. (in press). Coevolu-
    tionary disequilibrium and Pleistocene extinctions. In:
    P. S. Martin and R. G. Klein, eds., Quaternary
    Extinctions: A Prehistoric Revolution. Tucson, Univer-
    sity of Arizona Press.
GRAYSON, D. K. (in press). Explaining Pleistocene extinc-
    tions: thoughts on the structure of a debate. In: P. S.
    Martin and R. G. Klein, eds., Quaternary Extinctions: A
    Prehistoric Revolution. Tucson, University of Arizona
    Press.
GUILDAY, J. E. 1977. Sabertooth cat, Smilodon floridanus
    (Leidy), and associated fauna from a Tennessee Cave (40 DV
    40), the first American bank site. Journal Tennessee
    Academy of Science 52:84-94.
HANSEN, R. M. 1978. Shasta ground sloth food habits, Rampart
    Cave, Arizona. Paleobiology 4:302-319.
HAYNES, C. V. 1970. Geochronology of man-mammoth sites and
    their bearing on the origin of the Llano Complex. pp.
    77-92. In: Pleistocene and Recent Environments of the
    Central Great Plains, W. Dorr, Jr. and J. K. Jones, eds.,
    Lawrence, The University Press of Kansas.
HAYNES, C. V. 1982. Were Clovis progenitors in Beringia? pp.
    383-398. In: Paleoecology of Beringia, D. M. Hopkins, J.
    V. Matthews, Jr., C. E. Schweger and S. B. Young, eds.,
    New York, Academic Press.
HAYNES, C. V. (in press). Stratigraphy and late Pleistocene
    extinction in the United States. In: P. S. Martin and R.
    G. Klein, eds., Quaternary Extinctions: A Prehistoric
    Revolution. Tucson, University of Arizona Press.
HESTER, J. J. 1960. Pleistocene extinction and radiocarbon
    dating. American Antiquity 26:58-77.

HESTER, J. J. 1967. The agency of man in animal extinctions. pp. 169-200. In: Pleistocene Extinctions: The Search for a Cause, P. S. Martin and H. E. Wright, Jr., eds., New Haven, Yale University Press.

HO, T. Y., L. F. MARCUS, and R. BERGER. 1969. Radiocarbon dating of petroleum-impregnated bone from the tar pits at Rancho la Brea, California. Science 164:1051-1052.

INTERNATIONAL STUDY GROUP 1982. An inter-laboratory comparison of radiocarbon measurements in tree rings. Nature 298:619-623.

JANZEN, D. H. 1983. The Pleistocene hunters had help. The American Naturalist 121:598-599.

JELINEK, A. J. 1982. The Tabun Cave and Paleolithic man in the Levant. Science 216:1369-1375.

JELINEK, J. 1975. The Pictoral Encyclocpedia of the Evolution of Man. Hamlyn, London.

JONES, R. 1979. The fifth continent: problems concerning the human colonization of Australia. Annual Review of Anthropology 8:455-466.

KIERNAN, K., R. JONES and D. RANSON. 1983. New evidence from Fraser Cave for glacial age man in southwest Tasmania. Nature 301:28-32.

KLEIN, J., J. C. LERMAN, P. E. DAMON and E. K. RALPH. 1982. Calibration of radiocarbon dates. Radiocarbon 24:103-150.

KLEIN, R. G. 1973. Ice age hunters of the Ukraine. Chicago, University of Chicago Press.

KURTÉN, B. 1965. The Pleistocene Felidae of Florida. Bulletin Florida State Museum 9:215-273.

KURTÉN, B. and E. ANDERSON. 1980. Pleistocene mammals of North America. New York, Columbia University Press.

LONG, A. and P. S. MARTIN. 1974. Death of American ground sloths. Science 186:638-640.

MACARTHUR, R. H. and E. O. WILSON. 1967. The Theory of Island Biogeography. Princeton, Princeton University Press.

MACNEISH, R. S. 1976. Early man in the New World. American Scientist 64: 316-327.

MARCUS, L. and R. BERGER. (in press). The significance of radiocarbon dates for Rancho la Brea. In: P. S. Martin and R. G. Klein, eds. Quaternary Extinctions: A Prehistoric Revolution. Tucson, University of Arizona Press.

MARTIN, P. S. 1958. Pleistocene ecology and biogeography of North America. pp. 375-420. In: Zoogeography, American Association for the Advancement of Science Symposium volume, Carl Hubbs, eds., Washington, D. C.

MARTIN, P. S. 1967. Prehistoric overkill. In: P. S. Martin and H. E. Wright, Jr., Eds., Pleistocene Extinctions: A Search for a Cause. New Haven, Yale University press, pp. 75-120.

MARTIN, P. S. 1973. The discovery of America. Science
179:969-974.
MARTIN, P. S. (in press). Prehistoric overkill: a global
model. In: P. S. Martin and R. G. Klein, eds., Quaternary
Extinctions: A Prehistoric Revolution. Tucson, Univer-
sity of Arizona Press.
MARTIN, P. S. and R. G. KLEIN, eds. (in press). Quaternary
Extinctions: A Prehistoric Revolution. Tucson, University
of Arizona Press.
MARTIN, P. S., B. E. SABELS and R. SHUTLER, JR. 1961. Rampart
Cave coprolite and ecology of the Shasta ground sloth.
American Journal of Science 759:102-127.
MARTIN, P. S. and H. E. WRIGHT, eds. 1967. Pleistocene
Extinctions: A Search for a Cause. New Haven, Yale
University Press.
MELTZER, D. J. and J. I. MEAD. 1982. The timing of late
Pleistocene mammalian extinctions in North America.
Quaternary Research 19:130-135.
MORLAN, R. E. and J. CINQ-MARS. 1982. Ancient Beringians:
human occupation in the late Pleistocene of Alaska and the
Yukon Territory. In: Paleoecology of Beringia, D. M.
Hopkins, J. V. Matthews, Jr., C. E. Schweger and S. B.
Young, eds. New York, Academic Press. 353-381 pp.
MOSIMANN, J. E. and P. S. MARTIN. 1975. Simulating overkill
by Paleoindians. American Scientist 63:304-313.
PHILLIPS, A. M. 1977. Packrats, plants and the Pleistocene in
the Lower Grand Canyon. Ph.D. Dissertation. Tucson,
University of Arizona. 123 p.
PHILLIPS, A. M. (in press). Shasta ground sloth extinction:
Fossil packrat midden evidence from the western Grand
Canyon. In: P. S. Martin and R. G. Klein, eds.
Quaternary Extinctions: A Prehistoric Revolution. Tuc-
son, University of Arizona Press.
RAUP, D. M. and J. J. SEPKOSKI, JR. 1982. Mass extinctions in
the marine fossil record. Science 215:1501-1503.
SAVAGE, D. E. and D. E. RUSSELL. 1983. Mammalian Paleofaunas
of the World. Reading, Massachusetts. Addison-Wesley,
432 p.
SCHILPP, P. A. (ed). 1974. The philosophy of Karl Popper.
Open Court. La Salle, Illinois. (2 volumes).
SIMPSON, G. G. 1953. The Major Features of Evolution. New
York, Columbia University Press, 434 p.
SPAULDING, W. G. and P. S. MARTIN 1979. Ground sloth dung of
the Guadalupe Mountains. In: Biological Investigations
in the Guadalupe Mountains National Park, Texas. H. H.
Genoways and R. J. Baker, eds. pp. 259-269. U. S.
National Park Service Proceedings and Transactions Series
No. 4. Washington, D. C.

STAFFORD, D. 1979. Alluvial geology and archaeological poten-
   tial of the Texas southern High Plains. American
   Antiquity 46:548-565.
STANFORD, D. 1979. The Selby and Dutton sites: evidence for
   a possible pre-Clovis occupation of the High Plains. In:
   Pre-Llano Cultures of the Americas: Paradoxes and
   Possibilities. R. L. Humphrey and D. Stanford, eds. pp.
   101-123. The Anthropological Society of Washington.
STANLEY, S. M. and L. D. CAMPBELL. 1981. Neogene mass extinc-
   tion of western Atlantic molluscs. Nature 293:457-459.
TAYLOR, R. E. 1980. Radiocarbon dating of Pleistocene bone:
   toward criteria or the selection of samples. Radiocarbon
   22:69-79.
TAYLOR, R. E. and L. A. PAYEN. 1979. The role of archaeometry
   in American archaeology: approaches to the evaluation of
   the antiquity of Homo sapiens in California. Advances in
   Archaeological Method and Theory 2:239-283. New York,
   Academic Press.
TAYLOR, R. E., L. A. PAYEN, B. GEROW, D. J. DONAHUE, T. H.
   ZABEL, A. J. T. JULL, and P. E. DAMON. 1983. Middle
   Holocene age of the Sunnyvale human skeleton. Science
   220:1271-1272.
THOMPSON, R. S., T. R. VANDEVENDER, P. S. MARTIN, A. LONG and
   T. FOPPE. 1980. Shasta ground sloth (Nothrotheriops
   shastense Hoffstetter) at Shelter Cave, New Mexico:
   environment, diet and extinction. Quaternary Research
   14:360-376.
WEBB, S. D. 1969. Extinction-origination equilibria in late
   Cenozoic land mammals of North America. Evolution
   23:688-702.
WEBB. S. D. (in press). Ten million years of mammal extinc-
   tions in North America. In: P. S. Martin and R. G.
   Klein, eds. Quaternary Extinctions: A Prehistoric
   Revolution. Tucson, University of Arizona Press.
WEBSTER, D. 1981. Late Pleistocene extinction and human pre-
   dation: a critical overview. pp. 556-594. In: R. S. O.
   Harding and G. Teleki, eds. Omnivorous Primates. New
   York, Columbia University Press.
WEST, F. H. 1983a. Taphonomy and archaeology in the Upper
   Pleistocene of the northern Yukon Territory: a glimpse of
   the peopling of the New World (Morlan). Quarterly Review
   of Archaeology 4:13-16.
WEST, F. H. 1983b. The antiquity of man in North America.
   pp. 364-382. In: Late Quaternary Environments of the
   United States. H. E. Wright, Jr. ed. Volume 1, Univer-
   sity of Minnesota Press.
WYMAN, J. 1973. Freshwater Shell Mounds of the St. John's
   River, Florida. New York, AMS Press, Inc. (Reprint of
   1875 edition of Peabody Academy of Science, Salem, Massachusetts).

"NORMAL" EXTINCTIONS OF ISOLATED POPULATIONS

Jared M. Diamond

INTRODUCTION

Case studies of extinction fall along a continuum with respect to suddenness, extent, and identifiable causes of extinction. At one extreme, the dramatic end of the spectrum, are extinctions or extinction waves due to some clearly iden- tifiable event. Some of these dramatic extinctions were sud- den, in the cases of events that were themselves sudden rather than gradual. Some consisted of extensive waves of extinction, in the cases of events impinging on many species. Examples discussed elsewhere in this volume are the terminal-Cretaceous extinction wave attributed to an asteroid impact (Raup present volume), the late-Pleistocene continental waves and the Holo- cene island waves that followed the first arrivals of man (Mar- tin present volume), the late-Cretaceous plant extinctions and the late Pleistocene hominid extinctions due to evolution of competing taxa (Knoll present volume, Walker present volume), and extinctions of marine species and of swamp lycopods due to changes in climate and habitat (Stanley present volume, Knoll present volume).

At the opposite extreme are the extinctions that are con-
stantly befalling populations isolated on islands or on disjunct patches of habitat. Such extinctions eliminate populations one-by-one rather than in a wave. They have no "cause"
other than year-to-year fluctuations in the environment, or
even just those accidents in the lives of individuals that may
happen to eliminate all conspecifics (at least all those of one
sex) on the island within a short time. Somewhere in between
these two extremes lie the extinction waves due to fragmentation or insularization of habitat, as exemplified by modern
extinctions in Amazonian forest fragments (Lovejoy et al.
present volume) and post-Pleistocene extinctions in fragmented
patches of montane habitat (Patterson present volume).

In this chapter I shall review the less dramatic half of
the spectrum and discuss extinctions on islands or in island-
like situations. This material will help us to unravel the
dramatic extinctions, by showing what level of "background
extinction" to expect in the absence of dramatic events. I
begin by summarizing theoretical studies of what factors may
determine the risk of extinction for isolated populations.
There follow four sets of case studies:

1. Modern extinctions of bird populations on islands or
else on mainland census plots at equilibrium, in the absence of
major environmental change.

2. Modern extinctions of bird populations in habitat
patches created by fragmentation of a formerly continuous habitat.

3. Extinctions of mammal, bird, and lizard populations
due to late-Pleistocene fragmentation of land masses or of
habitats.

4. Extinctions of species in evolutionary time, as
reflected in a biota´s degree of endemism.

THEORY OF POPULATION LIFETIMES

The following oversimplified summary is based on treat-
ments by MacArthur and Wilson (1967, chapter 4), Richter-Dyn
and Goel (1972), and Leigh (1975, 1981), which may be consulted
for further details. Some additional complications are discussed by May et al. (1974).

Let us first ask how a population´s probability-per-unit-
time of extinction, e (in units of year^{-1}), varies with the
number of individuals (or male-female pairs) in the population,
N. Suppose that the probability-per-unit-time that a single
individual will die is p. Then, if the deaths of individuals
are independent of each other, e is simply p^N, implying a steep
decline in risk of extinction with increasing population size
(fig. 1). Correlations between deaths of individuals, or
effects of population size on each individual´s risk of death,
will alter the steepness. For instance, if individuals compete
with each other such that each individual´s chance of dying (p)
increases with population size N, the relation will be less
steep. Any environmental fluctuations will also tend to make
the relation less steep, since a bad year for one individual
tends to be bad for all. On the other hand, mutualism, as is
expected for social species, will make the relation more steep,
because an individual´s chance of dying decreases with population size N.

Instead of considering the probability that a population
will disappear within a short time, let us now ask how long the
population is expected to survive. First assume that the
environment is constant, and that population fluctuations arise
solely from demographic accidents (the random schedule of
births and deaths of individuals). With the further assumption
of geometric population growth for N less than the carrying
capacity K (the maximum population size that the island can
support), table 1 gives the expected lifetime T (measured in

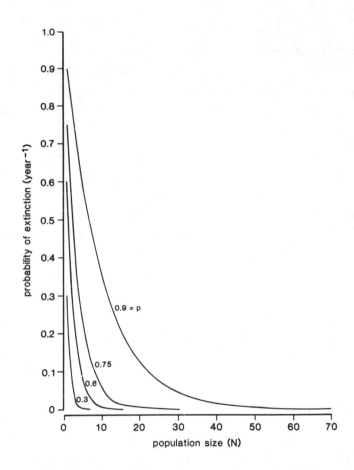

FIGURE 1. Predicted relation between the probability-per-unit time that a population will go extinct (ordinate) and the number of individuals or pairs constituting the population (abscissa). The curves are calculated as p^N, where N is the abscissa value and the number beside each curve is the value of p. This calculation in effect assumes that individuals or pairs die independently of each other with probability-per-unit time p.

generations) for a population now at K, as a function of K and of the intrinsic rate of population increase r. The lifetime is seen to increase steeply with K and with r. The proportional increase for a given K increases steeply with r, and vice versa. Since the values of table 1 are in generations

TABLE 1. Expected population lifetime. The numbers are the
expected lifetime (in generations) of a population at carrying
capacity, as a function of the carrying (K) and the intrinsic
rate of population increase (r). The environment is assumed
constant, and population fluctuations are assumed to arise
solely from the random schedule of briths and deaths. Data
are from table 2 of Leigh (1981). Note that expected lifetime increases with K and with r.

		K		
	10	20	30	40
0.1	46	197	925	4,897
0.2	109	2,844	103,750	4,386,342
0.3	414	92,184	29,218,650	1.057×10^{10}
0.4	2,312	5,222,731	1.64×10^{10}	5.843×10^{13}

(r labels the left-hand column)

rather than years, a population's lifetime also increases with
the generation time or lifetime of its individuals.

In fact, populations fluctuate much more widely than
expected if demographic accidents were the sole cause of fluctuations. That is, the major contribution to population fluctuations comes from fluctuations of the environment. The
effect of this on calculations such as those of table 1 can be
obtained by assuming that environmental fluctuations yield random variation in r. With this assumption, it turns out that
the higher the population's coefficient of variation (abbrevi-
ated CV), the shorter is its lifetime. The more susceptible a
population is to environmental fluctuations, the more slowly
its expected lifetime increases with K (Leigh 1981). For
highly susceptible populations, CV becomes more important than
K in determining population lifetime.

The intrinsic rate of increase r equals the difference
between the instantaneous birth rate λ and death rate μ, each
of which may depend on N. While population lifetime increases

with r, it also increases with λ/μ. That is, the lower birth and death rates for a given difference $\lambda - \mu = r$, the safer is the population (MacArthur and Wilson 1967). Since λ, μ, r, and generation time are interrelated, the predictions for dependence of population lifetime on r, generation time, and λ/μ are also interrelated.

In short, for populations exposed to a randomly fluctuating environment rather than to occasional catastrophes, one predicts that population lifetime will increase with:

1.   generation time or individual lifetime;

2.   carrying capacity K or population size N, which is proportional to the product of

        2a.   population density, times

        2b.   island area;

3.   intrinsic rate of increase r; and

4.   ratio of birth to death rate λ/μ.

Population lifetime will decrease with

5.   variability in population size (CV of N).

In effect, we have six separate predictions (1, 2a, 2b, 3, 4, and 5). Let us now compare these predictions with available data.

MODERN EXTINCTIONS OF BIRD POPULATIONS IN COMMUNITIES EXHIBITING TURNOVER AT EQUILIBRIUM

Numerous studies have tabulated the bird species breeding in each of a series of consecutive years on an island, or else on a mainland census plot. Some of these studies, such as the census reproduced in table 2 for Bardsey Island off the west coast of Britain from 1954 to 1969, have determined not only the breeding species in each year but also the number of breeding pairs of each species. Examples of such studies for islands are those for the California Channel Islands (Jones and Diamond 1976), the Farnes Islands off Britain (Diamond and May

1977), the Krunnit Islands off Finland (Vaisanen and Jarvinen
1977), and many British islands (Diamond 1980; Jones and Diamond, unpublished); for mainland census plots, those for
Trelease Woods in Illinois (Whitcomb et al. 1976, Kendeigh
1982), seven other eastern North American woodlands (Lynch and
Whitcomb 1978), northern European woodlands (Jarvinen 1979,
1980), and a British oak woodland (Williamson 1981).

All these studies have yielded the conclusion that about 1
- 30% of the breeding bird populations turn over per year on
islands not undergoing marked changes of habitat. That is,
bird species number in island and mainland bird communities
tends to be maintained in a state of dynamic equilibrium, as a
result of 1-30% of the breeding populations disappearing each
year and a similar number of new populations beginning to breed
or resuming breeding. Naturally, drastic habitat changes or
effects of man create an imbalance between extinctions and
immigrations and cause species number to change.

Such surveys permit one to calculate the probability e
that a population will become extinct within one year, as a
function of the average number N of pairs constituting the
population during years of breeding presence. For instance,
consider the five years of breeding presence documented in
table 2 for the Cuckoo on Bardsey from 1954 to 1968. (We
ignore the last survey year, 1969, for the purpose of this calculation, because a 1970 survey is unavailable and it is therefore unknown whether the 1969 population survived or became
extinct). Of those five years, three were followed by a year
of breeding absence, yielding e = 0.6 for the probability of
extinction within one year. The average population size of
Cuckoo in those five years was N = 1.4 pairs. Fig. 2 plots
(N,e) values for all breeding species of Bardsey. It is obvious that the risk of extinction falls very steeply with
increasing population size, at least as steeply as predicted by

TABLE 2. Breeding censuses of Bardsey Island. Breeding species and the number of breeding pairs are shown.

	1954	1955	1956	1957	1958	1959	1960	1961	1962	1963	1964	1965	1966	1967	1968	1969
Sparrowhawk (Accipiter nisus)	1	1	1													
Kestrel (Falco tinnunculus)								1	1	1	1	1	1	1	1	1
Corncrake (Crex crex)	2	2														
Moorhen (Gallinula chloropus)	1	1	1	1	1	2	2	4	5	4	5	4	4	7	6	8
Oystercatcher (Haematopus ostralegus)	37	35	35	35	27	35	40	44	39	44	44	34	40	52	55	55
Lapwing (Vanellus vanellus)		10	8	10	8	7	20	11	10	5	4	3	6	7	6	10
Ringed Plover (Charadrius hiaticula)															1	1
Curlew (Numenius arquata)										1	1	1	1	1	1	
Wood Pigeon (Columba palumbus)													1		1	2
Cuckoo (Cuculus canorus)		1						2	1		1	2				1
Little Owl (Athene noctua)	3	3	3	3	4	4	5	6	7	6	5	5	5	6	6	5
Skylark (Alauda arvensis)	5		2	3	3	4	4	4	4	6	7	5	6	7	7	7
Swallow (Hirundo rustica)	10	6	6	6	6	6	6	5	4	7	5	2	4	5	7	7
Raven (Corvus corax)	2	3	2	3	1	2	1	3	1	1	1	2	2	3	3	2
Carrion Crow (Corvus corone)	3	4	4	6	7	7	6	6	4	6	5	4	4	5	4	4
Jackdaw (Corvus monedula)	35	30	30	25	25	30	30	20	20	25	30	50	45	50	50	47
Chough (Pyrrhocorax pyrrhocorax)	2	2	2	2	2	1	2	2	2	3	4	4	4	4	4	3
Wren (Troglodytes troglodytes)	20	19	20	20	21	30	30	20	30	4	7	10	14	20	20	20
Song Thrush (Turdus philomelos)					2	2	4	2				1				
Blackbird (Turdus merula)	3	2	2	3	2	5	7	10	14	12	12	16	16	45	47	40
Wheatear (Oenanthe oenanthe)	6	6	2	4	5	9	3	12	8	12	5	6	10	17	20	20
Stonechat (Saxicola torquata)	10	8	3	4	6	8	15	12	6	5		2	3	7	8	6
Robin (Erithacus rubecula)	10	7	4	1	1		3	3	3		1	1	2	2	1	
Sedge Warbler (Acrocephalus schoenobaenus)	2		1									1	1	1	1	1
Whitethroat (Sylvia communis)	5	5	5	5	7	10	15	12	14	5	5	6	6	9	10	
Willow Warbler (Phylloscopus trochilus)														1		
Chiffchaff (Phylloscopus collybita)																1
Dunnock (Prunella modularis)	15	13	14	15	15	15	15	15	12	5	12	13	15	20	22	35
Meadow Pipit (Anthus pratensis)	100	80	55	60	80	100	100	100	95	25	42	45	47	50	48	45
Rock Pipit (Anthus spinoletta)	50	50	50	30	20	25	25	30	30	13	20	26	20	40	40	45
Pied Wagtail (Motacilla alba)	3	2	3	2	2	3	2	3	3	3					1	1
Starling (Sturnus vulgaris)									3	3	4	12	20	21	36	50
Linnet (Acanthis cannabina)	35	27	20	25	27	30	30	27	30	14	20	23	15	15	15	15
Chaffinch (Fringilla coelebs)					1							1				
Yellowhammer (Emberiza citrinella)			1	2	4	4	2	3	4	4	3	4	4	3	3	3
Reed Bunting (Emberiza schoeniclus)				2	2	2	2	4	3	4	4	1	1		2	2
House Sparrow (Passer domesticus)	12	+	+	10	10	15	30	30	28	30	30	25	25	20	20	12
S	24	24	23	25	25	25	25	27	27	26	26	30	28	27	30	29

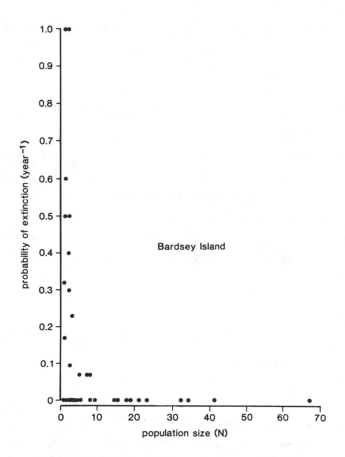

FIGURE 2. Observed relation between the probability-per-unit-time of extinction (ordinate) and the population size (abscissa), for the breeding birds of Bardsey Isle off Britain in the years 1954-1969. Compare this observed relation with the theoretical relation of figure 1. The abscissa is the average population size in years of breeding presence. The ordinate is calculated as the number of years of breeding presence that were followed by a year of breeding absence, divided by the total number of years of breeding presence. Each point represents one bird species. From analyses by H. L. Jones and J. M. Diamond, of breeding censuses evaluated by T. Reed.

the relation $e = p^N$. Similarly steep curves are obtained for 15 other British islands analyzed by Jones and Diamond (unpublished). Thus, the main predictor of extinction in these

studies was small populations size. Bird censuses on the California Channel Islands yield the same conclusion (Jones and
Diamond 1976, fig. 6).

Examination of graphs similar to fig. 2 for the 16 available British islands shows that certain bird species on island
after island tend to have e values lying above the general pattern for their N value, while certain other species tend to
have low e values for their N value on island after island.
Thus, there are species-specific determinants of extinction
proneness besides population size.

The species that are more extinction-prone than most other
species with the same population size turn out to share one or
more of four characteristics:

1. Many of them are small songbirds, which tend to be
short-lived.

2. Their populations tend to fluctuate widely in abundance (year-to-year CV of N > 0.4: e.g., wren, lapwing, reed
bunting, linnet, and whitethroat). CV was calculated as the
coefficient of variation for N from consecutive surveys on an
island or a mainland census plot.

3. Several of these species (wren, stonechat, song
thrush) are especially susceptible to harsh winters, which may
eliminate a whole population regardless of its size.

4. Several extinction-prone species of large body size
(lapwing, rock dove, wood pigeon) are ones that breed in loose
groups. Lack of social stimulation may make very small populations of these species prone to disappear.

Conversely, species that are more resistant to extinction
than most other species with the same population size turn out
to have one or both of two characteristics:

1. Most of them are large-bodied and long-lived (raven,
chough, crow, moorehen).

2. Some of them have very stable populations (year-to-

year CV of N > 0.3: raven and crow).

Alternatively, one can ask which trophic category of bird species is most prone to extinction in short-term island studies. The carnivores (hawks, owls, and shrike) prove to be nearly twice as extinction-prone as the average bird species. The probable explanation is that carnivores tend to live at low population densities.

To compare different islands, one can calculate for each island the average value of the percentage of its bird populations breeding in a given year that do not breed in the following year. This value is the average per-species extinction rate e^o. If one makes comparisons among northern European islands (fig. 3) or among the California Channel Islands (Jones and Diamond 1976) or among Panamanian islands (S. J. Wright, unpublished observations), e^o is seen to decrease with island area, i.e., with increasing population sizes. In addition, e^o is seen to increase with latitude when one compares the California Channel Islands ($33-34^oN$) with northern European islands ($50-65^oN$), or else when one compares various mainland census plots in northern Europe (Jarvinen 1979, 1980). The likely explanation is shorter individual lifetimes at high latitudes.

Summary of turnover studies.

Turnover studies at equilibrium confirm the theoretically predicted dependences of extinction probability on population density and island area (predictions 2a and 2b). When the overriding effect of population density is taken into account, the predicted effects of individual lifetime and population variability (predictions 1 and 5) are also confirmed. Predictions 3 and 4, concerning intrinsic rate of increase r and ratio of birth to death rate λ/μ, have not been tested. The predictions concerning population density and island area have also been confirmed by turnover studies on orb spiders (Toft

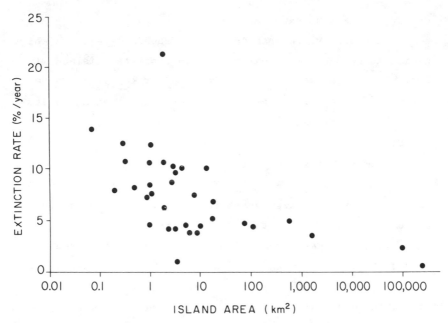

FIGURE 3. Risk of extinction as a function of island area, for breeding land birds of Northern European islands, on a time scale of one year. Ordinate: percentage of an island's breeding land bird populations that go extinct from one year to the next, on the average. Abscissa: island area. Note that risk of extinction decreases with island area. From analyses by H. L. Jones and J. M. Diamond, of breeding censuses evaluated by T. Reed.

and Schoener 1983). Comparisons of turnover studies for a range of organisms from protozoans and sessile marine organisms to arthropods, lizards, and birds show that extinction rates decrease approximately linearly with generation time (Schoener, 1983).

MODERN EXTINCTIONS OF BIRD POPULATIONS IN COMMUNITIES UNDERGOING HABITAT FRAGMENTATION

The previous section considered islands or habitat areas not undergoing drastic habitat changes, and hence maintaining species number more or less steady. In this section I instead

consider habitats that are being or have recently been fragmented. Reduction in area inevitably means a net loss of
species, due to an excess of extinction over immigrations. I
ask: can one generalize about which species are most prone to
disappear as a result of modern habitat fragmentation? Elsewhere in this volume Lovejoy et al. discuss the effect of
modern habitat fragmentation on an Amazonian rainforest biota.
The present chapter considers five other such studies.

    1. Southeastern Brazilian woodlots. Willis (1979, 1980)
studied bird distributions in three forest tracts on the Sao
Paulo plateau of southeastern Brazil. Over the past 150 years
the formerly unbroken forest that covered this plateau has been
largely cleared for agriculture, leaving only small and isolated forest "islands". The three tracts studied by Willis
were 1,400, 250, and 21 ha in area, and supported respectively,
175, 119, and 76 breeding species as of 1975-1978. Since the
original forest avifauna of the plateau consisted of about 203
species, the largest tract has lost about 28 species, the
medium-sized one 84 species, and the smallest one 127 species.
The large tract contains virtually all species of the medium-
sized one, which in turn contains virtually all species of the
small tract. Thus, the extinctions resulting from forest fragmentation occur in a fairly regular sequence.

    Some groups of birds have been more extinction-prone than
others. For instance, the smaller tracts have lost most
species of large-bodied canopy frugivores (parrots, toucans,
and cotingids), large-bodied terrestrial insectivores, and
small-bodied understory omnivores and insectivores and most
edge species. A generalization that makes sense of these
results is that risk of extinction in the small tracts
decreases with initial abundance, as assessed by current abundance in the largest tract (fig. 4). That is, the most
extinction-prone species are the rarest ones (Terborgh and

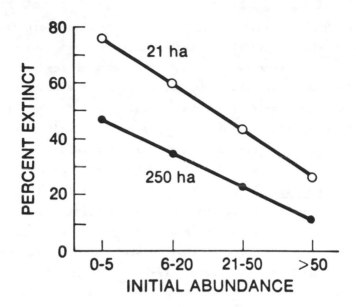

FIGURE 4. Risk of extinction as a function of population density and habitat area, for Brazilian forest birds, on a time scale of several decades. For two forest patches, one of area 21 ha, the other of 250 ha, initial population densities were estimated and expressed as bird individuals encountered per 100 hours of observation. Populations were then grouped into four classes on the basis of population density (abscissa). The ordinate gives the percentage of populations in each class that became extinct over the past few decades. Note that risk of extinction decreases with population density for each patch and is higher for the smaller patch. From Terborgh and Winter (1980), based on data of Willis (1979).

Winter 1980). In addition, forest species that readily fly across open country have been less likely to disappear in small tracts than sedentary species, presumably because populations of the former species are not truly isolated but can be replenished by colonizing individuals from other forest tracts.

   2. <u>Rio Palenque Field Station, Ecuador</u>. Mention should be made of Leck's (1979) study of an Ecuadorean forest patch that similarly became isolated by clearing of surrounding forest for agriculture. Of 170 forest bird species, 44 have

now disappeared, and 15 more declined and are likely to disappear. Among the lost species are nine very large birds and
five other rare birds, as well as several mammalian carnivores.

     3. Barro Colorado Island. The damming of the Chagras
River to create the Panama Canal and Lake Gatun converted many
former hilltops into islands in the lake. The best studied of
these islands is Barro Colorado (Willis 1974, Wilson and Willis
1975, Willis and Eisenmann 1979, Karr 1982a and 1982b, Wright
1984a and 1984b). Of the ca. 108 breeding species formerly
recorded on Barro Colorado, about 45 have disappeared. Many of
these disappearances are due to habitat changes (forest edge
and second-growth species eliminated by growth of forest).
However, about 13 of these documented former residents are
forest species whose disappearances cannot be attributed to
habitat changes and are probably due to insularization. The
actual number of species that disappeared may be as much as
three times higher (Karr, 1982a), because intensive studies of
Barro Colorado birds did not begin until well after Barro
Colorado was transformed from a hilltop into an island. Thus,
many populations are thought to have disappeared unnoticed.

     How can one explain which particular species disappeared?
Some of them were ground nesters and may have been eliminated
by terrestrial mammalian predators, which have become abundant
on Barro Colorado due to disappearance of top carnivores with
large area requirements (Willis 1974, Wilson and Willis 1975,
Terborgh and Winter 1980, Karr 1982a). When rarity is inferred
from its correlates of large body size, high trophic level, and
high metabolic requirements, extinction proneness correlates
poorly with inferred rarity (Wright 1984b). For birds catch-
able in mist-nets, abundance measured by mist-nets is also a
poor predictor of extinction (Karr 1982b). However, for the
whole avifauna, relative abundances estimated by Christmas
counts on the Panama mainland do have predictive value, the

rarer species being more extinction-prone (Wright 1984b). For
mist-netted species Karr (1984b) concluded that population
variability (CV of N) predisposes species to extinction. The
reason why inferred correlates of rarity are of low predictive
value may be that large species at high trophic levels are not
only rare; they also tend to be good overwater dispersers,
hence likely to buffer their Barro Colorado populations against
extinction through arrival of colonists from the Panama mainland.

     4. Banks Peninsula. When European settlement of New Zea-
land began in the early 19th century, the forests of South
Island's Banks Peninsula were already separated from the main
body of South Island forest by the grasslands of the Canterbury
Plains. During the late 19th century the peninsular forests
were heavily logged and fragmented, until today they exist only
as scattered patches, of which the largest is about 250 hec-
tares (Johnston 1969).

     Knowledge of Banks Peninsula birds has been summarized by
Turbott (1969), and I am indebted to Dr. Gordon Williams for
further information.

     Early European ornithologists recorded about 23 species of
native forest birds from the peninsular forests (table 3).
Only 11 of these species persist on the peninsula today. Four
of the 12 lost species disappeared completely or almost completely over the whole of New Zealand in the late 19th century,
due to introduced rats, mammalian predators, and other factors.
The other eight lost species are still widespread in large
tracts of New Zealand forest. Their disappearances on the peninsula, mainly in the decade after 1900, coincided with the
peak in forest destruction and fragmentation. Of the 11
species that survived, none is uncommon, and eight are small
passerines that rank as the most abundant bird species of South
Island. In contrast, six of the eight species lost through

TABLE 3. Forest birds of New Zealand's Banks Peninsula. The
data are from Turbott (1969), as evaluated by G. Williams.

1. Formerly present, now absent. The populations not only of
   the Banks Peninsula but also over the whole of New Zealand
   crashed during the 19th century:

Kokako	Callaeas cinerea
Saddleback	Philesturnus carunculatus
Bush Wren	Xenicus longipes
Thrush (Piopio)	Turnagra capensis

2. Formerly present, now absent. Still widespread in large
   tracts of New Zealand forest:

Weka	Gallirallus australis
Falcon	Falco novaeseelandiae
Red-crowned Parakeet	Cyanorhampus novaezelandiae
Yellow-crowned Parakeet	Cyanorhampus auriceps
Kaka	Nestor meridionalis
Long-tailed Cuckoo	Eudynamis taitensis
Robin	Petroica australis
Yellowhead	Mohoua ochrocephala

3. Still present:

Pigeon	Hemiphaga novaeseelandiae
Shining Cuckoo	Chrysococcyx lucidus
Morepork Owl	Ninox novaeseelandiae
Rifleman	Acanthisitta chloris
Fantail	Rhipidura fuliginosa
Tomtit	Petroica macrocephala
Brown Creeper	Finschia novaeseelandiae
Grey Warbler	Gerygone igata
Bellbird	Anthornis melanura
Tui	Prosthemadera novaeseelandiae
Silvereye	Zosterops lateralis

forest fragmentation live at lower densities, possibly lower
than that of any of the 11 species that survived. The disappearance of the two remaining species, the formerly common
robin and yellowhead, may be somehow related to their being
much more sedentary than any of the 11 survivors or than all of
the other lost species except the flightless weka. Perhaps the
ability to reverse extinctions in one forest patch by recolonization from other patches has been important to bird survival
in the fragmented Banks Peninsula forest.

    5. Eastern North American deciduous forest. The decidu-
ous forests of the eastern United States have become greatly

fragmented since European settlement. Whitcomb et al. (1981)
summarized extensive studies of bird distributions in relation
to the area and isolation of forest fragments and the life history properties of the bird species. The authors identified a
group of 15 species that are confined to the forest interior,
and that in addition prove to be virtually confined to forest
tracts exceeding 70 ha in area. Thus, these species tend to be
eliminated by forest fragmentation. Three of them (worm-
eating, hooded, and black-and-white warblers) have thus disappeared from entire 25-km^2 blocks.

The most remarkable finding is that 11 of these 15 species
are long-distance migrants that winter far to the south in the
neotropics and commute annually between breeding and wintering
grounds! One might have guessed a priori that fragmentation
would mainly affect sedentary permanent residents and least
affect long-distance migrants, since vagile species are the
ones that would most likely rapidly recolonize a forest patch
following a temporary extinction.

Whitcomb et al. (1981) explain this paradox in two ways.
First, banding recoveries show that returning adults of the
long-distance migrants tend to be philopatric. Thus, the long
migration flight between winter and summer grounds may be
irrelevant to colonizing of new summer territories: these
species are functionally sedentary if one is concerned with
breeding sites. Second, philopatry also means that individuals
replacing territory-holders that died since the last breeding
season tend to come from nearly forest patches. For example,
breeding censuses are available for Cabin John forest before
and after destruction of adjacent forest. The populations of
neotropical migrants increased in the year following destruction of adjacent forest (as its returning territory-holders
moved to Cabin John), but then declined drastically in subsequent years due to the permanent loss of neighboring sources of

colonists. In contrast, populations of permanent resident
species were steady throughout this period.

Summary of modern fragmentation studies. These five studies of modern habitat fragmentation differ from the turnover
studies discussed in the preceding section in an important
respect. The turnover studies were concerned with year-to-year
extinction, documented by absence of a breeding population of a
species in a year following a year of breeding presence for the
same species. The extinction was still counted as such for the
purposes of the analysis even if the species then bred again
the next year. In contrast, the fragmentation studies merely
ask what species were present before fragmentation many years
ago but are now absent. Absence now requires not only that the
species have become extinct but also that it not have subsequently recolonized. Thus, species differences in persistence
today cannot be be interpreted unequivocally in terms of
differences in resistance to extinction: they may also mean
differences in ability to recolonize.

It is certain that recolonization plays at least some role
in the results of most or all of these studies. For eastern
North American forest patches Whitcomb et al. (1981) explicitly
consider species differences in recolonization as the
overwhelming determinant of species differences in persistence.
Recolonization was noted as the cause of some continued presences of species on the southeastern Brazilian woodlots, Barro
Colorado, and Rio Palenque.

Persistence correlates with population density in four of
these five studies (all except the last). It correlates with
area in the Brazilian study, and inversely with population
variability on Barro Colorado. The other three theoretical
predictions about extinction listed earlier were not tested.
The area effect in the Brazilian study is the strongest indication that at least some of the patterns reflect differing

resistance to extinction, not just differing ability to
recolonize. The correlation between population density and
persistence is compatible with the extinction interpretation
but also with an interpretation based on recolonization: abundant mainland species produce more colonists. Haila et al.
(1979) were able to interpret species differences in persistence on Finland's Aland Archipelago on the latter basis.

In order to decide the relative importance of species
differences in extinction and recolonization for interpreting
these fragmentation studies, it will be necessary to identify
which species are actually capable of dispersing across open
country (or Lake Gatun) between forest patches. For species
incapable of such dispersal, persistence does provide unequivocal evidence of resistance to extinction. Wright (1984b) has
begun to analyze the Barro Colorado avifauna from this point of
view.

A further consideration in these fragmentation studies
concerns ways of assessing the composition of the pre-
fragmentation avifauna. Clearly, the ideal way is to have
available a survey before fragmentation, for the same forest
patch left standing after fragmentation. Two of the eastern
North American patches, Cabin John and Trelease Woods, were
actually surveyed yearly for several decades, and World
Wildlife Fund is now doing so for Amazonian patches under study
(Lovejoy et al. present volume). Multiple surveys are also
available for Barro Colorado and Rio Palenque, but many species
may have disappeared from both in the early years of fragmentation, before surveys began (Karr 1982a). When a pre-
fragmentation survey for the patch itself is not available,
there are two alternative ways to assess the pre-fragmentation
fauna: to equate it with the pre-fragmentation fauna of a
larger region including the patch, as available for the
southeast Brazilian and Banks Peninsula studies; or to equate

it with the fauna of a much larger forest in the vicinity
today, as Whitcomb et al. (1981) did for some eastern North
American patches. Both of these alternatives are imperfect, in
that a small patch would not start out with all the species of
a larger tract in which it was embedded. However, one can calculate the magnitude of this error from the so-called continental species/area relation for the fauna and region studied (a
graph of species number against area for nested census areas).

EXTINCTIONS OF MAMMAL POPULATIONS ON LAND-BRIDGE ISLANDS AND
MONTANE COMMUNITIES FRAGMENTED AT THE END OF THE PLEISTOCENE
    The end of the Pleistocene fragmented species ranges in
two ways. First, sea level rose more than 100 m due to glacial
melting, converting coastal lowlands into shallow seas and
thereby dissecting many land masses. Examples include the
dissection of Britain from Europe, of Trinidad from South America, of Fernando Po from Africa, of Tasmania from Australia,
and of Ceylon, Japan, Taiwan, Hainan and the Greater Sunda
Islands from Asia (figs. 5, 8, 11, 13). More than a century
ago Alfred Russel Wallace recognized that the presence of
flightless mammals and other taxa with poor water-crossing
ability on these islands was a legacy of the now-submerged
Pleistocene land bridges. For instance, it was over such a
bridge that rhinoceroses walked to what is now the island of
Java.
    Second, late-Pleistocene rising temperatures and altered
rainfall patterns fragmented continental expanses of habitat
into habitat patches. For example, habitats now distributed
disjunctly on mountain tops were continuous at lower elevations
during cool periods of the Pleistocene. The mystery of how the
same species of flightless montane animals and plants with
heavy seeds came to occupy the tops of distant mountains, such
as the Pyrenees and Alps and Caucasus, was solved by Forbes

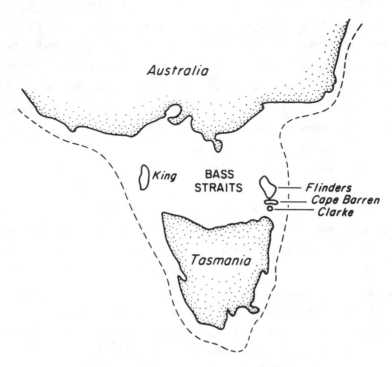

FIGURE 5. Map of Bass Strait, which separates Tasmania from
Australia today. The dashed line represents the coast line at
Pleistocene times of low sea level, when Bass Strait was dry
land and Tasmania was part of the Australian mainland. Rising
sea level flooded most of the Bass Strait platform except for
the highest hills that became modern islands, with the result
that Tasmania is now cut off from Australia.

(1846), who pointed out that dispersal had formerly been possible.

These late-Pleistocene fragmentations of land masses and
habitats sundered species ranges. Some of the resulting fragments retained more of their initial biota than did others, and
some species survived on more fragments than did others. Post-
Pleistocene extinctions have either been documented directly by
fossil remains of species at a site where the species no longer
occurs, or else inferred from modern discontinuous distributions. Such studies are available for mammals, birds, and

lizards. I begin with the mammal studies, because they are
easier to interpret for two reasons. First, fossil evidence is
far better for mammals than for birds and lizards, so that mammal extinctions are often documented rather than inferred.
Second, the poorer dispersal abilities of mammals permit one to
be more confident that modern disjunct distributions are the
product of differential extinction alone, not of extinctions
partly reversed by immigrations. I shall discuss three sets of
studies for mammals.

  1. Tasmania and the Bass Strait islands. Bass Strait,
which now separates Tasmania from Australia, nowhere exceeds
100 m in depth. Thus, the entire strait was a land platform at
low-sea-level times of the Pleistocene (fig. 5). Rising sea
levels submerged most of this platform, leaving one large
island (Tasmania, 67,900 km^2), four islands of 100 to 1,500 km^2
(Flinders, King, Cape Barren, and Clarke), and many smaller
islands. Hope (1973) has reported the extant and recent fossil
mammals of these islands. Her study is a particularly clean
study of differential extinction, because there is fossil evidence for former presence of almost all modern Tasmanian mammal
species on smaller islands now lacking those mammals; the fossils permit approximate dating of some of the extinctions; the
approximate time when various land connections were severed is
known; and humans were among the first species to disappear on
all islands except Tasmania, so that extinctions of other mammals due to fragmentation are not confounded by effects of man.
In addition, most of the modern water gaps are too wide to be
crossed by most of the mammal species involved, so that modern
presence of a mammal on many islands implies resistance to
post-Pleistocene extinction rather than good overwater colonizing ability.

  The largest island (Tasmania, 67,900 km^2), second largest
(Flinders, 1,330 km^2), and third largest (King, 1,110 km^1)

retained respectively the most (25), second most (13), and
third most (12) native flightless mammal species. Fig. 6 shows
that the number of herbivorous marsupials increases with island
area: Tasmania retained 10 species, the four islands in the
size range 100-1,500 km^2 retained 4-7, most islands of 1.4 to
10 km^2 retained 1 or 2, and no island smaller than 1.4 km^2
retained any.

Species varied greatly in their resistance to extinction
following habitat fragmentation (fig. 7). Species confined to
a few islands are generally on the largest islands, while those
on many islands are also on numerous small islands. At one
extreme, the rat-kangaroo Aepyprymnus rufescens and the mouse
Pseudomys novaehollandiae disappeared from all islands and

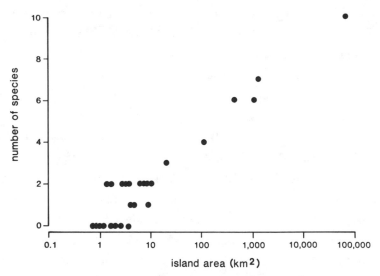

Herbivorous marsupials on Bass Strait islands

FIGURE 6. Number of species of herbivorous marsupials on the
islands of Bass Strait in modern times, as a function of island
area. Note that species number increases with island area, so
that the largest island (Tasmania) has 10 species while islands
smaller than 1.4 km^2 have no species. Data are from Hope
(1973). The pattern was produced by differential extinction,
small islands suffering more extinctions than large islands.

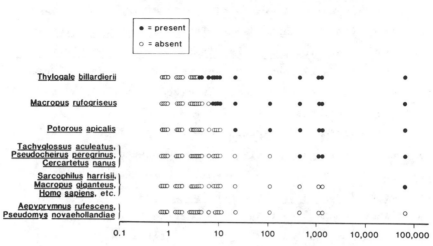

FIGURE 7. Distributions of the flightless mammals named on the
left, on islands of Bass Strait, as a function of island area.
Species tend to be distributed from the largest island down to
islands of a lower size limit that varies with the species.
The species that occupies the largest number of islands and
that reaches the smallest islands is at the top, while the next
to the bottom line depicts species confined to the largest
island (Tasmania), and the bottomline depicts two species that
disappeared from all the islands and are now confined to the
Australian mainland. Data are from Hope (1973). This pattern
was produced by differential extinction, some species being
more susceptible than others.

survived only on the Australian mainland. The marsupial "cat"
Dasyurus viverrinus, Homo sapiens, and nine other species did
little better, surviving on Tasmania and no other island. At
the opposite extreme, the wallaby Thylogale billardierii survived on 17 islands, including one of only 1.4 km^2.

How can one explain why some mammals were so much more
susceptible to effects of habitat fragmentation than were others? Three generalizations emerge:

(a) Carnivores were more susceptible than herbivores.
Among mammals weighing over 1 kg, three of the four marsupial
carnivores (the Tasmanian "wolf" Thylacinus cynocephalus, the
Tasmanian devil Sarcophilus harrisii, and Dasyurus viverrinus)
survived only on Tasmania, while seven of the nine marsupial
herbivores in this weight range survived on 5-17 islands,
including islands as small as 1.6 or 1.4 km^2.

(b) Large carnivores were more susceptible than small carnivores. The largest carnivores (T. cynocephalus and S.
harrisii) survived only on Tasmania, while the smallest carnivores (Smithopsis leucopus and Antechinus minimus) survived
on islands as small as 6 and 9 km^2, respectively. The
omnivorous Homo sapiens, the largest flightless mammal of Bass
Strait, also survived only on Tasmania. (The Tasmanians lacked
watercraft capable of voyages exceeding a few miles). For herbivores, however, there is not a clear inverse relation between
survival and size. For instance, the third and fourth largest
herbivores, the wallabies Macropus rufogriseus and Thylogale
billardierii, are the ones on the largest number of islands (11
and 17, respectively), far more than species one-tenth their
weight.

(c) Habitat specialists were more susceptible than habitat
generalists. Two small rodents of specialized habitats,
Mastacomys fuscus and Pseudomys higginsi, survived only on
Tasmania. The platypus Ornithorhynchus anatinus, which is confined to fresh water, survived on only Tasmania and two other
large islands.

Thus, the main pattern visible for Bass Strait Mammals is
that risk of extinction decreased with inferred population
size. This is why large islands retained more species than
small islands; why herbivores, habitat generalists, and small
carnivores survived on more islands than did carnivores, habitat specialists, and large carnivores; and why the latter three

types of species, which tend to live at low population density,
survived usually just on the largest island(s).

2. <u>Islands of the Sunda Shelf</u>. It was the rhinoceroses
of Java and Sumatra that brought Alfred Russel Wallace to
appreciate the importance of former land connections for the
modern distributions of species blocked by water gaps. Java,
Sumatra, Borneo, and many adjacent smaller islands are
separated from each other and the Asian mainland by the shallow
waters of the Java Sea and South China Sea. In the Pleistocene
the entire Sunda Shelf was an extension of the Asian mainland.
Rising sea-level fragmented the shelf into its modern configuration of sea and islands (fig. 8).

Fig. 9 (from Wilcox 1980) depicts the number of flightless
extant mammal species, S, as a function of island area for the
islands of the Sunda Shelf. For all islands S is lower than in
an equivalent area of the adjacent Asian mainland. The smaller
the island, the lower is the proportion that the island´s mammal fauna bears to the continental fauna of an equivalent area.
This suggests that post-Pleistocene extinctions have proceeded
further on the small islands than on the large islands. This
interpretation is confirmed for 10 big mammals of the Greater
Sunda Islands by fossil evidence. Today these 10 mammals
(tiger, orangutan, Javan and Sumatran rhinoceroses, elephant,
gibbon, banteng, leopard, Malay tapir, and Malay bear) are pat-
chily distributed on the three largest islands (Borneo, Sumatra, Java), each species being on only one or two of the three
islands. Of 30 possible populations (3 species x 10 islands),
only 17 are extant. However, in nine of the 13 cases of
species presently missing, the species is known as a Pleistocene fossil from the same island (Hooijer, in Terborgh 1974).
Thus, modern absence does mean past extinction rather than
non-arrival.

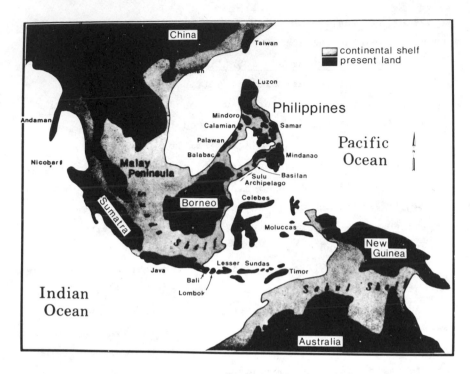

FIGURE 8. Map of the region from Southeast Asia to Australia, depicting modern land configurations today as well as land configurations at Pleistocene times of low sea level. Sea-level lowering converted the Sunda Shelf into an extension of Southeast Asia, and joined New Guinea, Australia, and the Sahul Shelf into a single continent. Rising sea level fragmented both shelves into archipelagoes of islands and separated New Guinea from Australia.

A systematic analysis to evaluate which species were most susceptible to extinction has not been done. It is obvious that some small mammals fared much better than any of the 10 just-mentioned big mammal species. None of the 10 big mammals managed to survive even on all three of the largest islands. In contrast, some squirrels and other small mammals survived not only on all three of the largest islands but also on islands that were too small to retain any of the big mammals.

3. Mountains of western North America. During cool periods of the Pleistocene, habitats today confined to higher

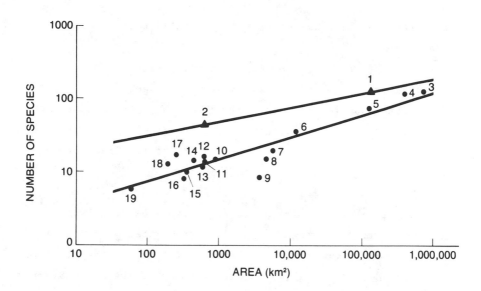

FIGURE 9. Lower line and points: the species/area relation for flightless mammals on islands of the Sunda Shelf, which was part of the Asian mainland at Pleistocene times of low sea-level. Upper curve and points: species/area relation for flightless mammals on pieces of the Southeast Asian mainland of varying areas. As a result of post-Pleistocene extinctions, S on all islands today is lower than in an equivalent area of the Asian mainland, and the smaller islands have lost proportionately more of their original mainland fauna and contain a lower proportion of the mammal fauna found in an equivalent mainland area. From Wilcox (1980); see Wilcox for identification of islands and mainland areas by number.

elevations of western North American mountains extended to lower elevations and lower latitudes. Flightless mammals characteristic of these habitats were then able to occupy the basin floors and to disperse among mountain ranges. Rising temperatures drove the habitats and their mammals up the mountains, leaving them unable to disperse through the deserts of the basin floor and yielding the disjunct distributions that we see today. The isolated populations were then subjected to a process of differential extinction. Fossils confirm the former presence of montane mammal species in lowland or southern areas or on certain mountains where the species no longer occur today.

Two sets of studies have been carried out on this differential extinction of montane mammals. Elsewhere in this volume Patterson reports his studies for 28 ranges of the southern Rocky Mountains. His results agree with and extend those of Brown (1971, 1978) for 19 ranges of the Great Basin. Brown's findings will be summarized here.

The montane mammals on the isolated mountain "islands" of the Great Basin are ultimately derived from the much larger "mainland" mountain ranges of the Sierra Nevadas to the west and of the Rocky Mountains to the east (fig. 10). Fig. 10 demonstrates, as did fig. 9 for the islands of the Sunda Shelf, that the number of montane mammal species on an isolated mountain range is lower than in a comparable area of the Sierra Nevada "mainland". The smaller the mountain, the lower the proportion that its mammal fauna bears to that in an equivalent Sierran area. This implies that extinction has proceeded further on the smaller mountains.

Table 4 shows that some species fared much better than did others. The chipmunk _Eutamias umbrinus_ survived on 17 of 19

FIGURE 10.   Above: map of the Great Basin of western North America, outlining mountain ranges at the 7500-ft. contour. The Great Basin today consists of mountain "islands" separated by deserts of the basin floor. Below: species/area relation for small flightless montane mammals on mountains of the Great Basin (lower curve), and for sample areas of various sizes in the continuous plateau of the Sierra Nevada (upper curve). As a result of extinction since the Pleistocene, the mountain "islands" contain fewer mammal species than equivalent Sierran areas, and the smaller mountain ranges have lost proportionately more species than the large ranges. From Brown (1971): see Brown for identification of "islands" and "mainland" areas by number.

Montane Mammal Species

on "Mountain Islands" of the Great Basin

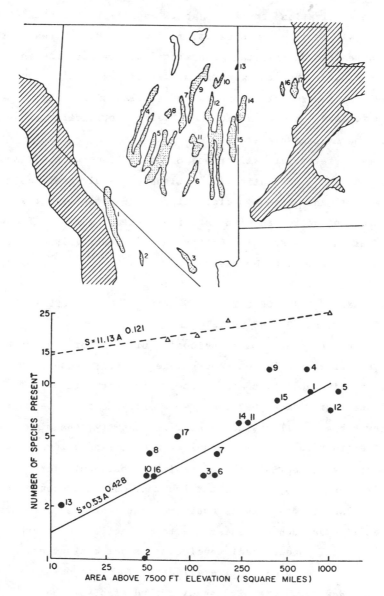

mountains (all but the two smallest mountains), while the hare
Lepus townsendi survived only on a single large mountain.
Three generalizations emerge. Habitat specialists (labelled S
in table 4), confined to streams, meadows, or rock piles, fared
much worse than did habitat generalists of similar size and
trophic status. Habitat generalist carnivores fared worse than
did habitat generalist herbivores of similar size. Big mammals
tended to fare worse than did small mammals of similar trophic
status and habitat preference.

The preferential extinctions of populations on small mountains, and the preferential extinctions of carnivores, habitat
specialists, and large mammals, all fit the pattern that risk
of extinction decreases with inferred population size. These
same four patterns describe Patterson's (present volume) study
for the southern Rocky Mountains.

EXTINCTIONS OF BIRD POPULATIONS ON LAND-BRIDGE ISLANDS FRAG- MENTED AT THE END OF THE PLEISTOCENE

Flightless mammals are obviously suitable for studies of
differential extinction on land-bridge islands, because their
water-crossing abilities are so obviously poor. It may at
first seem surprising that comparable analyses could be carried
out for birds at all. Since most birds can fly, one might
expect extinction of a bird population on a land-bridge island
to be highly susceptible to reversal by subsequent overwater
colonization. Thus, one might think that modern presences of
birds on land-bridge islands would reflect overwater colonization ability as much as resistance to extinction and therefore
could not yield unequivocal conclusions about extinction.

At the level of an entire avifauna, this reasoning is
correct. However, some bird species (and also some bat
species) that are capable of flight nevertheless refuse to
cross water gaps (Diamond 1976, 1981). Such species afflicted

TABLE 4. Differential extinction of mammals due to post-Pleistocene habitat fragmentation. Modern distributions of small flightless mammal species of pinon-juniper woodland, on 19 mountain ranges rising from the Great Basin of western North America. Woodland is now disjunctly distributed on montane "islands" above 7500 feet, separated by deserts of the basin floor. During cool wet periods of the Pleistocene the woodlands were continuously distributed across the basin, and small mammals could disperse between mountains. Habitat fragmentation since the Pleistocene has subjected mammal populations to differential extinction, resulting in modern absences of many species from many mountains. The body weight, diet (H = herbivore, C = carnivore), and habitat preference (G = habitat generalist; S = confined to a specialized habitat such as streams, meadows, or talus) are given for each species. Note that large animals, carnivores, and habitat specialists disappeared on more islands (−), especially on the smaller islands, than did small animals, herbivores, and habitat generalists. That is, rare animals were more prone to extinction following habitat fragmentation than were common animals. Large habitat islands (last row: area) retained more species (next-to-last row) than did small islands. From Brown (1971, 1978).

Species	Number of islands per species	Weight (in grams)	Diet	Habitat	Tolyabe	Ruby	White-Inyo	Snake	Toquima	Schell Creek	Deep Creek	White Pine	Desatoya	Spring	Stansbury	Oquirrh	Grant	Diamond	Spruce	Roberts Creek	Sheep	Pilot	Panamint
Eutamias umbrinus	17	60	H	G	+	+	+	+	+	+	+	+	+	+	+	+	+	+	+	+	+	+	−
Neotoma cinerea	17	300	H	G	+	+	+	+	+	+	+	+	+	+	+	+	+	+	+	−	+	+	+
Eutamias dorsalis, E. panamintinus	16	55	H	G	+	−	+	+	+	+	+	−	+	+	+	+	+	+	+	−	+	+	+
Spermophilus lateralis	14	170	H	G	+	+	+	+	+	+	+	+	+	+	+	+	+	+	−	−	−	+	−
Microtus longicaudus	13	45	H	G	+	+	+	+	+	+	+	+	+	+	+	−	+	−	−	−	−	−	−
Sylvilagus nuttallii	12	800	H	G	+	+	+	+	+	+	+	+	−	+	−	−	+	−	−	−	−	−	−
Marmota flaviventris	10	3,000	H	G	+	+	+	+	−	+	+	+	+	+	+	+	−	−	−	−	−	−	−
Sorex vagrans, S. tenellus	8	7	C	G	+	+	+	+	+	+	+	+	+	−	−	−	−	−	−	−	−	−	−
Sorex palustris	6	14	C	S	+	+	+	+	+	−	−	−	+	−	+	−	−	−	−	−	−	−	−
Ochotona princeps	5	120	H	S	+	+	−	+	+	−	+	−	−	+	−	+	−	−	−	−	−	−	−
Zapus princeps	4	25	H	S	+	+	+	+	−	−	+	−	−	−	−	+	−	−	−	−	−	−	−
Mustela erminea	4	50	C	G	+	+	+	+	+	−	−	−	+	−	+	−	−	−	−	−	−	−	−
Spermophilus beldingi	3	300	H	S	−	+	+	−	+	−	−	−	−	−	−	−	−	−	−	+	−	−	−
Lepus townsendii	1	3,000	H	S	−	+	−	−	−	−	−	−	−	−	−	−	−	−	−	−	−	−	−
number of species per mountain					13	12	11	10	10	8	8	7	7	6	6	6	5	4	4	4	3	3	3
mountain area above 7500 feet (sq. miles)					684	364	738	417	1178	1020	223	262	83	125	56	82	150	159	49	52	54	12	47

Mountain Ranges

by fear of flying overwater constitute an increasing percentage
of avifaunas as one approaches the equator. The non-water-
crossers represent only a few percent of northern European
birds, about 20% of southern California birds, and the majority
of New Guinea birds. There are hundreds, perhaps thousands of
tropical bird species that live in coastal lowlands but have
never been recorded from any island lacking a Pleistocene land
bridge to the mainland: not even from islands only a few miles
offshore. These species include all broadbills (Eurylaimidae),
malkohas (Phaenicophaeus), pheasants, partridges, forktails,
whistling thrushes, and song babblers of tropical Asia, and
most or all species of the families Furnariidae, Formicariidae,
Dendrocolaptidae, Pipridae, Bucconidae, Ramphastidae, and Gal-
bulidae in the New World tropics. The non-water-crossers are
as dependent on land bridges for access to islands, and as
suitable material for study of differential extinction, as are
rhinoceroses. MacArthur et al. (1972) and Diamond and Gilpin
(1983) discuss criteria for identifying non-water-crossing
species in the avifauna of Panama and the Malayan subregion,
respectively.

I shall summarize two studies of the effects of post-
Pleistocene fragmentation on birds, and briefly mention some
other such studies.

1. Solomon Islands. In the northern chain of the Solomon
Archipelago in the tropical southwest Pacific, all islands from
Buka and Bouganville through Shortland, Fauro, Choiseul, and
Ysabel to Ngela (Florida) and possibly Guadalcanal are
separated today by shallow water gaps and were joined into a
single huge island ("Greater Bukida": fig. 11) in the Pleisto-
cene (Diamond and Mayr 1976, Diamond 1983). There are numerous
other Solomon islands that were not connected to Greater
Bukida, some of them over 3000 km^2 in area and separated from
Greater Bukida by water gaps of less than 20 km.

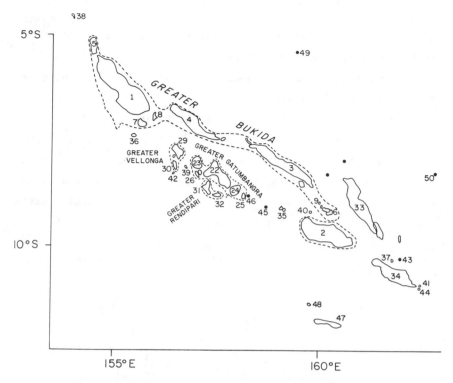

FIGURE 11. Map of the Solomon Archipelago in the Southwest Pacific Ocean, showing modern island outlines (solid lines) and also island outlines at Pleistocene times of low sea level (dashed lines). Sea-level lowering converted what are today shallow straits into dry land, joining numerous sets of modern islands into single larger islands. Rising sea level then fragmented the Pleistocene islands. The largest of these Pleistocene islands was Greater Bukida, whose fragments today extend from Buka Island in the northwest to Ngela (Florida) and possibly Guadalcanal in the southeast. From Diamond (1983); see Diamond and Mayr (1976) for identification of islands by number.

Not surprisingly, the endemic giant rats (Uromys and Solomys) of the Solomons are confined to the largest islands derived from Greater Bukida. Most Solomon bird and bat species cross water readily and occur not only on Greater Bukida fragments but also on other islands. However, 13 bird species endemic to the Solomons, as well as the endemic bats Pteralopex atrata, Pteropus mahaganus, and Anthops ornatus, are now confined to one or more islands that represent fragments of Greater Bukida. These species are evidently unable (in the case of one flightless bird species) or unwilling (in the case of the bats and the other birds) to cross water gaps. They must have been distributed over Greater Bukida when it was a single land mass. Their present distributions (summarized in table 5 for the birds) reflect the extent to which they have become extinct on the fragments of Greater Bukida in the ca. 10,000 years since it was dissected by rising sea-level. Table 5 yields the following conclusions:

TABLE 5. Distribution of land-bridge relict bird species on the post-Pleistocene fragments of Greater Bukida, Solomon Islands.

Island	Area (km²)	Halcyon leucopygia	Zosterops metcalfii	Corvus woodfordii	Nesoclopeus woodfordi	Pitta anerythra	Accipiter imitator	Nesasio solomonensis	Halcyon bougainvillei	Rhipidura drownei	Pachycephala implicata	Stresemannia bougainvillei	Meliphaga inexpectata	Microgoura meeki
Bougainville	8591	✓	✓	✓	✓	✓	✓	✓	✓	✓	✓	✓		
Guadalcanal	5281	✓		✓	✓				✓	✓	✓		✓	
Ysabel	3877	✓	✓	✓	✓	✓	✓	✓						
Choiseul	2966	✓	✓	✓	✓	✓	✓	✓						✓
Buka	611	✓	✓											
Ngela	368	✓	✓											
Shortland	233	✓	✓											
Wagina	90.7			✓										
Fauro	69.6	✓												
Buena Vista	14.0	✓												
Molakobi	7.67	✓	✓											
Fara	7.25	✓												
Arnavon	5.65													
Bates	5.23		✓											
Piru	2.95													
Oema	2.85													
Nusave	0.534													
Bagora	0.326													
Nugu	0.149													
Samarai	0.091													
New	0.071													
Dalakalonga	0.067													
Elo	0.055													
Kukuvulu	0.040													
Tapanu	0.0161													
Kanasata	0.0091													
Near New	0.0070													

The number of relict populations rises steeply with increasing island area, until the largest island (Bouganville, 8590 km^2) has all but two of the 13 relicts (fig. 12). Islands of 250-650 km^2 retained only two relicts. Not a single relict population survived on any of the numerous ornithologically explored Greater Bukida fragments of less than 5 km^2.

Some species are much more prone to extinction than others, even after we remove from consideration the ground pigeon Microgoura meeki (whose distribution may have become restricted by feral cats before ornithological exploration began) and the five montane species Meliphaga inexpectata, Stresemannia

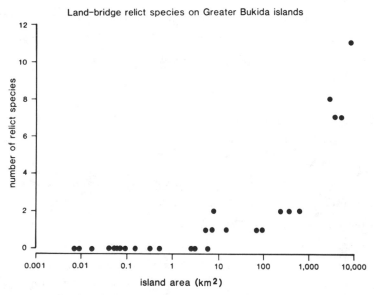

FIGURE 12. Species/area relation for land-bridge relict bird species on modern Solomon islands derived from fragmentation of the large Pleistocene island Greater Bukida by rising sea level. The ordinate gives for each island the number of bird species that are unwilling or unable to fly across water gaps and that are confined to islands derived from Greater Bukida. The populations of these bird species today are relicts of populations distributed over Greater Bukida during the Pleistocene period (Diamond 1983).

bougainvillei, Pachycephala implicata, Rhipidura drownei, and
Halcyon bougainvillei (now confined to either or both of the
two islands with the highest mountains, but possibly also formerly on medium-high islands when Pleistocene cool climates
lowered the altitudinal limits of montane vegetation). Of the
remaining seven species, four (the rail Nesoclopeus woodfordi,
the pitta Pitta anerythra, the hawk Accipiter imitator, the
large owl Nesasio solomonensis) are now confined to three or
all four of the four islands with areas exceeding 2500 km^2.
Three species (the kingfisher Halcyon leucopygia, the white-eye
Zosterops metcalfii, the crow Corvus woodfordi) have survived
on eight islands each, including most islands with areas of 230
km^2 or greater plus a few islands with areas of 5-90 km^2. The
former four species, which must be considered extinction-prone,
have considerably lower population densities than any of the
latter three species, which are evidently more resistant to
extinction.

The increase in species retained per island with island
area, and the increase in surviving populations per species
with abundance, both mean that risk of extinction decreases
with population size.

2. New Guinea land-bridge islands. New Guinea and Australia lie on the Sahul Shelf (fig. 13). Today the shallow
Arafura Sea separates New Guinea from Australia. However, at
late-Pleistocene times of low sea level New Guinea, Australia,
and the whole Sahul Shelf were a single land mass that was then
dissected by rising sea level. Of the modern islands near New
Guinea, some (e.g., Aru, Japen, Misol) are land-bridge islands
that were just pieces of the New Guinea mainland until they
became dissected away. Others (e.g., Biak, New Britain, Ceram)
are "oceanic" islands that have had no recent land connections
to New Guinea.

Fig. 14 shows that all the large land-bridge islands (open circle) have about twice as many lowland species as oceanic islands of comparable area and proximity to New Guinea (filled circle), but many fewer species than equal-sized pieces of the New Guinea mainland (X) (Diamond 1972). The excess of species over the number on oceanic islands arose because the land-bridge islands started off with the full species complement of the mainland. The species deficit compared to modern mainland areas arose because populations that died out after the land bridges were severed either could not be restored at all (in the case of non-water crossing species), or else had to be restored by colonization overwater rather than from adjacent mainland areas (in the case of water-crossing species). On the smallest land-bridge island (A=0.93 km^2) the species number is no larger than on a comparable-sized oceanic island (see last sentence of next paragraph for explanation).

Alternatively, one can focus on those 134 New Guinea lowland species that are incapable of crossing water gaps. These species occur today only on land-bridge islands, not on oceanic islands. However, their number decreases sharply with area of land-bridge island: 36-45 such species on land-bridge islands of area 1,600-7,800 km^2; 26 on an island of 450 km^2; 3 on an island of 145 km^2; and none on an island of 0.93 km^2 (which nevertheless has 14 water-crossing species). The explanation is that extinction rates increase with decreasing island area, hence all Pleistocene bird populations have disappeared in the past 10,000 years on very small land-bridge islands. Their avifauna consists entirely of post-Pleistocene overwater colonists, and their species composition as well as species number are indistinguishable from those on comparable-sized oceanic islands.

Among the non-water-crossing species, some fared much better than others on land-bridge islands since the end of the

Pleistocene. At the on extreme (fig. 13), some species, such
as the black cockatoo Probosciger aterrimus and frilled monarch
Monarcha telescophthalmus, have survived on all seven land-
bridge islands exceeding 450 km^2 in area (but none smaller).
At the opposite extreme, 32 species disappeared from all land-
bridge islands, including the largest island (7,800 km^2). Most
of these 32 species fit into one or more of four categories:
(a) big birds with enormous territories, hence small initial
populations. Examples: the New Guinea harpy eagle (Harpyopsis
novaeguineae), Doria´s goshawk (Megatriorchis doriae),
Pesquet´s parrot (Psittrichas fulgidus). (b) Small birds that
occur in forest but are rare, hence small initial populations.
Examples: the cuckoo-shrike Campochaera sloetii, flycatcher
Monarcha rubiensis, and honey-eater Timeliopsis griseigula.
(c) Non-forest species with specialized habitat requirements,
hence small initial populations. Examples: the rail Megacrex
inepta, wren-warbler Malurus alboscapulatus, and whistler
Pachycephala aurea. (d) Species that depend for food on patchy
and ephemeral fruits, seeds, and flowers, hence populations
fluctuate greatly. Examples: the cuckoo Eudynamis parva, the
honey-eater Meliphaga flavirictus, and four species of grass-
finches (Lonchura).

FIGURE 13. Distribution of the flycatcher Monarcha
telescophthalmus (shaded islands). The dashed line outlines
the Sahul Shelf, which was all dry land at Pleistocene times of
low sea level. Rising sea level fragmented the shelf into
islands, isolating populations of flightless animals and birds
unwilling to fly across water. The flycatcher Monarcha
telescophthalmus today occurs on every large island fragmented
from the Sahul Shelf, but on no small fragment (as a result of
its extinction on small islands), nor on oceanic islands off
the Sahul Shelf (as a result of its inability ever to reach
these islands) (Diamond 1975).

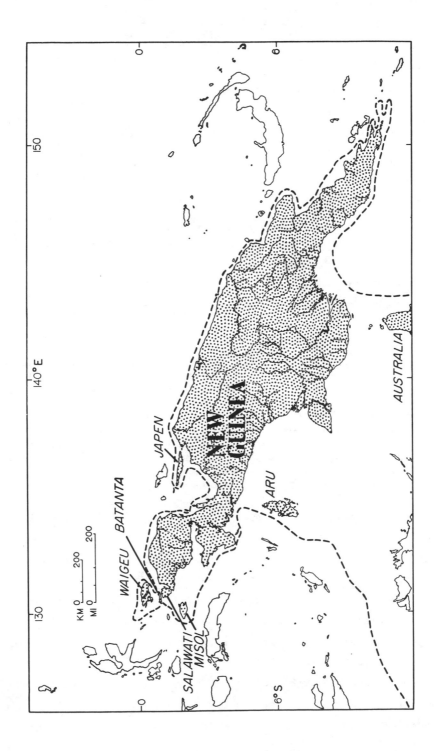

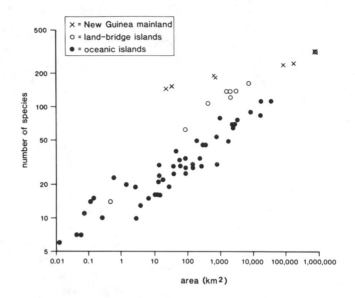

Species/area relation for New Guinea region

FIGURE 14. Species/area relation for bird species on oceanic islands (●) and land-bridge islands (o) of the New Guinea region, and for areas of various sizes on the New Guinea mainland (x). Note that land-bridge islands have fewer species than equivalent-sized areas of the New Guinea mainland, as a result of extinctions since the end of the Pleistocene period. Oceanic islands have fewer species than equivalent-sized land-bridge islands, except that very small land-bridge islands do not differ in species number from oceanic islands because of very high post-Pleistocene extinction rates.

Thus, small population size (small size of island or low population density of the species) is again the best predictor of proneness to extinction. Population variability appears important in a few cases.

3. Other studies. Studies of differential extinction of birds on land-bridge islands, based on analysis of total species number, are those of Terborgh (1974, 1975) for neotropical islands, Diamond (1975) for the Bismarck island of New Hanover, and Terborgh and Winter (1980) for five large islands off four continents. Studies based on non-water-crossing species alone are those of MacArthur, Diamond, and Karr (1972)

for Panamanian islands, and of Diamond and Gilpin (1983) for
greater Sunda islands. All of these studies concluded that
extinction rates are higher on smaller islands.

EXTINCTIONS OF LIZARD POPULATIONS ON LAND-BRIDGE ISLANDS FRAG-
MENTED AT THE END OF THE PLEISTOCENE
     Post-Pleistocene extinctions of lizards on land-bridge
islands in the Gulf of California have been studied by Soule
and Sloan (1966), Case (1975), and Wilcox (1978, 1980, 1983).
These analyses yielded the following conclusions:
     1. Species losses decreased with island area, just as in
the studies of birds and mammals on land-bridge islands (fig.
15).
     2. The Gulf islands differ in time since the land bridge
was severed, from 6,000 to 12,000 years. Wilcox (1978) was
able to show, after partialling out variation in S due to area
and latitude, that S decreases with time since severing of the
land bridge: i.e., that extinction increases with time (fig.
16). This conclusion is to be expected, but there is no other
set of Pleistocene land-bridge islands where it has been
tested.
     3. As usual, some species fared much better than others
(Case 1975). Where abundances have been measured directly,
abundant lizards such as Uta stansburiana and Cnemidophorus
tigris are on many more islands than are rare lizards. Alternatively, if one correlates persistence with habits without
considering abundance, one finds that species on few islands
tend to be habitat specialists (e.g., Coleonyx variegatus,
Streptosaurus mearnsi, Xantusia vigilis, Phrynosoma coronatum)
or else species at high trophic levels (the lizard-eating
lizards Crotophytus wislizenii and C. collaris).
     4. If one compares calculated extinction rates for
lizards on the Gulf islands with those for birds on neotropical

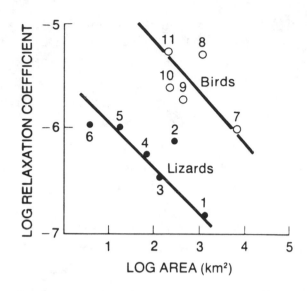

FIGURE 15. Risk of extinction (log relaxation coefficient: ordinate), as a function of island area (abscissa), for birds and lizards, on a time scale of 10,000 years. Extinction rates since the end of the Pleistocene were calculated for species on land-bridge islands of the New World. Note that risk of extinction decreases with area for both birds and lizards, but that bird populations go extinct over 10 times faster than lizard populations on an island of the same area (Wilcox 1980).

islands or mammals on western North American mountain tops, the values for lizards are an order of magnitude lower (Case 1975, Wilcox 1980; see fig.15). In fact, for birds on Gulf islands there is no difference between oceanic and land-bridge islands: all the Pleistocene populations of the land-bridge islands have disappeared, and the present avifauna consists entirely of sub-sequent overwater colonists (Wilcox 1983, Cody 1983). Thus, lizards are much less extinction-prone than birds and mammals on the same islands or on islands of similar area. The reasons are that lizards have much lower metabolic rates, tend to have higher population densities, and are far better able to survive

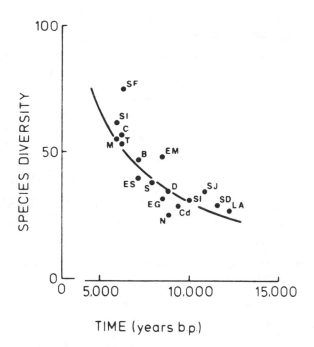

FIGURE 16. Calculated losses of lizard species on land-bridge islands near Baja California as a function of number of years elapsed since rising sea level severed the land bridge between each island and the Baja California mainland. The ordinate gives the number of lizard species corrected for variation due to area and latitude. Note that species number decreases with time because extinctions proceed with time. From Wilcox (1978): see Wilcox for identification of islands by letter.

long periods without food than are similar-sized birds and mammals (Wilcox 1978, 1980).

SUMMARY OF MAMMAL, BIRD, AND LIZARD STUDIES ON LAND-BRIDGE ISLANDS

Studies of extinction following late-Pleistocene fragmentation raise the same two methodological issues as did studies of extinction following modern fragmentation: assessing the initial biota, and separating the relative contributions of recolonization, and of resistance to extinction, in explaining modern presence.

Ideally, one would like to have the initial biota documented by fossils. The familiar difficulties in sampling the
fossil record will generally frustrate this ideal. Among
post-Pleistocene fragmentation studies to date, only the mammal
studies have been able to draw on fossil evidence. In the
absence of fossil evidence the initial biota must be inferred
on the basis of the biota of similar-sized mainland areas
today. Naturally, the mainland biota itself will have changed
somewhat in the 10,000 years since the end of the Pleistocene.
However, for the three studies involving mammals and with availability of fossils, it turns out that the fossils do not significantly alter any of the conclusions that would have been
drawn if fossils had been unavailable.

Comparison of modern distributions and inferred late-
Pleistocene ones yields unequivocal conclusions about extinction only if recolonization has been negligible. In the studies of mammals this assumption appears to be justified. The
assumption would not be justified for an entire avifauna or
herpetofauna. However, by confining attention to species
unable to cross water gaps (as inferred from field observations
and from absence from islands lacking Pleistocene land
bridges), one can isolate sets of bird and lizard species that
yield as unequivocal conclusions about extinction as do mammals. The analyses of Gulf of California lizards need reexami-
nation from this point of view. The analysis of bird distributions on land-bridge islands by Terborgh and Winter (1980)
encompassed all breeding land bird species, not just the non-
water-crossers. This may explain why that analysis did not
find clear relations between presence on land-bridge islands
and expected correlates of resistance to extinction.

All studies of mammal, bird, and lizard extinctions on
land-bridge islands have shown that populations on small
islands are at greater risk than those on large islands.

Resistance to extinction correlated with direct estimates of
abundance in three studies (Solomon birds, New Guinea birds,
Gulf of California lizards), and with correlates of abundance
(herbivory, small body size, generalized use of habitat) in
four studies (Tasmanian, Sundan, and North American mammals and
Gulf of California lizards). A few New Guinea bird species
illustrated the expected dependence of extinction on population
variability. Other expected correlates of extinction have not
been tested in these studies of land-bridge islands.

EXTINCTIONS IN EVOLUTIONARY TIME, AS ESTIMATED FROM ENDEMISM

Some oceanic islands, such as Hawaii, Galapagos, and New
Zealand, are famous for the endemism of their biotas, which
consist mostly of endemic species and even genera and families.
Other islands, such as the New Hebrides, Bismarcks, and Palau,
lack such fame and share most of their species with the neighboring mainland or archipelago. What can be learned from these
differences in endemism?

One can show that the number of species on an archipelago
(or island) depends both on immigration rates and extinction
rates, but that the percentage of an archipelago's species that
are endemic to the archipelago depends only on extinction
rates. That percentage, for some natural group of species such
as birds, varies inversely with the average extinction rate for
the group's species in the archipelago. The reason is that if
populations go quickly extinct, few survive long enough to
evolve into an endemic species or genus. Let the colonist pool
outside the archipelago consist of P species with the probability p per unit time of colonizing the archipelago; and let q be
the probability per unit time that a species present in the
archipelago will go extinct. Then the number of species in the
archipelago at any instant is $Pp/(p + q)$, a function of both
the immigration probability p and the extinction probability q.

However, the fraction of the archipelago's species that survive
for time t (e.g., for the time necessary to evolve into a distinct species) is simply e^{-qt}, a function only of the extinction probability q. The comparisons of archipelagoes (or
islands) with respect to their percentages of endemics permits
one to compare the risk of extinction among the archipelagoes.

At least five caveats require mention. First, the calculation obviously must exclude islands recently risen from the
sea (e.g., Krakatoa and Surtsey), whose biota has had no time
to differentiate and is entirely non-endemic for reasons unrelated to extinction. Second, one must similarly exclude
islands recently covered by glaciers (e.g., Iceland); the biota
of such islands is also necessarily recent. Third, one must
exclude all Pleistocene land-bridge islands, on which endemism
is very low because the island was a piece of the mainland so
recently. A fourth point is that immigration does influence
endemism insofar as gene flow from the mainland inhibits subspeciation and development of reproductive isolation. However,
once reproductive isolation has been achieved, subsequent differentiation beyond the level of endemic allospecies (to the
level of endemic full species, genus, or family) is not
directly affected by immigrants. (Immigration rates may, however, have an indirect effect, by raising equilibrium species
number and hence extinction rates.) Finally, while subfossil
endemic bird species exterminated by the first Polynesian
colonists are known for New Zealand and Hawaii, similar extinct
subfossil endemics probably await discovery on other remote
islands (Olson and James 1982). When subfossil avifaunas are
better explored, consideration of them is expected to
strengthen rather than change the conclusion drawn from fig.
17. Fig. 17 shows that the highest percentage of presently-
known endemics is on large remote archipelagoes. It is precisely these archipelagoes, with their absence of native

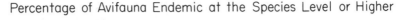

Percentage of Avifauna Endemic at the Species Level or Higher

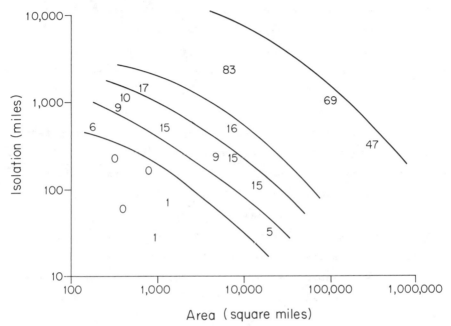

Area (square miles)

FIGURE 17. Numbers on the graph give, for some Pacific island or archipelago, the percentage of its breeding land bird species that are endemic at the level of full species or higher. Location of number gives the island's area (square miles, abscissa) and distance from nearest major colonization source (miles, ordinate). For instance, 16% of the species of Fiji, with an area of 7055 square miles and distance of 520 miles from the New Hebrides, are endemic full species or belong to endemic genera. Curves are drawn by hand to group islands with similar endemism.. Note that endemism increases with island area and isolation. Since percentage of endemics is an inverse measure of the risk of extinctions, this means that extinction rates over evolutionary time are lowest on the largest, most remote islands (Diamond 1980).

mammals, that are most likely to have radiations of endemic birds that suffered extinctions when man arrived with his cats, rats, and pigs.

Fig. 17 shows how the percentage of endemic birds increases with archipelago area and isolation for Pacific

island avifaunas (Diamond 1980). The Pacific islands with a
high percentage of endemics are the huge, somewhat isolated
islands of New Zealand (69%, including extinct subfossils),
Australia (49%), and New Guinea (47%),and the medium-sized,
very remote Hawaiian archipelago (83%; even higher when extinct
subfossils are included). There is only a modest percentage of
endemics on the large but close Solomons (15%) and Bismarcks
(5), and on the remote but small Societies (17%) and Marquesas
(9%). The reason why endemism increases with area is that
extinction rates decrease with area over geological time, just
as over shorter times (figs. 3, 4, 6, 9, 10, 12, 14, 15).
Endemism increases with isolation because more remote archipelagoes receive fewer immigrants, hence fewer species at
equilibrium, less competition, and lower extinction rates.

There are also differences in degree of endemism of various bird groups on the same island. For instance, of New
Guinea's hawks, most (65%) belong to extralimital species, and
only 10% belong to endemic genera, while the majority of New
Guinea songbirds belong to endemic species and even genera.
These differences become even more marked when one compares
birds with other groups. For instance, Australia has numerous
Gondwanaland relicts among its insects and plants, but almost
all its endemic songbirds are products of a radiation from a
post-Gondwanan colonization (Sibley and Ahlquist 1984). New
Caledonia is a geologically old island on which volcanism
ceased about 80 million years ago. It has endemic tribes of
beetles and families of plants. Probable Gondwanan relicts
include its mayflies and many beetles, and its podocarps, arau-
carias, Nothofagus, and Proteaceae among its plants (Holloway
1979). In contrast, among its 71 breeding land bird species
only one (the kagu Rhinochetus jubatus) is even conceivably a
Gondwanan relict, while 66 are not generically distinct, 52 are

not specifically distinct, and 26 are not even subspecifically
distinct.

   These comparisons suggest that birds are much more
extinction-prone than beetles, which have lower metabolic rates
and higher population densities, and than many plant groups
with longer lifetimes and higher population densities. The
hawk-vs.-songbird comparison for New Guinea suggests higher
extinction rates for hawks due to their lower population densities. However, it is risky to assess extinction proneness of
different groups on the same island by means of differences in
levels of endemism alone without fossil evidence. The very low
endemism of New Guinea hawks may be due to high immigration
rates preventing achievement of reproductive isolation. The
same factor may explain why endemism is so much lower in
Hawaiian ferns than Hawaiian insects. Molecular evidence from
protein and DNA clocks makes it obvious that taxa of the same
nominal level of endemism in different groups can be of very
different ages, e.g., species of frogs or rodents considered
congeneric on morphological grounds are far more distinct than
congeneric bird species (Wilson et al. 1977; Sibley and
Ahlquist 1982). In short, since we do not know whether songbirds can differentiate to the level of being considered an
endemic genus more rapidly than can hawks or ferns and less
rapidly than can beetles, the intergroup comparisons of endemism are equivocal indicators of proneness to extinction. This
objection does not apply to comparison of the same group in
different archipelagoes.

CONCLUSIONS
   I began with six theoretical predictions about population
lifetimes (resistance to extinction): that they would increase
with generation time or individual lifetime, population density, area, intrinsic rate of increase, and ratio of birth to

death rate, and that they would decrease with variability in population size. The data base for testing these conclusions comes from studies of turnover in communities at equilibrium, modern habitat fragmentation, late-Pleistocene land or habitat fragmentation, and endemism. How well do the predictions stand up?

All studies confirm that risk of extinction decreases with area available to the population. (The increase in habitat diversity as well as population size with area surely contributes to this decrease in the risk of extinction.)

Studies of turnover, modern fragmentation, and late-Pleistocene fragmentation confirm that risk of extinction decreases with population density, either measured directly or else inferred from its correlates of trophic position, body size, and habitat niche width.

The prediction concerning variability in population size is confirmed by turnover studies, and supported by fragmentary data from the Barro Colorado fragmentation study and the New Guinea land-bridge island study.

The prediction concerning individual lifetime is confirmed by turnover studies.

The predictions concerning intrinsic rate of increase and ratio of birth to death rate have not been tested.

I suggest two steps for carrying these analyses of extinction further:

First, if one compares populations of different species on the same island, the effect of population density on risk of extinction is so steep (fig. 2) that it will be impossible to discern effects of other factors until the effect of this overriding factor has been removed. Indirect correlates of population density (trophic position, body size, and habitat niche width) will not suffice for this purpose. The first step

should therefore be direct measurement of population density
and construction of an e-vs.-N graph like fig. 2.

   Second, one may then try to interpret species with devi-
antly high or low values on e-vs.-N graphs in terms of the
species' lifetime or generation time, population variability,
intrinsic rate of increase, and birth and death rates. Some of
this life-history information can already be culled from the
literature. Thus, I have hopes that we can make progress soon
in understanding how species differ in susceptibility to
extinction, in terms of biological attributes of the species.

   It is a pleasure to acknowledge my debt to Lee Jones,
Egbert Leigh, Jr., Robert May, Timothy Reed, the late Gordon
Williams, and S. Joseph Wright for valuable information and
discussion.

LITERATURE CITED

BROWN, J. H. 1971. Mammals on mountaintops: nonequilibrium
    insular biogeography. American Naturalist 105:467-478.
BROWN, J. H. 1978. The theory of insular biogeography and the
    distribution of boreal birds and mammals. Great Basin
    Naturalist Memoirs 2:209-227.
CASE, T. J. 1975. Species numbers, density compensation, and
    colonizing ability of lizards on islands in the Gulf of
    California.. Ecology 56:3-18.
CODY, M. L. 1983. The land birds. In: Biogeography of the
    Gulf of California, eds. T. J. Case and M. L. Cody.
    University of California Press, Berkeley, in press.
DIAMOND, J. M. 1972. Biogeographic kinetics: estimation of
    relaxation times for avifaunas of Southwest Pacific
    islands. Proc. Nat. Acad. Sci. 69, 3199-3203.
DIAMOND, J. M. 1975. Assembly of species communities. In:
    Ecology and Evolution of Communities, eds. M. L. Cody and
    J. M. Diamond. Pp. 342-444. Harvard University Press, Cam-
    bridge.
DIAMOND, J. M. 1976. Relaxation and differential extinction
    on land-bridge islands: applications to natural preserves.
    Proc. 16th Intern. Ornith. Congr., pp. 616-628.
DIAMOND, J. M. 1980. Species turnover in island bird communi-
    ties. Proc. 19th Intern. Ornith. Congr., pp. 777-782.

DIAMOND, J. M.   1981.   Flightlessness and fear of flying in
    island species. Nature
    293, 507-508.
DIAMOND, J. M.   1983.   Report of a 1974 ornithological expedi-
    tion to the Solomon Islands: survival of bird populations
    stranded on land-bridge islands. Nat. Geog. Soc. Research
    Reports, 15:127-141.
DIAMOND, J. M. and M. E. GILPIN.   1983.   Biogeographic umbilici
    and the evolution of the Philippine avifauna. Oikos, 41:in
    press.
DIAMOND, J. M. and R. M. MAY.   1977.   Species turnover rates on
    islands: dependence on census interval. Science 197, 266-
    270.
DIAMOND, J. M. and E. MAYR.   1976.   Species-area relation for
    birds of the Solomon Archipelago. Proc. Nat. Acad. Sci.
    73, 262-266.
FORBES, E.   1846.   Geol. Suv. G. B. Eng. Wales 1, 336-432.
HAILA, Y., O. JARVINEN and R. A. VAISANEN.   1979.   Effect of
    mainland population changes on the terrestrial bird fauna
    of a northern island. Ornis Scandinavica 10, 48-55.
HOLLOWAY, J. D.   1979.   A Survey of the Lepidoptera,
    Biogeography and Ecology of New Caledonia. Junk, The
    Hague.
HOPE, J. H.   1973.   Mammals of the Bass Strait Islands. Proc.
    Roy. Soc. Vict. 85, 163-196.
JARVINEN, O.   1979.   Geographical gradients of stability in
    European land bird communities. Oecologia 38, 51-69.
JARVINEN, O.   1980.   Dynamics of North European bird communi-
    ties. Proc. 19th Intern. Ornith. Congr., 770-776.
JOHNSTON, W. B.   1969.   Modification of the natural environment
    by man. In: The Natural History of Canterbury, ed. G. A.
    Knox, pp. 77-94. Reed, Wellington.
JONES, H. L. and J. M. DIAMOND.   1976.   Short-time-base studies
    of turnover in breeding birds of the California Channel
    Islands. Condor 76, 526-549.
KARR, J. R.   1982a.   Avian extinction on Barro Colorado Island
    Panama: a reassessment. Amer. Natur. 119,220-239.
KARR, J. R.   1982b.   Population variability and extinction in
    the avifauna of a tropical land-bridge island. Ecology 63,
    1975-1978.
KENDEIGH, S. C.   1982.   Bird populations in east central Illi-
    nois: fluctuations, variations, and development over a
    half-century period. Ill. Biol. Mongr. 52.
LECK, C. F.   1979.   Avian extinctions in an isolated tropical
    wet-forest preserve, Ecuador. Auk 96, 343-352.
LEIGH, E. G., JR.   1975.   Population fluctuations, community
    stability, and environmental variability. In: Ecology and
    Evolution of Communities, eds. M. L. Cody and J. M. Dia-
    mond, pp. 51-73. Harvard University Press, Cambridge.

LEIGH, E. G., JR. 1981. The average lifetime of a population
    in a varying environment. J. Theor. Biol. 90, 213-239.
LYNCH, J. F. and R. F. WHITCOMB. 1978. Effects of the insu-
    larization of the eastern deciduous forest on avifaunal
    diversity and turnover. In: Classification, Inventory, and
    Analysis of Fish and Wildlife Habitat, ed. A. Marmelstein,
    pp. 461-489. U.S. Fish and Wildlife Service, Washington,
    D. C.
MacARTHUR, R. H., J. M. DIAMOND and J. R. KARR. 1972. Density
    compensation in island faunas. Ecology 53, 330-342.
MacARTHUR, R. H. and E. O. WILSON. 1967. The Theory of Island
    Biogeography. Princeton University Press, Princeton.
MAY, R. M., G. R. CONWAY, M. P. HASSELL and T. R. E. SOUTHWOOD.
    1974. Time delays, density dependence, and single species
    oscillations. J. anim. Ecol. 43, 747-770.
OLSON, S. L. and H. F. JAMES. 1982. Prodromus of the fossil
    avifauna of the Hawaiian Islands. Smithsonian Contr.
    Zool. 365:1-59.
RICHTER-DYN, N. and N. S. GOEL. 1982. On the extinction of a
    colonizing species. Theor. Pop. Biol. 3, 406-433.
SCHOENER, T. W. 1983. Rate of species turnover decreases from
    lower to higher organisms: a review of the data. Oikos,
    41:in press.
SIBLEY, C. G. and J. E. AHLQUIST. 1982. The relationships of
    the Yellow-breasted Chat (Icteria virens) and the alleged
    slowdown in the rate of macromolecular evolution in birds.
    Postilla 187.
SIBLEY, C. G. and J. E. AHLQUIST. 1984. The phylogeny and
    classification of the passerine birds, based on comparison
    of the genetic material, DNA. Proc. 20th Intern. Ornith.
    Congr., in press.
SOULE, M. and A. J. SLOAN. 1966. Biogeography and distribu-
    tion of the reptiles and amphibians on islands in the Gulf
    of California, Mexico. Trans. San Diego Soc. Nat. Hist.
    14, 137-146.
TERBORGH, J. 1974. Preservation of natural diversity: the
    problem of extinction-prone species. BioScience 24, 715-
    722.
TERBORGH, J. 1975. Faunal equilibria and the design of
    wildlife preserves. In: Tropical Ecological Systems:
    Trends in Terrestrial and Aquatic Research, eds. F. B.
    Golley and E. Medina, pp. 369-380. Springer, New York.
TERBORGH, J. and B. WINTER. 1980. Some causes of extinction.
    In: Conservation Biology, eds. M. E. Soulé and B. A. Wil-
    cox, pp. 119-134. Sinauer, Sunderland.
TOFT, C. A. and T. W. SCHOENER. 1983. Abundance and diversity
    of orb spiders on 106 Bahamian islands: biogeography at an
    intermediate trophic level. Oikos, 41:in press.

TURBOTT, E. G. 1969. Native birds. In: The Natural History of
    Canturbury, ed. G. A. Knox, pp. 426-434. Reed, Wellington.
VAISANEN, R. A. and O. JARVINEN. 1977. Dynamics of protected
    bird communities in a Finnish archipelago. J. anim. Ecol.
    46, 891-908.
WHITCOMB, R. F., J. F. LYNCH, P. A. OPLER and C. S. ROBBINS.
    1976. Island biogeography and conservation: strategy and
    limitations. Science 193, 1030-1032.
WILCOX, B. A. 1978. Supersaturated island faunas: a species-
    age relationship for lizards on post-Pleistocene land-
    bridge islands in the Gulf of California. Science 199,
    996-998.
WILCOX, B. A. 1980. Insular ecology and conservation. In:
    Conservation Biology, eds. M. E. Soulé and B. A. Wilcox,
    pp. 95-118. Sinauer, Sunderland.
WILCOX, B. A. 1983. Comparative island biogeography of ver-
    tebrates on islands in the Gulf of California. In:
    Biogeography of the Gulf of California, eds. T. J. Case
    and M. L. Cody. University of California Press, Berkeley,
    in press.
WILLIAMSON, M. 1981. Island Populations. Oxford University
    Press, Oxford.
WILLIS, E. O. 1974. Populations and local extinctions on
    Barro Colorado Island, Panama. Ecol. Mongr. 44, 153-169.
WILLIS, E. O. 1979. The composition of avian communities in
    remanescent woodlots in southern Brazil. Papéis Avulsos
    Zool., S. Paulo 33, 1-25.
WILLIS, E. O. 1980. Species reduction in remanescent woodlots
    in southern Brazil. Proc. 19th Intern. Ornith. Congr.
    783-786.
WILLIS, E. O. and E. EISENMANN. 1979. A revised list of birds
    on Barro Colorado Island, Panama. Smithsonian Contrib.
    Zool. 291, 1-31.
WILSON, A. C., S. S. CARLSON and T. J. WHITE. 1977. Biochemi-
    cal evolution. Ann. Rev. Biochem. 46, 537-639.
WILSON, E. O. and E. O. WILLIS. 1975. Applied biogeography.
    In: Ecology and Evolution of Communities, eds. M. L. Cody
    and J. M. Diamond, pp. 522-534. Harvard University Press,
    Cambridge.
WRIGHT, S. J. 1984a. The avifauna of islands in Lake Gatun,
    Panama. Ms in preparation.
WRIGHT, S. J. 1984b. Population size and the distribution of
    birds on islands in Gatun Lake, Panama. Ms in prepara-
    tion.

MAMMALIAN EXTINCTION AND BIOGEOGRAPHY IN THE
SOUTHERN ROCKY MOUNTAINS

Bruce D. Patterson

INTRODUCTION

    Mammals on mountaintops in the American Southwest offer a
uniquely documented system for examining historical factors in
biogeography. Mountaintop habitats of forest and meadow have
distinctly insular distributions, and are isolated from each
other and from the Southern Rocky Mountains by saxicolous vegetation, grasslands, and deserts at lower elevations. The disjunct distributions of boreal plants and animals on isolated
ranges apparently represent formerly larger, now relictual distributions dating from Pleistocene climatic changes. A
detailed reconstruction of the biogeographic history of this
region has emerged from studies of botany, zoology, palynology,
and paleontology. The reconstruction is probably unique in
being based on: 1) numerous paleobotanical studies of late
Wisconsin-Recent times, 2) an abundance of mammal fossils, 3) a
detailed understanding of the current distributions of montane
habitats, and 4) thorough knowledge of distributions, ecolo-
gies, and to a lesser extent, evolutionary relationships of
mammals.

The following historical reconstruction is suggested.
Although currently disjunct, montane habitats in the Southwest
were formerly joined via displacements of montane vegetation to
lower altitudes and latitudes during "pluvial" periods of the
Pleistocene. Thus joined by montane habitats at lower elevations, mountain ranges exchanged component species. With the
inception of interglacial intervals and concomitant drier climates, montane habitats disappeared in lowland areas, finding
refuge at higher altitudes and latitudes. Consequentially,
faunas restricted to montane habitats became disjunct,
separated from one another by inhospitable "seas" of low-lying
desert and grassland. Once isolated, montane biotas suffered
extinctions of component species in accordance with island
biogeographic theory: mountain ranges limited in area and habitat diversity support a correspondingly lower diversity of montane species. After some 10,000 years of interglacial climates, one now finds relict faunas on isolated mountain ranges
that comprise non-random subsets of the species that inhabited
these ranges at the start of the Holocene.

The present paper evaluates this reconstruction and the
hypotheses on which it is based. A number of hypotheses are
expressly formulated, and literature relevant to their evaluation is reviewed. Additionally, an expanded data set is
described herein and is used to test some of the hypotheses.
Using this approach, I hope to establish what is known of the
biogeographic history of this region, and what remains to be
determined. I conclude with a brief discussion of fruitful
avenues for future research.

THE DATA SET
In the present analysis, mountain ranges were identified
and defined as areas of montane vegetation (associations of
alpine tundra, spruce-fir forest, mountain meadow grassland,

mixed coniferous forest, and pine forest), as mapped by A. W.
Kuchler (1964) in "The potential natural vegetation of the con-
terminous United States, 1:3,168,000". Twenty-seven areas supporting one or more of these associations were selected from a
region embracing southern Wyoming, Utah east of the Green and
Colorado Rivers, Arizona south of the Grand Canyon, Colorado,
and New Mexico (fig. 1). Previous studies of mammals (Kelson,
1951; Durrant, 1952; Cockrum, 1960; Armstrong, 1972, 1977;
Findley et al., 1975) have shown these ranges all lie within a
relatively homogeneous faunal province comprising the Southern
Rocky Mountains and its faunal derivatives. Data from my own
studies of the Organ Mountains in south-central New Mexico were
also included, so that the present analysis is based on 28
ranges.

An element of subjectivity is introduced when mountains
are defined by vegetational formations rather than by elevation
(e.g., Brown, 1971). This method requires a delimitation of
montane versus non-montane vegetation, and permits an analytical resolution no greater than that which is available in vegetational maps. The resolution of vegetational formations is
far less than that developed for topographic features. However, montane vegetation provides an integrated summary of a
variety of proximate factors that probably limit mammalian distributions, among them slope, exposure, soil type and texture,
temperature, and precipitation. In this region, striking contrasts may be found in the flora and fauna inhabiting north-
facing and south-facing slopes of a canyon at a single elevation. In addition, Hopkin's bioclimatic law (i.e., that the
cooling effects of 1000 feet in elevation are approximated by
the cooling of 100 miles in latitude) suggests that a single
elevation has quite different biotic effects at the northern
and southern limits of the study area, which spans 1200 km of
latitude. Montane vegetation, in contrast, seems more directly

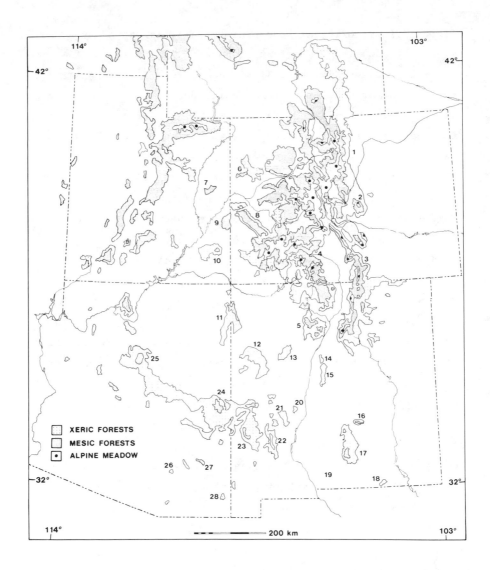

FIGURE 1. Distributions of montane vegetation in the American Southwest, (modified from Kuchler, 1964). Mountain ranges analyzed are indicated by numbers; physical and biotic characteristics are given in Table 1.

pertinent to the distributions of mammal species. A map of
distributions of montane vegetation is given in figure 1.

For each mountain range, the following characteristics
were determined: area of all montane habitats (defined above),
area of mesic montane habitats (excluding Pinus and Pinus-
Pseudotsuga associations), elevation of the highest peak
included within montane habitats, and its latitude and longitude. Areal measures were taken from Kuchler's map with a com-
pensating polar planimeter (27 ranges) or were estimated from
field notes (Organ Mountains). In order to express the
integrity of regional topographic features, I arbitrarily
divided certain continuous forest areas in the Southern Rocky
Mountain of Colorado and the Mogollon Rim of Arizona and New
Mexico at natural barriers (river or isthmus). The most sub-
jective of these, the Southern Rocky Mountains "mainland"
(range 1 of figure 1, table 1), consists of the Front, Laramie,
and Park ranges and the Gore, Sawatch, and Elk mountains.
Other instances of arbitrary delimitation of montane habitats
are ranges 2, 3, 4, 8, and 24 (see fig. 1). Elevations and
coordinates were taken from U.S. Geological Survey topographic
maps. The latter variables were recorded in degrees and
decimals rather than degrees and minutes for regression analyses. These data are presented in table 1.

The American Southwest harbors a strikingly rich mammalian
fauna variously derived from the Great Basin, Mohave, Sonoran
and Chihuahuan deserts, the Great Plains, the Sierra Madre
Occidental, and the Southern Rocky Mountains (see Durrant,
1952; Cockrum, 1960; Armstrong, 1972, 1977; Findley et al.,
1975). A detailed study of the biogeographic relationships of
this fauna is outside the scope of the present paper. However,
only the Sierra Madre Occidental and the Southern Rocky Mountains have contributed importantly to the mammal faunas now
restricted to Southwestern mountain ranges, and of these the

boreal influence is certainly the stronger. This study focuses
on montane mammals derived from the Southern Rocky Mountains or
in situ, and leaves untouched some fascinating questions
related to the presence of the cliff chipmunk (Eutamias
dorsalis), southern pocket gopher (Thomomys umbrinus), Mexican
woodrat (Neotoma mexicana), and Mexican vole (Microtus
mexicanus) on many southwestern mountain ranges. How and when
such species reached these ranges, and possible effects they
may have had on boreal colonists or residents, must await
future study.

I considered as "montane" those species that are more or
less restricted in geographic and ecological distribution
within this region to areas supporting montane vegetation.
Species with southern affinities (see above), eurytopic species
inhabiting montane and nonmontane habitats (e.g., the western
harvest mouse, Reithrodontomys megalotis, and the long-tailed
weasel, Mustela frenata), and montane "fringe" species (e.g.,
the rock squirrel, Spermophilus variegatus, and the brush
mouse, Peromyscus boylii) were excluded. Also excluded were
volant and aquatic forms (i.e., bats, beaver, otter), species
whose distributions have been greatly affected by human agency
(i.e., ungulates and large carnivores), and one species
suspected of having grossly incomplete distributional records
(i.e., Merriam's shrew, Sorex merriami).

The distributions of 26 boreal montane taxa were assembled
from the literature (see above) and are presented in table 2.
The distributions of two subspecies, Eutamias minimus operarius
(the southern least chipmunk) and Peromyscus maniculatus
rufinus (the Southern Rocky Mountain deer mouse) are given
because each is a distinctive Rocky Mountain race bordered by
one or more lowland subspecies; records for P. maniculatus
nebrascensis from ranges 6 and 7 were admitted because its distribution falls within mapped montane vegetation. Also,

TABLE 1. Physical and biotic characteristics of 28 Southwestern mountain ranges. Range numbers correspond to those in figure 1. Latitude and longitude are in degree-decimal notation for regression analyses.

		elevation of highest peak (m)	latitude of highest peak (decimal)	longitude of highest peak (decimal)	area of all montane habitats (km^2)	area of mesic montane habitats (km^2)
1.	Rocky Mts. "mainland"	4345	40.25	105.62	58,508	37,321
2.	Pike's Peak Massif	4300	38.83	105.05	17,169	791
3.	Sangre de Cristo Mts.	4372	37.57	105.48	19,604	5,205
4.	San Juan Mts.	4272	37.83	107.98	33,120	22,831
5.	Jemez Mts.	3524	35.88	106.59	3,288	913
6.	Rabbit Hills	2755	39.63	108.77	2,161	244
7.	Tavaputs Plateau	2894	39.18	109.77	639	639
8.	Uncompaghre Plateau	2966	38.43	108.50	2,953	1,553
9.	LaSal Mts.	3877	38.45	109.23	791	791
10.	Abajo Mts.	3463	37.83	109.47	1,826	122
11.	Chuska Mts.	2989	36.47	109.10	3,257	518
12.	Zuni Mts.	2821	35.17	108.09	2,892	---
13.	Mt. Taylor	3445	35.22	107.61	852	---
14.	Sandia Mts.	3256	35.21	106.45	183	---
15.	Manzano Mts.	3078	34.59	106.45	791	---
16.	Capitan Mts.	3118	33.56	105.27	487	183
17.	Sacramento Mts.	3659	33.38	105.84	3,531	396
18.	Guadalupe Mts.	2667	31.57	104.85	244	---
19.	Organ Mts.	2704	32.33	106.57	50	---
20.	Magdalena Mts.	3123	34.01	107.19	183	---
21.	San Mateo Mts.	3083	33.89	107.50	670	---
22.	Black Range	3051	33.14	107.85	1,583	---
23.	Mogollon Mts.	3320	33.32	108.65	3,531	365
24.	White Mts.	3533	33.91	109.56	18,630	670
25.	San Francisco Mts.	3865	35.35	111.68	18,630	578
26.	Santa Catalina Mts.	2803	32.45	110.79	122	---
27.	Pinaleño Mts.	3267	32.68	109.87	244	---
28.	Chiricahua Mts.	2986	31.88	109.30	122	---

TABLE 2. Distributions of 26 montane mammals on 28 Southwestern mountain ranges. Presence (+) and absence (0) determined from various literature sources; see text for qualifications. Letters appended to taxa refer to trophic-habitat groups: I, insectivore; M, mesic forest and meadow herbivore; X, xeric forest herbivore; C, carnivore.

MOUNTAIN RANGES	Sorex cinereus (I)	Sorex monticolus (I)	Sorex nanus (I)	Sorex palustris (I)	Microsorex hoyi (I)	Ochotona princeps (M)	Lepus americanus (M)	E. minimus operarius (M)	E. quadrivittatus complex (X)	Marmota flaviventris (M)	Spermophilus elegans (M)	Spermophilus lateralis (X)
1. Rocky Mts. "mainland"	+	+	+	+	+	+	+	+	+	+	+	+
2. Pikes Peak Massif	+	+	+	+	0	+	+	+	+	+	0	+
3. Sangre de Cristo Mts.	+	+	+	+	0	+	+	+	+	+	0	+
4. San Juan Mts.	+	+	+	+	0	+	+	+	+	+	0	+
5. Jemez Mts.	+	+	+	+	0	+	+	+	+	0	0	+
6. Rabbit Hills	0	+	0	+	0	0	0	0	+	+	0	+
7. Tavaputs Plateau	0	+	0	0	0	0	0	0	+	+	0	0
8. Uncompaghre Plateau	0	+	0	+	0	0	0	+	+	+	0	+
9. LaSal Mts.	0	+	0	+	0	+	0	+	+	+	0	0
10. Abajo Mts.	0	+	0	+	0	0	0	+	+	0	0	0
11. Chuska Mts.	0	+	0	0	0	0	0	+	+	0	0	+
12. Zuni Mts.	0	+	0	0	0	0	0	0	+	0	0	0
13. Mt. Taylor	0	+	0	0	0	0	0	0	+	0	0	0
14. Sandia Mts.	0	+	+	0	0	0	0	+	+	0	0	0
15. Manzano Mts.	0	+	+	0	0	0	0	0	+	0	0	0
16. Capitan Mts.	0	+	0	0	0	0	0	0	+	0	0	0
17. Sacramento Mts.	0	+	+	0	0	0	0	+	+	0	0	0
18. Guadalupe Mts.	0	0	0	0	0	0	0	0	+	0	0	0
19. Organ Mts.	0	0	0	0	0	0	0	0	+	0	0	0
20. Magdalena Mts.	0	+	0	0	0	0	0	0	+	0	0	0
21. San Mateo Mts.	0	+	0	0	0	0	0	0	+	0	0	0
22. Black Range	0	+	0	0	0	0	0	0	+	0	0	+
23. Mogollon Mts.	0	+	0	0	0	0	0	0	+	0	0	+
24. White Mts.	0	+	0	+	0	0	0	+	+	0	0	+
25. San Francisco Mts.	0	+	0	0	0	0	0	0	+	0	0	+
26. Santa Catalina Mts.	0	+	0	0	0	0	0	0	0	0	0	0
27. Pinaleno Mts.	0	+	0	0	0	0	0	0	0	0	0	0
28. Chiricahua Mts.	0	+	0	0	0	0	0	0	0	0	0	0

Sciurus aberti (X)	Tamiasciurus hudsonicus (X)	Thomomys talpoides complex (M)	Peromyscus maniculatus rufinus (X)	Neotoma cinerea (X)	Clethrionomys gapperi (M)	Phenacomys intermedius (M)	Microtus montanus (M)	Microtus longicaudus (X)	Zapus princeps (M)	Martes americana (C)	Mustela erminea (C)	Gulo gulo (C)	Lynx canadensis (C)
+	+	+	+	+	+	+	+	+	+	+	+	+	+
+	+	+	+	+	+	+	+	+	+	0	+	0	0
+	+	+	+	+	+	+	0	+	+	+	+	+	+
+	+	+	+	+	+	+	+	+	+	+	+	+	+
+	+	+	+	+	+	0	+	+	+	0	+	0	0
0	+	+	+	+	+	0	0	+	+	0	0	0	0
0	0	+	+	+	0	0	0	+	0	0	0	0	0
0	+	+	+	+	0	0	+	+	+	0	0	0	0
0	+	+	+	+	0	0	0	+	+	+	0	0	0
+	+	+	+	+	0	0	0	+	0	0	0	0	0
+	+	+	+	+	0	0	0	+	0	0	0	0	0
+	+	0	+	0	0	0	0	+	0	0	0	0	0
+	+	+	+	0	0	0	0	+	0	0	0	0	0
+	+	0	+	0	0	0	0	+	0	+	0	0	0
+	+	0	+	0	0	0	0	+	0	0	0	0	0
0	+	0	+	0	0	0	0	+	0	0	0	0	0
0	+	0	+	0	0	0	0	+	0	0	0	0	0
0	0	0	0	0	0	0	0	0	0	0	0	0	0
0	0	0	0	0	0	0	0	0	0	0	0	0	0
+	0	0	+	0	+	0	0	0	0	0	0	0	0
+	+	0	+	0	+	0	0	0	0	0	0	0	0
+	+	0	+	0	0	0	0	+	0	0	0	0	0
+	+	0	+	0	+	0	+	+	0	0	0	0	0
+	+	0	+	0	+	0	+	0	0	0	0	0	0
+	+	0	+	0	0	0	0	+	0	0	0	0	0
+	0	0	+	0	0	0	0	0	0	0	0	0	0
0	+	0	+	0	0	0	0	+	0	0	0	0	0
0	0	0	+	0	0	0	0	0	0	0	0	0	0

records for two species complexes, Eutamias quadrivittatus complex ("Colorado chipmunks", including E. quadrivittatus, E.
rufus, E. cinereicollis, and E. canipes) and Thomomys
talpoides complex (northern pocket gophers, including taylori,
fossor, and durranti) were treated as single entries because
they represent geographically replacing but ecologically similar forms.

FORMULATIONS AND TESTS

Hypothesis I. During glacial periods, altitudinal and
latitudinal displacements of montane vegetation took place,
resulting in the establishment of "montane" habitats in lowland
areas.

Meteorological data indicate global consequences of boreal
ice sheet accumulations (e.g., Emiliani, 1958). Global climates became generally cooler (Emiliani, 1955; Ericson et al.,
1964), and correspondingly more mesic in many temperate
regions. The interplay of temperature, precipitation, and
their seasonal variation in the Pleistocene of the Southwest
remains uncertain, but it is generally agreed that annual conditions were effectively more mesic.

Antevs (1954) suggested that lower temperatures and higher
precipitation (especially snowfall) prevailed during the Cary
glaciation (Wisconsin II stage) in New Mexico 24,000+ years BP;
the effects of greater precipitation were presumed to have
increased importance southward. In their study of cave faunas
in central New Mexico, Harris and Findley (1964) postulated
cooler temperatures, especially during summer months, and
spring (vs. summer) precipitation roughly twice present levels.
Galloway (1970) proposed the term "minevaporal" (cf. "pluvial")
for Southwestern climates during Pleistocene glacial advances.
He suggested that even with reduced precipitation rates (80-90%
of present values), the 10-11 C lower temperatures which

prevailed during the Wisconsin glacial would have reduced eva-
poration rates to half their current levels, making climates
effectively more mesic. Dalquest et al. (1969) suggested that
Wisconsin ice-sheets would have lowered summer temperatures and
moderated winter conditions in the Southwest, and Smartt (1977)
concluded that summer and winter precipitation would have been
more or less equal.

In his study of changes in Quaternary plant remains in
woodrat middens in the eastern Grand Canyon, Cole (1982) noted
impressive similarities between full-glacial Grand Canyon and
modern northern Utah. He stated (1982:1144) that "...a latitudinal shift in climatic values provides a better model for
inferring the nature of fullglacial climates than does an
elevational depression and that the full-glacial climate of the
Grand Canyon was colder in all seasons than it is today, had a
wider range between summer means and winter means (less temperate) and had a mean annual precipitation approximating
modern values. Unlike the present biseasonal regime ..., the
precipitation fell predominantly in winter." Wells (1977:71)
concluded from work in the northern Chihuahuan Desert that
"enhancement of precipitation and its effectiveness were the
prime climatic factors determining the pluvial expansion of
woodland...."

Whatever the proximate cause, the expansions of woodland
and forest habitats during glacial advances are well documented
by both plant macrofossil and pollen analyses. The maximum
displacement of montane vegetation during the Wisconsin
apparently occurred 21,000 to 15,000 years ago, when most plant
species in the Grand Canyon extended 600 to 1000 m below their
current limits (Cole, 1982). Pinyon-oak- juniper woodlands in
the Chisos Mountains of Trans-Pecos Texas may have extended
nearly 800 m below their current lower limits at 1400 m (Wells,
1966). Xerophilous woodlands probably extended to the Pecos

River (1075 m) in the vicinity of the nearby Guadalupe Mountains (Van Devender et al., 1977), invading areas that today
support Chihuahuan desert-scrub (see also Van Devender and
Everitt, 1977).

Altitudinal expansions of montane forest also occurred at
this time, although its vertical displacement appears generally
not as great as that for woodland habitats. 13,000 years ago,
the Guadalupe Mountains supported a well-developed subalpine
forest at 2000 m that included spruce, Douglas fir, and
southwestern white pine (Van Devender et al., 1979). Pleistocene pollens of spruce and fir have been recorded from the San
Augustin Plains of the Mogollon Rim (Clisby and Sears, 1956).
In the Grand Canyon, Utah juniper, Douglas fir, white fir, and
spruce occurred 600 to 800 m lower during the full glacial, and
limber pine may have extended 1000 m below its present lower
limits (Cole, 1982). Engelmann spruce and Douglas fir are
known to have been present 12,000 years BP in portions of
Utah's Colorado Plateau that now support well-developed
pinyon-juniper woodlands (Spaulding and Van Devender, 1977).
The replacement of early Holocene forests of Douglas fir, Rocky
Mountain juniper, and limber pine by pinyon-juniper woodlands
in the San Juan Basin of northern New Mexico is documented by
Betancourt and Van Devender (1981). However, the extent of
glacial displacements of the "Transition Zone" dominant, ponderosa pine, has not been determined and may have been comparatively minor (Van Devender et al., 1979).

Latitudinal displacements of montane vegetation during
glacial advances are also apparent. Spruce pollen has been
documented in Pleistocene lake sediments near Mexico City, far
beyond its current southern limits in Chihuahua and Durango,
where it occurs at 2300- 2500m (Sears et al., 1955). Martin
(1958) postulated that the range of spruce and its associated
biota extended south into the Sierra Madre Occidental from the

Mogollon Rim during Pleistocene glacial periods. The most
likely route of such colonization would have been via the
Peloncillo Mountains, which currently support far more xeric
associations. In the adjacent Chiricahua Mountains, spruce is
restricted to north-facing canyons above 2580 m (Martin, 1958),
so that both altitudinal and latitudinal displacements of mesic
vegetation are suggested. Van Devender et al. (1979) found
Pleistocene remains of manzanita (Arctostaphylos sp.), dwarf
juniper (Juniperus communis), spruce (Picea), and raspberry
(Rubus strigosus) in the Guadalupe Mountains. None of these
taxa is present in the current flora of the Guadalupes, and
their presence 13,000 years ago documents geographic range
changes that involve a significant latitudinal component (see
also Cole, 1982).

It is important to note that Pleistocene montane communities in this region differ significantly from those of today.
As Harris has repeatedly asserted (Harris and Findley, 1964;
Harris, 1970, 1977), the traditional, simplistic view that
entire montane communities (especially forests) simply invaded
lowland areas is untenable. A greater co-mingling of "life
zone" species is apparent. Pleistocene woodland associations
in the Chihuahuan Desert region show less zonation with elevation than comparable associations in the Sonoran and Mohave
deserts (Wells, 1977), and the late pluvial subalpine forest
atop the Guadalupe Mountains "... was a mixture of Hudsonian
(Picea sp., Juniperus communis), Canadian (Pseudotsuga
menziesii, Pinus strobiformis), Transition (Quercus gambelii,
Ostrya knowltonii), and Upper Sonoran (Pinus edulis, Juniperus
sp.) Life Zone elements" (Van Devender et al., 1979:

The responses of each montane species to altered climatic
changes during Pleistocene stages were apparently individualis-
tic. Presumably, species whose distributions are limited by
climatic factors (e.g., precipitation, temperature) were most

strongly influenced by changing climates, while those limited
by other factors (e.g., edaphic factors) were only indirectly
affected. Collectively, however, vegetational shifts caused by
Pleistocene climatic changes led to the establishment of a
mosaic of more-or-less "montane" habitats in lowland areas,
which would have permitted colonization of isolated mountain
ranges by mammal species restricted to boreal habitats.

Hypothesis II. Boreal mammal species colonized currently
isolated mountain ranges during Pleistocene glacial advances.
Supporting data for this hypothesis are indirect, as
nowhere in the Southwest do uninterrupted fossil strata extend
from one interglacial stage through the succeeding glacial
advance. Many Pleistocene mammal deposits have been reported
from the Southwest. Early studies of Pleistocene fossils from
Burnet and Williams caves of the Guadalupe Mountains (Schultz
and Howard, 1935; Ayer, 1936) revealed that nearly half of the
cave faunas represented either extinct or extralimital species.
Fossils from caves and other deposition sites (summarized by
Findley et al., 1975) establish the occurrence of such northern
montane taxa as the vagrant shrew (Sorex monticolus), dwarf
shrew (Sorex nanus), Merriam's shrew (Sorex merriami), yellow-
bellied marmot (Marmota flaviventris), northern pocket gopher
(Thomomys talpoides), bushy-tailed woodrat (Neotoma cinerea),
montane vole (Microtus montanus), and long-tailed vole
(Microtus longicaudus) in southernmost New Mexico during the
latest Wisconsin stage. None of these species is found at such
low latitudes or altitudes today (cf. current distribution in
tables 1 and 2), and collectively they indicate far more
widespread distributions during glacial maxima. Range expansions during glacial advances are also apparent far to the
south in Nuevo Leon, Mexico, where Cushing (1945) reported
Pleistocene marmots (Marmota), pocket gophers (Thomomys), and

voles (<u>Microtus</u>), and Findley (1953) reported masked shrews
(<u>Sorex</u> <u>cinereus</u>). Additional extralimital records for Pleistocene fossils are also available for areas to the west (Wells
and Jorgenson, 1964) and northwest (Grayson, 1977, 1981; Thompson and Mead, 1982) of the study region.

These reports document the Pleistocene occurrence of montane mammals in southern lowland areas. Many of the deposition
sites now support habitats that are less favorable to montane
mammals than those present on any of the mountain ranges under
study. Because the species represented by fossils occupy a
wide variety of montane habitats, it seems certain that a
variety of montane species colonized each of the mountain
ranges during glacial advances. Furthermore, the data suggest
that glacial colonists of these ranges may have included a
majority of those species now occupying montane habitats in the
Southern Rocky Mountains.

Brown (1971:475) also concluded that "all the islands
[major mountain ranges in the Great Basin] were inhabited by a
common pool of species at some time in the past ...." However,
the universal absence on these mountains of species restricted
to higher elevation habitats led him to believe that the glacial source pool consisted only of lower elevation forms. The
subsequent discoveries of fossils of Holocene heather voles
(<u>Phenacomys</u>) in Nevada (Grayson, 1981) and pikas (<u>Ochotona</u>) in
Nevada and Utah (Thompson and Mead, 1982) indicate that Brown
may have underestimated the extent of glacial colonizations of
these ranges (and thus the extent of Recent extinctions).
Colonizations in the Southwest are documented by an abundance
of Wisconsin fossils and by more detailed paleobotanical studies.

Hypothesis III. Montane mammal populations on isolated
ranges are relicts of formerly larger, continuous
distributions; there is no recurrent colonization of isolated
ranges by montane mammals.

The extensive ranges of many montane mammals during glacial periods are documented by fossils (cited above). These
species have since disappeared from lowland areas and from some
mountain ranges where they presumably occurred during glacial
maxima. For example, Phenacomys cf. intermedius was present
5300 years BP in central Nevada (Grayson, 1981) where it no
longer exists (Hall, 1946). Thompson and Mead (1982) reported
late Wisconsin Ochotona princeps in the Great Basin, inferring
that pikas inhabited "most of the nonlacustrine portions of
intermountain valleys of the eastern Great Basin through the
Late Wisconsin"(p. 48). Comprehensive collecting at lower
elevations by a variety of researchers (see locality records
for non-montane taxa in Durrant, 1952; Durrant et al., 1955;
Cockrum, 1960; Armstrong, 1972; Findley et al., 1975) have
failed to demonstrate the occurrence of montane species (table
2) in areas joining their current disjunct distributions.

An indirect approach to this hypothesis was taken by Brown
(1971) in his study of montane mammals on isolated ranges in
the Great Basin. He proposed that if recurrent colonization of
isolated mountain ranges by montane mammals occurs, then the
number of montane species on these ranges should be related to
variables describing their current isolation. Brown tested
this alternative by relating species number on islands to: 1)
distance to the nearest mainland (Sierra Nevada or Rocky Mountains), 2) distance to the nearest mountain range with more
species, and 3) elevation of the highest pass connecting ranges
to potential source areas. None of these variables contributed
significantly to a multiple regression employing montane area
and peak elevation (Brown, 1971), nor is any significant (P <

0.05) in bivariate correlations with boreal species numbers (my
analysis of data in Brown, 1971: highest pass, r = 0.312;
nearest island, r = -0.108; nearest mainland, r = 0.001).

   Hypothesis IV. Montane mammal populations became locally
extinct on some isolated mountain ranges during the Holocene,
and, by inference, preceding interglacial periods.
   SPECIES DISTRIBUTIONS. The climatic similarities of the
Recent to Pleistocene interglacials have led many researchers
(e.g., Opik, 1952; Emiliani, 1958) to consider the Recent as an
interglacial period properly belonging to the Pleistocene
epoch. Certainly, climatic interpretation of deep-sea cores
(Ericson et al., 1964) supports such a conclusion. Thus,
postglacial changes in plant and animal distributions probably
paralleled those that occurred during earlier interglacial
periods.
   Late Wisconsin fossils of certain montane species in the
Organ and Guadalupe mountains (Findley et al., 1975:342-344),
coupled with their current absence on these ranges (table 2),
establishes their post-glacial extinction. The effects of
extinction on other species populations on other mountain
ranges must be extrapolated. Brown (1971:472) proposed that
evidence for post-glacial extinctions could be found in
species-area curves. He argued that because there is negligible immigration of montane species to isolated ranges, the
number of species on ranges is primarily dependent on extinction rates. Extinction rates are thought to be related to area
through population size. A large slope to the species-area
curve should result (see also MacArthur and Wilson, 1967:16).
The slope of the curve he obtained for montane mammals in the
Great Basin ($z = 0.43$) falls above the range of values characteristic of equilibrial insular situations ($z = 0.20-0.40$), and
accords well with his predictions. A comparable value resulted

from a study involving a similar set of species in New Mexico
(z = 0.427; Patterson, 1980a), although the inclusion of additional taxa derived from both the Rocky Mountains and the
Sierra Madre Occidental lessened the dependence of species
number on area (z = 0.23). Patterson attributed the latter
relationship to his less restrictive definition of montane mammals (including species excluded here as "fringe" species), and
to the "gradual replacement of northern boreal species with
others at successively lower latitudes" (Findley, 1969:113).

The relation between number of boreal montane species and
area of all montane habitats in the Southern Rocky Mountains
(tables 1 and 2) is presented in figure 2.

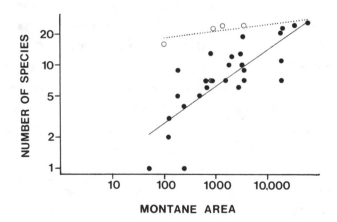

FIGURE 2. Regression of number of montane mammal species
versus area of montane habitats, in square kilometers (log-
transformed variables). The least-squares regression line
shown is given by: log S = -0.267 + 0.357 log A; r = 0.802 (P
< 0.01). See text for discussion.

The correlation of log-transformed variables (see MacArthur and
Wilson, 1967), r, equals 0.80 (P < 0.01) and describes 64% of
the variation in species number. The slope of this equation,
0.36, is lower than that obtained for similar sets of species
by Brown (1971) and Patterson (1980a) and is near the upper
limit of values for islands having real immigration rates.
However, Connor and McCoy (1979) have argued that the biological interpretation of such regression parameters is at best
complex, and the present slope offers no convincing argument
for the prevalence of post-glacial extinctions.

    The model´s apparent lack-of-fit, especially for the
smaller southern ranges, may be attributable to the exclusion
of montane species having affinities with Mexican forms that
comprise significant fractions of the smaller faunas (see
Patterson, 1980a). It is probably also influenced by elevation
(table 1). In fact, elevation of the highest peak accounts for
fully as much variation in species number as does montane area
(figure 3); correlation of species number with elevation is

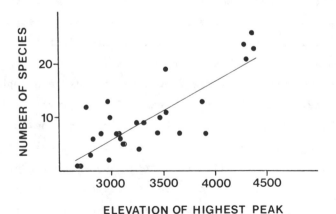

FIGURE 3.   Regression of number of montane mammal species
versus elevation of that range´s highest peak, in meters.   The
least-squares regression line shown in given by: S = -26.160 +
0.11 E; r = 0.809 (P < 0.01).   See text for discussion.

species number with elevation is 0.81 (P < 0.01), and the
regression describes 65% of the total variation. Tall ranges
tend also to be large, and, given altitudinal zonation of habitats, present more habitats, as well as greater areas of these,
than small ranges. Together, area (entered as an untransformed
variable) and elevation account for 71% of the variation in
species number (F = 31.74; P < 0.01).

Better evidence for Recent extinctions in montane assemblages dating from the Pleistocene is evident in the distributions of individual species. As reasoned above, species are
supposedly limited in distribution to those ranges which are
large enough to support viable populations throughout the
period of their isolation. Individual species should thus be
distributed on a non-random subset of mountain ranges, specifically the largest ranges. Ranking the 28 ranges by area of all
montane habitats, and breaking ties with elevation of the
highest peak (table 1), one can compare range occurrences
(table 2) on a species-by-species basis using the Mann-Whitney
test (Siegel, 1956). Results of these tests are presented in
table 3. No species is distributed randomly with respect to
montane area; all occur on ranges which are significantly
larger than those on which each is absent.

One can examine the distributions of individual species in
another way. Brown (1971:472) reasoned as follows: extinction
rates should be related to population size, because large population size hedges against ecological and genetical accidents
leading to local extinction (MacArthur and Wilson, 1967:22).
Extinction rates should therefore be related to a variety of
factors influencing population size. Brown (1971) emphasized
three of the more important ones: body size, trophic level,
and habitat specialization. Using trophic level and habitat
specialization to stratify species, Brown (1971: figure 3)
found that larger species tended to occur on fewer isolated

TABLE 3. Tests for nonrandomness in the distributions of 26 montane
mammal species on 28 mountain ranges in the American Southwest. Ranges
were ranked by montane area (ties broken by peak elevation) and the
ranks of ranges supporting populations of mammals were compared to
those on which species were absent. Tabulated values include total
occurrence, Mann-Whitney U statistics, z values, and associated
probabilities. No species is distributed randomly with respect to
montane area.

SPECIES	NO. RANGES	U	z	α
Microsorex hoyi	1	0	-1.6713	.05
Spermophilus elegans	1	0	-1.6713	.05
Gulo gulo	3	0	-2.7854	.005
Lynx canadensis	3	0	-2.7854	.005
Martes americana	4	13	-2.2979	.025
Phenacomys intermedius	4	2	-3.0201	.005
Lepus americanus	5	6	-3.0892	.001
Sorex cinereus	5	6	-3.0892	.001
Mustela erminea	6	24	-2.3515	.01
Ochotona princeps	6	17	-2.7435	.005
Microtus montanus	7	14	-3.1568	.001
Marmota flaviventris	8	37	-2.1868	.025
Sorex nanus	8	34	-2.3393	.01
Zapus princeps	8	26	-2.7462	.005
Clethrionomys gapperi	10	36	-2.5891	.005
Sorex palustris	10	26	-3.0686	.001
Neotoma cinerea	11	40	-2.5167	.01
Eutamias minimus operarius	12	31	-3.0175	.001
Spermophilus lateralis	12	9	-4.0389	.001
Thomomys talpoides complex	12	44	-2.4140	.01
Sciurus aberti	18	47	-2.0617	.025
Microtus longicaudus	22	5	-3.4153	.001
Tamiasciurus hudsonicus	22	4	-3.4713	.001
Eutamias quadrivittatus group	25	6	-2.3398	.01
Sorex monticolus	26	4	-1.9625	.025
Peromyscus maniculatus rufinus	26	4	-1.9625	.025

ranges than smaller species of the same trophic-habitat class.
However, the limited numbers of montane species in the Great
Basin prevented him from establishing this as a well-defined
faunal pattern.

The same analysis can be applied to the richer assemblage
of species in the Southern Rocky Mountains. The 26 species
were classified into the following categories: insectivores
(five species of shrews), carnivores (four species), xeric
forest herbivores (those with significant portions of their
distributions in pine and mixed coniferous forests; seven
species of rodents), and mesic forest herbivores (those restricted to spruce-fir forests or alpine meadows and tundra; 10
species of rodents and lagomorphs). Results are plotted in
figure 4.

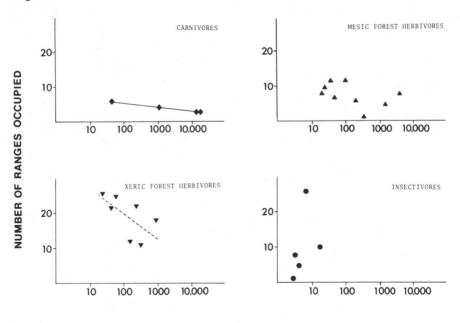

BODY SIZE (g)

FIGURE 4. Number of mountain ranges occupied by 26 mammal
species shown as a function of log body size, in grams.
Species have been stratified by trophic-habitat groups.
Least-squares fitted equations are shown for carnivores (solid
line, N = 7.674 - 1.139 log W; r = -0.989, P < 0.02) and xeric
forest herbivores (dashed line, N = 35.036 - 7.347 log W; r =
-0.664, P = 0.1). See text for discussion.

No relationship is demonstrable for the insectivores.
Although a least-squares fit of these data has a positive,
rather than negative, slope, it describes only 15% of the variation in range occurrences and is non-significant (P >> 0.05).
Xeric forest herbivores do show the expected negative relationship between range occurrences and body size. Although the
regression slope is marginally non-significant (P = 0.1), the
correlation is strong (-0.66) and moderately descriptive (R2 =
0.44). At most a poorly defined relationship is evident among
mesic forest herbivores. In carnivores, however, the relationship between body size and range occurrences is so strong (r =
-0.989), that statistical significance (P < 0.05) results from
a regression based on only four data points!

Thus, the predicted negative relationship is documented
for one data set and approximated by another, but is absent in
the third and perhaps contradicted by the fourth. The apparent
positive relationship in insectivores seems attributable to the
different habitat preferences of masked and vagrant shrews
(Sorex cinereus and S. monticolus, respectively). Although
both are widespread in Coloradan mountains (Armstrong, 1972),
S. cinereus is "restricted [in New Mexico] to hydrosere communities, usually above 9,500 feet" (Findley et al., 1975:11),
whereas S. monticolus inhabits ponderosa pine forests as low as
7,400 feet. Other instances of differences in habitat affinity
between species of a given category (Ochotona princeps vs.
Thomomys talpoides), or even between different populations of a
single species on different mountain ranges (Eutamias minimus
operarius, Neotoma cinerea), limit the resolution of this
analysis. Nonetheless, these results are broadly consistent
with the hypothesis that extinction governs the occurrence of
populations on mountain ranges.

Additional evidence for extinction is apparent in the
biotic composition of isolated mountain ranges in the Southern

Rocky Mountains. If post-glacial extinction has occurred, and
is responsible for the current assemblages of species found on
mountain ranges, then there should be progressive, cumulative
effects of extinction in the derivation of increasingly depauperate island biotas from a common, species-rich faunal pool.
To test this hypothesis, mountain ranges were grouped according
to species richness into the following classes: 1-5 species,
6-10 species, 11-15 species, 16-20 species, 21-25 species, and
the faunal pool (26 species). Numbers of ranges in these
classes are 7, 12, 4, 1, 3, and 1, respectively. The proportion of each range's fauna in each of the four trophic-habitat
groups was then calculated. Averages for species richness
classes are presented in figure 5, which shows that with progressive faunal diminution, the proportions of both carnivores
and mesic forest and meadow herbivores in montane assemblages
declines. While the proportion of insectivores appears largely
independent of faunal size, there is a concomitant increase in
the fraction of herbivore species occupying xeric forest habitats.

The greater proportion of species inhabiting xeric forests
on smaller ranges is a logical consequence of habitat distribution. On any of these ranges, there exists a greater area
between 2000-2500 m elevation than in the 2500 to 3000 m interval, this difference being especially great for smaller ranges.
Given an altitudinal zonation of habitats, there is a greater
area of xeric than of mesic forests, with predictable consequences for the mammal species which occupy them (Patterson,
1982).

The significance of changing faunal proportions can be
established as follows. X2 tests of homogeneity, conducted on
proportions of the habitat-trophic groups in ranges of each
species-richness class, indicate that these classes, although
established for analytical convenience, are not internally

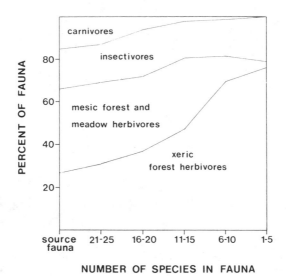

FIGURE 5. Faunal composition of southwestern mountain ranges
(in percent) plotted as a function of faunal size (in number of
species). Average values for ranges in each species richness
interval are shown; sample sizes for these intervals are:
source fauna (1 range), 21-25 species (3 ranges), 16-20 species
(1 range), 11-15 species (4 ranges), 6-10 species (12 ranges),
and 1-5 species (7 ranges).   Through selective extinction,
carnivores   and   mesic   forest and meadow herbivores are
disproportionately eliminated from smaller montane faunas.

heterogeneous (P > 0.05). Occurrences of species (table 2)

were then entered in an r x c table, where rows correspond to

trophic-habitat groups and columns represent species-richness

classes. Implicit in this classification is the assumption

that a species' presence or absence on a given mountain range

is independent of its occurrence elsewhere. A X2 test of

independence, testing whether the proportions of trophic-

habitat groups remain constant across species richness classes,

demonstrates a significant (P < 0.005) overall relationship

between these variables (table 4).

TABLE 4. Observed and expected (in parentheses) occurrences of montane species belonging to four trophic-habitat groups classified by the number of species in montane assemblages. The lower table contains X^2 tests of independence for each trophic-habitat class (5 d.f.) and for all species (15 d.f.). Differences in summations are due to rounding error.

SPECIES NUMBER CLASSES

	source fauna	21-25	16-20	11-15	6-10	1-5	
Insectivore	5 (4.74)	12 (12.41)	4 (3.28)	8 (8.94)	16 (16.79)	5 (3.83)	50
Carnivore	4 (1.52)	9 (3.97)	1 (1.05)	1 (2.86)	1 (5.37)	0 (1.23)	16
xeric forest herbivore	7 (12.91)	21 (33.75)	7 (8.93)	23 (24.32)	63 (45.66)	15 (10.42)	136
mesic forest herbivore	10 (6.90)	26 (18.05)	7 (5.04)	17 (13.01)	12 (24.42)	1 (5.57)	73
Total	26	68	19	49	92	21	275

TROPHIC-HABITAT GROUPS

Insectivores $0.014 + 0.014 + 0.156 + 0.099 + 0.037 + 0.356 = 0.675$
Carnivores $4.057 + 6.370 + 0.003 + 1.211 + 3.558 + 1.226 = 16.425*$
Xeric forest herbivores $2.702 + 4.818 + 0.419 + 0.072 + 6.581 + 2.009 = 16.601*$
Mesic forest herbivores $1.391 + 3.501 + 0.759 + 1.226 + 6.318 + 3.754 = \underline{16.948*}$
                                                                    $50.649**$

* P 0.01   ** P 0.005

The basis for this dependency between variables can be
identified by rank correlation analysis of the number of
species in each montane biota versus the proportion of its
species in each trophic-habitat class. Spearman's coefficient,
corrected for tied observations (Siegel, 1956), was used. The
proportion of carnivores shows a positive ($rs = 0.67$) and significant ($P < 0.01$) correlation with species number, as does
that for mesic forest and meadow herbivores ($rs = 0.86$; $P <
0.01$). In contrast, the proportion of xeric forest herbivores
is inversely correlated with species number ($rs = -0.78$; $P <
0.01$), while the fraction of insectivores in montane biotas
appears independent of faunal size ($rs = 0.05$; n.s.).

These results suggest the importance of extinction in the
determination of current montane biotas in the Southwest. A
richer and more mesic fauna existed during the Wisconsin on the
most xeric and southernmost mountain ranges under consideration
(the Organ and Guadalupe Mountains; Findley et al., 1975: table
3), and undoubtedly on less marginal ranges as well. With the
return of effectively more xeric climates and the disjunction
of species' ranges by retreating montane forests, isolated biotas underwent extinctions which selectively eliminated certain
species. Species groups which sustained the highest extinction
rates (i.e., whose proportions are significantly lower on
smaller ranges than in the complete source fauna) are those
whose trophic habits (carnivores) or habitat restrictions
(mesic forest and meadow herbivores) led to small population
size and hence vulnerability to extinction. Species in other
groups fared better: thus, all seven species of xeric forest
herbivores are found in the Chuska Mountains, which retains
fewer than half the source fauna. The catholic food and habitat requirements of Sorex monticolus are apparently responsible
for viable populations of this shrew on 26 of the 28 ranges.
Such conclusions intimate a "nested subset" relationship among

mountain ranges, in which species found on smaller ranges are
proper subsets of these found on progressively larger ranges.

A formal test of the "nested subset" relationship has not
been attempted here because of its logical (and mathematical)
complexity. The hypothesis states that the species that
currently occupy smaller mountain ranges are not at all a "random draw" from the total species pool inhabiting the Southern
Rocky Mountains "mainland" or those that inhabited isolated
ranges at the end of the Wisconsin glaciation. Instead,
species on smaller ranges are drawn from progressively smaller
sets of "survivors" which currently inhabit larger ranges or
which previously inhabited smaller ranges during post-glacial
times. To evaluate this hypothesis, a full-scale simulation
experiment is apparently necessary to construct the sample
space with which to compare observed patterns.

It is noteworthy, however, that the nested subset
hypothesis is supported by several lines of argument. First,
species-area curves (figure 2) demonstrate richer faunas on
larger ranges. Second, tests of species occurrences against
area (table 3) demonstrate the universal association of species
occurrences with larger mountain ranges; no boreal mammal
species which is found on smaller ranges is absent on larger
ones (contrast with "super-tramps" of Diamond, 1975: 358).
Third, physiographically similar mountain ranges tend independently to support similar mammal assemblages. In a study of
New Mexican mountain ranges, Patterson (1980a) found that a
distance matrix based on forested area, elevation, latitude,
and longitude was positively and significantly related to a
distance matrix based on mammalian species composition ($r =$
0.65, $P < 0.001$). A cluster analysis showed that four widely
separated yet physiographically similar mountain ranges (the
Peloncillo, Animas, Organ, and Guadalupe mountains) supported
similar mammal faunas, each independently derived from a

presumably common Wisconsin stock (Patterson, 1980a). Additional, correlative support for the nested subset hypothesis is
evident in the orderly changing proportions of species on
ranges of progressively smaller size (table 4).

TAXONOMIC DIVERGENCE
    Additional evidence for selective extinction can be found
in patterns of taxonomic diversification within the study area.
The existence of two or more subspecies of a species constitutes prima facie evidence of their respective resistance to
extinction throughout the period in which such divergence
occurred. Assuming that subspecies divergence occurred on isolated mountain ranges during interglacial and/or post-glacial
periods (cf. Findley, 1969; Patterson, 1982), the number of
subspecies within specific lineages should reflect their varying susceptibility to interglacial or post-glacial extinction,
as well as their overall evolutionary potentials.
    Numbers of subspecies in the study area were determined
for 22 taxa using Hall (1981) and other sources. Four taxa
were excluded from the analysis because, by definition, they
can have only one subspecies here: the pygmy shrew (Microsorex
hoyi) and the elegant ground squirrel (Spermophilus elegans)
are both restricted to a single studied range, whereas Eutamias
minimus operarius and Peromyscus maniculatus rufinus are themselves subspecies. Species were grouped according to trophic-
habitat classes, as before. Insectivores exhibit an average of
1.5 subspecies within the region, with a standard deviation of
1, carnivores, one subspecies (s.d. = 0), xeric forest herbivores, four subspecies (s.d. = 1.79), and mesic forest herbivores, 2.75 subspecies (s.d. = 1.28). Differences in numbers
of subspecies among trophic-habitat groups are significant ($F =$
5.30, $P < 0.01$); the least significant difference value ($P <$
0.05) for group means is 1.65.

Patterns in taxonomic diversification thus parallel those
found in species occurrences. Because of the greater area of
xeric as compared to mesic habitats on these ranges, species
inhabiting xeric forests (xeric forest herbivores; Sorex
monticolus) have sustained populations sufficiently large to
persist long enough for taxonomic diversification. Species
inhabiting higher elevation habitats, although more isolated,
exhibit fewer subspecies because of their greater susceptibility to extinction.

That differences between species groups are due to differential interglacial and post-glacial survivorship and not to
differences in evolutionary potential is seen in comparisons of
subspecies number divided by the number of ranges in which they
presently occur. This measure, reflecting the number of subspecies per range occurrence per species, takes the following
average values for trophic-habitat groups: insectivores, 0.14
(s.d. = 0.04), carnivores, 0.27 (s.d. = 0.08), xeric forest
herbivores, 0.22 (s.d. = 0.06), and mesic forest herbivores,
0.36 (s.d. = 0.15). A Kruskal-Wallis test conducted on the
incidence of subspecies in these groups show there are significant differences among them (H = 10.67; P < 0.025). However,
these values argue against the greater evolutionary potential
of xeric forest herbivores. In fact, a Mann-Whitney test of
the incidence of subspecies in six species of xeric forest herbivores and eight species of mesic forest herbivores shows
that, per range occurrence, mesic forest species have a higher
incidence of subspecies (U = 9; P = 0.03). This greater
incidence of subspeciation may be due to greater genetic or
temporal isolation, or to greater differences among higher
elevation habitats. Whatever the reason, there is no reason to
believe that xeric forest herbivores possess greater evolutionary potential than other species. Their present subspecific
diversity can be attributed to their interglacial and/or post-

glacial persistence on a variety of mountain ranges, and conse-
quent divergence via natural selection or genetic drift (see
also Patterson, 1982:389).

   Hypothesis V. Because of higher extinction probabilities,
species restricted to specific montane habitats are expected to
occur solely on the largest mountain ranges.

   This hypothesis was developed to account for the restricted distribution of Eutamias minimus operarius in New Mexico and Arizona, where it occurs exclusively on large mountain
ranges which support extensive coniferous forests (Patterson,
1981). Mann-Whitney tests of species occurrences and montane
area (table 3), which demonstrate significant relationships for
every species under present consideration, establish this as a
general phenomenon for species of all habitats. A more
detailed, if less definitive, analysis is possible if montane
elevation is also considered. Both area and elevation are
individually correlated with montane species number, and
together account for 71% of its variation.

   The occurrence of 24 montane species is shown graphically
in figure 6 as a function of both range area and elevation (the
remaining species, Microsorex hoyi and Spermophilus elegans,
are restricted to the largest, tallest range). Individual
species differ widely in their habitat requirements, and this
is reflected in the number of occurrences. However, it is
obvious that occurrences are variably clustered in the upper
right of each plot, as would unrealistically be expected if all
species had colonized all ranges, and all extinctions were
mediated by uniform populational effects of area and elevation.

   Plots in figure 6 show little evidence of deterministic
thresholds for extinction (i.e., areas or elevations above
which a species is ubiquitous and below which it is universally
absent). Substantial variation exists among species on ranges

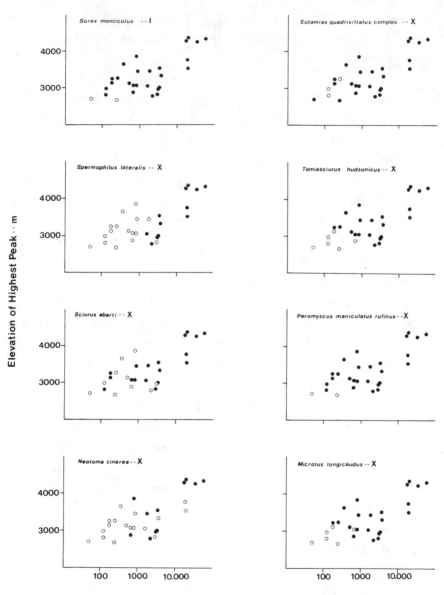

Area supporting Montane Vegetation -- km^2

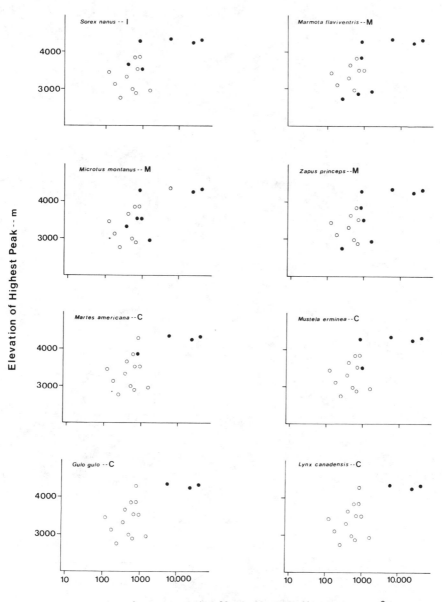

Elevation of Highest Peak -- m

Area supporting Mesic Montane Vegetation -- km²

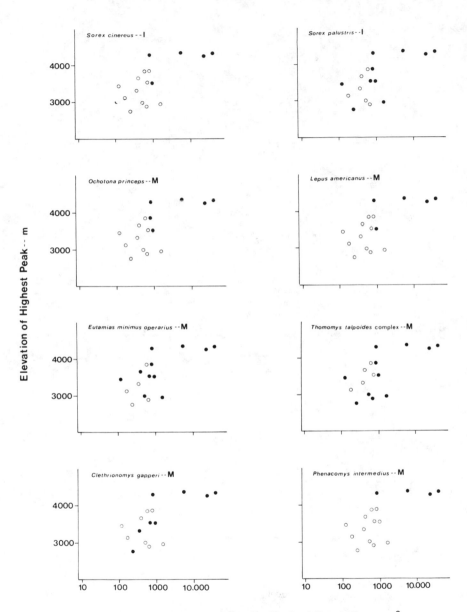

Elevation of Highest Peak -- m

Area supporting Mesic Montane Vegetation -- km²

of intermediate size. In part, this variation can be attributed to the latitudinal effects of Hopkin´s bioclimatic law
and the latitudinal spectrum of the present study. Strongest
departures from the predicted relationship are apparent in the
following species: Eutamias quadrivittatus complex, Sciurus
aberti, Neotoma cinerea, Sorex palustris, Eutamias minimus
operarius, Thomomys talpoides complex, Clethrionomys gapperi,
Marmota flaviventris, and Microtus montanus.

However, specific departures from the predicted relationship can be expected. Extinction is a probabilitistic process,
and slight irregularities in the specific distribution of
occurrences with area and elevation should result. Additional
irregularities may result from 1) the failure of species to
colonize all mountain ranges during the latest glacial stage,
and 2) distinctive synecologies of various populations of a
species on different mountain ranges. With regard to glacial
colonizations, it should be noted that several species showing
departures from the predicted relationship are known (by fossils) to have colonized even marginal mountain ranges.
Together, these plots of species occurrences provide support
for orderly, selective extinction.

FIGURE 6. Occurrence of mammal species as a function of range
area and elevation.   Plotted points indicate the area and
highest elevation of mountain ranges; presence (closed circles)
and absence (open circles) on these ranges is given for each
species. Trophic-habitat affinities are given with the plots:
I, insectivore; X, xeric forest herbivore; M, mesic forest and
meadow herbivore; C, carnivore. Note the different abscissas
used for species having different habitat affinities.   The
occurrence of Mustela erminea on the Sandia Mountains is not
indicated because this range has no mapped mesic forest habitat
(cf. Kuchler, 1964). See text for discussion.

Hypothesis VI. Only populations inhabiting the largest
mountain ranges are expected to have persisted throughout the
extended interglacial periods necessary for taxonomic
divergence; the development of endemic faunas is thus
restricted to these larger ranges.

Patterson (1982) formulated this hypothesis in his
analysis of systematic relationships within the Eutamias
quadrivittatus species complex. The distributions of the two
southern derivative species, E. cinereicollis and E. canipes,
are centered in the Mogollon Rim and the Sacramento Mountains,
respectively, which are the most likely southern ranges for the
interglacial persistence of montane populations. Both montane
areas support extensive areas of high elevation habitats.

The extension of this hypothesis to the entire assemblage
of species is made difficult by the lack of congruence in both
distribution and taxonomy of montane species, and by the impos-
sibility, in all cases of multiple range occupation, of determining the range on which a given subspecies originated. Some
headway can be made if it is assumed that subspecies originated
on the largest range included within their distributions. It
should be noted, however, that this assumption would bias an
analysis in the predicted direction of greater endemism on
larger ranges. The opposite bias is introduced when one considers that more or less extended interglacial survival is a
Divergent selection pressures related to differing ecological
demands are apt to increase in strength towards the distributional margins, which, in the Southern Rocky Mountains (figure
1), often consist of smaller ranges. Thus, small ranges such
as the Organ Mountains may harbor Wisconsin relicts that differ
more from their progenitors than older isolates living under
less extreme environmental conditions (cf. Patterson, 1980b).
The potential effects of these biases are so great that no formal analysis is undertaken.

It may be observed, however, that 56 subspecies have been described for the 22 taxa treated in Hypothesis IV above. Nine of the species are considered monotypic within this region, including three species of shrews, all of the carnivores, and two mesic forest herbivores. Each of the remaining 13 species is represented by a subspecies in the Rocky Mountains of northern Colorado, and one or more presumed derivatives. Taxonomic divergence among populations inhabiting ranges 1-5 (the main block of the Southern Rocky Mountains) is characteristic of species inhabiting higher elevation habitats and not occurring appreciably farther south (i.e., Ochotona princeps, Marmota flaviventris). Other species having distinctive subspecies within this area (Sciurus aberti, Tamiasciurus hudsonicus, Thomomys talpoides, Clethrionomys gapperi, and Microtus montanus) exhibit a different subspecies in the Rocky Mountains of southern Colorado and northern New Mexico (San Juan and Sangre de Cristo Ranges). The Southern Rocky Mountain form can be restricted to these northern ranges (races of S. aberti, C. gapperi, M. montanus) or extend farther to the west (T. talpoides) or south T. hudsonicus). Of the 17 subspecies restricted to Arizona or New Mexico south of ranges 3-5, the ranges of eight include or are restricted to the Mogollon Rim of Arizona and New Mexico, three to the Sacramento Mountains, two to the Pinaleno Mountains, and one each to Mt. Taylor, and the Chuska, Organ and Guadalupe mountains.

Hypothesis VII. Montane satellites of larger ranges were colonized during succeeding glacial periods by populations originating in regional centers of interglacial persistence.
This hypothesis was advanced by Patterson (1982) to account for regional patterns of differentiation within the Eutamias quadrivittatus complex (figure 7). Regional clusters of ranges support a single taxon of this complex, and these

FIGURE 7. Eutamias quadrivittatus, an intermediate-sized diurnal rodent inhabiting xeric forests and woodlands. Distributed on many Southwestern mountain ranges, this species complex (which includes E. rufus, E. cinereicollis, E. durangae, and E. canipes) shows patterns of divergence which are thought to characterize those of other montane elements.

clusters are each associated with a large mountain mass on which interglacial divergence was presumed to have taken place (Patterson, 1982:393). Concordant patterns of divergence are found in several montane species (e.g., Spermophilus lateralis, Tamiasciurus hudsonicus, Clethrionomys gapperi), although the distributions of regional endemics are not fully congruent. For example, the range of Sorex m. monticolus, which inhabits the Mogollon Rim of Arizona and Mew Mexico, extends northward to include the Chuska and Zuni mountains and Mt. Taylor (Hennings and Hoffmann, 1977). In contrast, E. cinereicollis, which inhabits the ranges of the Mogollon Rim, does not occur appreciably north of that area and is replaced on more northern ranges by E. quadrivittatus (Findley et al., 1975).

Metcalf (1977:55) substantiates this hypothesis in his discussion of montane mollusk distributions, proposing that

"The Sacramento, Guadalupe, Davis, and Chisos mountains may
have served as major insular "staging areas" of an archipelago
between the Southern Rocky Mountains and the Sierra Madre
Oriental of Mexico." He goes on to suggest that, in response
to "pluvial" climates, there were faunal "movements both down-
ward and southward from a number of refugia until concentric
fronts of dispersal probably merged" (p. 64).

This hypothesis is contingent on the validity of the
hypothesis that large and tall ranges served as faunal refuges
during interglacial periods. The predictions of the hypothesis
concur with traditional views of biotic dispersal based on distance and local adaptation, and its applicability to the
present situation should therefore be expected.

Hypothesis VIII. Because this historical reconstruction
is based on vicariance during interglacial periods,
characteristic patterns of distribution and of divergence in
montane biotas should be evident.

Patterson (1980a) described well-defined patterns in the
distribution of montane mammals in New Mexico that are consistent with a vicariant explanation. A multiple regression,
involving the area, elevation, latitude and longitude of mountain ranges was found to account for 92% of the variation in
species number. Such well defined patterns are necessary, but
not sufficient for the vicariance explanation, as similar patterns may also be obtained in equilibrial situations (cf. Connor and McCoy, 1979). However, his demonstration of a significant correlation between these variables and the specific composition of mammalian assemblages provides further evidence for
vicariance. The relationship was interpreted as reflecting the
independent derivation of montane biotas from a common source
pool inhabiting these ranges during the Wisconsin glacial
period (Patterson, 1980a).

Common geographic patterns of divergence should also be
evident for montane species suffering range disjunctions during
Pleistocene climatic fluxes, although actual amounts of divergence (and corresponding taxonomic levels) will vary with the
many factors known to affect evolutionary potential (Patterson,
1982). This is reflected in the homogeneity of faunal proportions belonging to different trophic-habitat groups (Hypothesis
IV above), and the similarity of species belonging to these
groups in terms of subspecies number and incidence. Patterns
evident in the distributions of subspecies (hypothesis VI
above) also support this contention. One can look to the subspecies of Sorex monticolus inhabiting the Southern Rockies
(obscurus), the Mogollon Rim (monticolus) and the Sacramento
Mountains (neomexicanus) and find insectivoran counterparts to
corresponding species within the Eutamias quadrivittatus complex (i.e., quadrivittatus, cinereicollis and canipes, respectively). The shrews have attained lower levels of divergence,
presumably because of their higher trophic position but perhaps
because of other aspects of their biology, but the overall
congruence of the pattern seems to be too striking to be
accidental.

CONCLUSIONS AND PROSPECTUS

The results of this analysis complement those of earlier
studies employing different sets of mammal species (Patterson,
1980a) or a different geographic theater (Brown, 1971, 1978).
All suggest that the current distributions of montane species
on isolated ranges are relictual, dating from the inception of
interglacial intervals. Because such distributions were once
continuous between ranges, and involved the simultaneous disjunction of both populations and their habitats, the process
producing them has been termed "nonequilibrium" insular

biogeography (Brown, 1971, 1978) or more descriptively "Pleistocene vicariance" (Patterson, 1980a, 1982). The qualitatively
and quantitatively similar results of different studies of
Southwestern biogeography serve to establish the robustness of
the several conclusions.

Post-glacial extinction has played a major role in determining the distributions of individual species and the species
richness of individual mountain ranges. Presumably extinction
played a similar role in preceding interglacials as well. Significant predictions of the effects of extinction are possible
using quite indirect measures of population size, for example
the overall area of a mountain range, the body size of mammal
species, or their trophic habits and habitat affinities.
Mechanistically, however, it is still unknown whether extinction is directly related to population size or rather to its
temporal variability (cf. Karr, 1982). Significant improve-
ments in our ability to detect extinction may be expected with
a fuller understanding of the mechanism of extinction.

In general, the distributional corollaries of the vicariant explanation seem reasonably well supported for montane mammals. The search for concordant patterns of distribution
should be extended to other groups of species, for example
boreal insects or plants. The study of species-area relationships, especially inferences concerning its slope, would benefit greatly if a richer assemblage of species were available
for analysis. Thorough studies of the distributions of invertebrates having obligate plant hosts might also add to our
knowledge of the specific composition of habitats which existed
in lowland areas during glacial periods, and indicate their
geographical continuity.

The applicability of this reconstruction might also be
investigated in general ecological studies. For example, a
replacement of mesic plant communities by more xeric ones has

been regarded as a principal factor in the post-glacial extinction of mammalian species, leading to reduced population size
and greater vulnerability to local extinction. Evidence for
such changes might be sought in survivorship tables of long-
lived plant species. During field work in the Organ Mountains
I observed far fewer saplings of the mesic-adapted tree
Juniperus deppeana than would be expected if this species were
reproducing at a rate sufficient to maintain its population
there.

This analysis suggests other ecological studies on the
mammal species themselves. How are total population density
(rarity vs. abundance) and temporal variability in density
related to extinction probabilities? Demographic studies of
population dynamics of species in the Southern Rocky Mountains
could serve to address these questions. How do food-use and
space-use by montane mammals change as a function of the
extinctions of other species? Does a "density compensation"
mechanism exist by which surviving species attain greater population densities following the extinction of competitors? If
so, extinction could be shown to be a self-regulating process,
controlled by a negative feedback loop involving the ecological
responses of surviving species. Comparative resource-use studies, particularly of niche shifts, are urgently needed.

Finally, refined studies of evolutionary divergence among
isolated populations of many taxa will be necessary. Although
the characters on which such studies will be based must vary
according to taxon, the studies should be directed towards 1)
determination of phyletic patterns, 2) determination of
phenetic patterns, and 3) relations between the two. Phyletic
and phenetic patterns need not be congruent, especially if
divergence due to isolation is greatly accelerated by selection
and drift. What is the relative importance of drift versus
selection in the divergence of montane isolates? Does any

macromolecule provide the basis for a "molecular clock," with
which to measure the length of time various populations have
been isolated? With reference to populations in the Southern
Rockies, do montane isolates show tendencies towards "K selection"? Is there evidence of in situ divergence of montane
populations on a single mountain range? How is the evolutionary divergence of montane populations influenced by the extinction of other faunal elements, especially mesic-adapted boreal
forms? Answers to these and other questions will be necessary
before our understanding of montane biogeography in the
Southwest can be considered comprehensive.

ACKNOWLEDGMENTS

     I wish to thank John W. Fitzpatrick and Robert F. Inger
for insightful discussions on distributional patterns, and
Jared M. Diamond for particularly instructive comments on a
previous draft of the manuscript. James S. Ashe, Robert M.
Timm, and two anonymous reviewers also contributed materially
to the expression of this work. Rosanne Miezio drew the chipmunk in figure 7, and Sarah D. Bruner typed the initial draft
of the manuscript. Finally, K. E. Freas assisted the study in
many ways.

LITERATURE CITED

ANTEVS, E. 1954. Climate of New Mexico during the last
     glacio-pluvial. Journal of Geology, 62:182-191.
ARMSTRONG, D.M. 1972. Distribution of mammals in Colorado.
     Monographs of the Museum of Natural History, University of
     Kansas, 3:1-415.
ARMSTRONG, D.M.. 1977. Distributional patterns of mammals in
     Utah. Great Basin Naturalist, 37:457-474.
AYER, M.Y. 1936. The archeological and faunal material from
     Williams Cave, Guadalupe Mountains, Texas. Proceedings of
     the Academy of Natural Sciences, Philadelphia, 88:599-618.

BETANCOURT, J.L., and T.R. VAN DEVENDER. 1981. Holocene vegetation in Chaco Canyon, New Mexico. Science, 214:656-658.

BROWN, J.H. 1971. Mammals on mountaintops: nonequilibrium insular biogeography. American Naturalist, 105:467-478.

BROWN, J.H.. 1978. The theory of insular biogeography and the distribution of boreal birds and mammals. Great Basin Naturalist Memoirs, 2:209-227.

CLISBY, K.H., and P.B. SEARS. 1956. San Augustin Plains - Pleistocene climatic changes. Science, 124:537-538.

COCKRUM, E.L. 1960. The Recent mammals of Arizona: their taxonomy and distribution. Tucson: University of Arizona Press. 276 pp.

COLE, K. 1982. Late Quaternary zonation of vegetation in the eastern Grand Canyon. Science, 217:1142-1145.

CONNOR, E.F., and E.D. McCOY. 1979. The statistics and biology of the species-area relationship. American Naturalist, 113:791-833.

CUSHING, J.E., Jr. 1945. Quaternary rodents and lagomorphs of San Josecito Cave, Nuevo Leon, Mexico. Journal of Mammalogy, 26:182-185.

DALQUEST, W.W., E. ROTH, and F. JUDD. 1969. The mammal fauna of Schulze Cave, Edwards County, Texas. Bulletin of the Florida State Museum, Biological Sciences, 13:205-276.

DIAMOND, J.M. 1975. Assembly of species communities. in M.L. Cody and J.M. Diamond, eds. Ecology and evolution of communities. Cambridge: Belknap Press. Pp. 342-444.

DURRANT, S.D. 1952. Mammals of Utah, taxonomy and distribution. University of Kansas Publications, Museum of Natural History, 6:1-549.

DURRANT, S.D., M.R. LEE, and R.M. HANSEN. 1955. Additional records and extensions of ranges of mammals from Utah. University of Kansas Publications, Museum of Natural History, 9:69-80.

EMILIANI, C. 1955. Pleistocene temperatures. Journal of Geology, 63:538-578.

EMILIANI, C.. 1958. Ancient temperatures. Scientific American, 198(2): 55-63.

ERICSON, D.B., M. EWING, and G. WOLLIN. 1964. The Pleistocene epoch in deep-sea sediments. Science, 146:723-732.

FINDLEY, J.S. 1953. Pleistocene Soricidae from San Josecito Cave, Nuevo Leon, Mexico. University of Kansas Publications, Museum of Natural History, 5:633-639.

FINDLEY, J.S.. 1969. Biogeography of Southwestern boreal and desert mammals. in J. K. Jones, Jr., ed. Contributions in mammalogy. Miscellaneous Publications, University of Kansas Museum of Natural History 51, Pp. 113-128.

FINDLEY, J.S., A.H. HARRIS, D.E. WILSON, and C. JONES. 1975. Mammals of New Mexico. Albuquerque: University of New Mexico Press. 360 pp.

GALLOWAY, R.W. 1970. The full glacial climate in the
    southwestern United States. Annals of the Association of
    American Geographers, 60:245-256.
GRAYSON, D.K. 1977. On the Holocene history of some northern
    Great Basin lagomorphs. Journal of Mammalogy, 58:507-513.
GRAYSON, D.K.. 1981. A mid-Holocene record for the heather
    vole, Phenacomys cf. intermedius, in the central Great
    Basin and its biogeographic significance. Journal of Mam-
    malogy, 62:115-121.
HALL, E.R. 1946. Mammals of Nevada. Berkeley: University of
    California Press. 710 pp.
HALL, E.R. 1981. The mammals of North America. New York:
    John Wiley and Sons. 1:1-600 + 90; 2:601-1181 + 90.
HARRIS, A.H. 1970. The Dry Cave mammalian fauna and late plu-
    vial conditions in southeastern New Mexico. Texas Journal
    of Science, 22:3-27.
HARRIS, A.H.. 1977. Wisconsin Age environments in the north-
    ern Chihuahuan Desert: evidence from higher vertebrates.
    in R.H. Wauer and D.H. Riskind, eds. Transactions of the
    symposium on the biological resources of the Chihuahuan
    Desert. National Park Service Proceedings and Transac-
    tions Series 3. Pp. 23-52.
HARRIS, A.H., and J.S. FINDLEY. 1964. Pleistocene-Recent
    fauna of the Isleta Caves, Bernalillo Co., New Mexico.
    American Journal of Science, 262:114-120.
HENNINGS, D., and R.S. HOFFMANN. 1977. A review of the taxon-
    omy of the Sorex vagrans species complex from western
    North America. Occasional Papers, Museum of Natural His-
    tory, University of Kansas, 68:1-35.
KARR, J.R. 1982. Population variability and extinction in the
    avifauna of a tropical land bridge island. Ecology,
    63:1975-1978.
KELSON, K.R. 1951. Speciation in the rodents of the Colorado
    River drainage. University of Utah Biological Series,
    11:1-125.
KUCHLER, A.W. 1964. The potential natural vegetation of the
    conterminous United States, 1:3,168,000. Special Publica-
    tions, American Geographical Society, 36:1-37.
MACARTHUR, R.H., and E.O. WILSON. 1967. The theory of island
    biogeography. Princeton: Princeton University Press.
    203 pp.
MARTIN, P.S. 1958. Pleistocene ecology and biogeography of
    North America. in C.L. Hubbs, ed. Zoogeography. Ameri-
    can Association for the Advancement of Science Publication
    51. Pp. 375-420.

METCALF, A.L. 1977. Some Quaternary molluscan faunas from the
    northern Chihuahuan Desert and their paleoecological
    implications. in R.H. Wauer and D.H. Riskind, eds. Tran-
    sactions of the symposium on the biological resources of
    the Chihuahuan Desert. National Park Service Proceedings
    and Transactions Series, 3. Pp. 53-66.
OPIK, E.J. 1952. The Ice ages. Irish Astronomical Journal,
    2:71-84.
PATTERSON, B.D. 1980a. Montane mammalian biogeography in New
    Mexico. Southwestern Naturalist, 25:33-40.
PATTERSON, B.D.. 1980b. A new subspecies of Eutamias
    quadrivittatus (Rodentia: Sciuridae) from the Organ Moun-
    tains, New Mexico. Journal of Mammalogy, 61:455-464.
PATTERSON, B.D.. 1981. Morphological shifts of some isolated
    populations of Eutamias (Rodentia: Sciuridae) in different
    congeneric assemblages. Evolution, 35:53-66.
PATTERSON, B.D.. 1982. Pleistocene vicariance, montane
    islands, and the evolutionary divergence of some chipmunks
    (genus Eutamias). Journal of Mammalogy, 63:387-398.
SCHULTZ, C.B., and E.B. HOWARD. 1935. The fauna of Burnet
    Cave, Guadalupe Mountains, New Mexico. Proceedings of the
    Academy of Natural Sciences, Philadelphia, 87:273-298.
SEARS, P.B., F. FORMAN, and K.H. CLISBY. 1955. Palynology in
    southern North America. Bulletin of the Geological
    Society of America, 66:471-530.
SIEGEL, S. 1956. Nonparametric statistics for the behavioral
    sciences. New York: McGraw-Hill. 312 pp.
SMARTT, R.A. 1977. The ecology of late Pleistocene and Recent
    Microtus from south-central and southwestern New Mexico.
    Southwestern Naturalist, 22:1-19.
SPAULDING, W.G., and T.R. VAN DEVENDER. 1977. Late Pleisto-
    cene montane conifers in southeastern Utah. Southwestern
    Naturalist, 22:269-286.
THOMPSON, R.S., and J.I. MEAD. 1982. Late Quaternary environ-
    ments and biogeography in the Great Basin. Quaternary
    Research, 17:39-55.
VAN DEVENDER, T.R., and B.L. EVERITT. 1977. The latest Pleis-
    tocene and Recent vegetation of the Bishop's Cap, south-
    central New Mexico. Southwestern Naturalist, 22:337-353.
VAN DEVENDER, T.R., P.S. MARTIN, A.M. PHILLIPS, III, and W.G.
    SPAULDING. 1977. Late Pleistocene biotic communities
    from the Guadalupe Mountains, Culberson County, Texas. in
    R.H. Wauer and D.H. Riskind, eds. Transactions of the
    symposium on the biological resources of the Chihuahuan
    Desert. National Park Service Proceedings and Transac-
    tions Series, 3. Pp. 107-113.

VAN DEVENDER, T.R., W.G. SPAULDING, and A.M. PHILLIPS, III.
    1979. Late Pleistocene plant communities in the Guadalupe
    Mountains, Culberson County, Texas. in H.H. Genoways and
    R.J. Baker, eds. Biological investigations in the Gua-
    dalupe Mountains National Park, Texas. National Park Ser-
    vice Proceedings and Transactions Series 4. Pp. 13-30.
WELLS, P.V. 1966. Late Pleistocene vegetation and degree of
    pluvial climatic change in the Chihuahuan Desert. Sci-
    ence, 153:971-975.
WELLS, P.V. 1977. Post-glacial origin of the present
    Chihuahuan Desert less than 11,500 years ago. in
    R.H.Wauer and D.H. Riskind, eds. Transactions of the sym-
    posium on the biological resources of the Chihuahuan
    Desert. National Park Service Proceedings and Transac-
    tions Series, 3. Pp. 67-83.
WELLS, P.V., and C.D. JORGENSEN. 1964. Pleistocene wood rat
    middens and climatic change in the Mohave Desert: a
    record of juniper woodlands. Science, 143:1171-1174.

ECOSYSTEM DECAY OF AMAZON FOREST REMNANTS

Thomas E. Lovejoy, Judy M. Rankin,
R. O. Bierregaard, Jr., Keith S. Brown, Jr., Louise H. Emmons,
and Martha E. Van der Voort

INTRODUCTION

With the exception of some island studies, interpretations of the causes of the past extinctions have only occasionally included the factor of area -- of the world of a species simply no longer being big enough. Perhaps this is because of the difficulty in paleontology of separating area effects from other possible causes.

Today, however, the area factor looms large as a cause of extinction. This is because fragmentation of once continuous wild areas is a major way in which people are altering the landscape and biology of the planet, although it is a less obvious alteration than sheer habitat destruction. While there is no worldwide measure of the degree of fragmentation, in most parts of the world natural habitats are being fragmented, whether in Wisconsin (Curtis 1956, Levenson 1980), Maryland (Whitcomb et al. 1981, Lynch and Whigham 1983), New Jersey (Forman et al. 1976), or the Brazilian state of Sao Paulo (Willis 1979, Oedekoven 1980).

Wilcox (1980) defines habitat fragmentation as including two components, namely the habitat destruction itself which is a requisite part of creating fragments, and the isolation which

is the result. Both components result in the loss of animals
and plants (Wilcox and Murphy, ms.). It is theoretically possible, however, for habitat destruction to take place only by
reduction of the extent of a wild area rather than creating
isolated fragments from the former continuum. For example a
forested region could be reduced by some amount as opposed to
being broken into a number of fragments totalling the same
reduced area. More importantly, with habitat destruction per
se, animals and plants are lost for different reasons than
those causing loss from the isolation of fragments. Hence, it
is our preference to consider habitat fragmentation as applying
specifically to the state of being a fragment and its consequences (i.e., the isolation factor), rather than also including the habitat destruction necessary to create the fragments.
This difference in terminology is not a serious problem as long
as the distinction in usage is clear.

It is clear from a number of lines of evidence that fragments lose species subsequent to isolation. This follows from
consideration of the theory of island biogeography (Diamond
1972, Diamond and May 1976, Terborgh 1974, Wilson and Willis
1975), as well as from consideration of species/area curves
(Lovejoy and Oren 1981). It also can be deduced from studying
continental islands (those connected to a mainland prior to the
rise to modern sea level) and existing forest remnants. Diamond (this volume), in particular, has made important contributions to the understanding of the species loss process from
considering present day islands.

The particular contributions of such approaches are in
providing some notion about the rates of species loss and final
("equilibrium") species number, as well as some idea about
which kinds of species are likely to be lost (Diamond this
volume; Terborgh and Winter 1983). Very often it is difficult
to state with much certainty why particular species have been

lost, or to discern much about the processes involved. This is
because all that is observed is the endpoint; lost to history
is how the particular isolate reached it. Even on Barro
Colorado island, which was studied (for other reasons) during
the species loss process, the details were largely overlooked,
in large part because the actual species loss was only apparent
with hindsight.

    This species loss process can be thought of as analogous
to decay of a radioactive mineral where radioactivity is shed
in the process of approaching a simpler, more stable state. In
this case, the ecosystem is shedding plants and animals to the
point where it sends entire species and approaches a less
diverse state that is more stable in the sense of change in
number of constituent species. It is slightly more complicated
because isolation is not total and species can enter the
ecosystem; it is considerably more complicated because in contrast to radioactive particles, each species is different.
What is needed is an opportunity to study the species loss process in a systematic way.

THE MINIMUM CRITICAL SIZE OF ECOSYSTEMS PROJECT
    The Minimum Critical Size of Ecosystems Project (Lovejoy
1980) was established to serve such a purpose. It is a joint
project of Instituto Nacional de Pesquisas de Amazonia (INPA)
and World Wildlife Fund-U.S., which is interested in the implication for design and management of conservation areas. It
takes advantage of a Brazilian requirement that 50% of the land
in any development project remain in forest and tree cover. In
a region 80 km north of Manaus (state of Amazônas), ranchers
have agreed that the 50% of the land where they are establishing cattle ranches by cutting and burning primary forest can be
arranged to provide a size series of reserves, from 1 to 1000
ha with replicates in each size class. These reserves are

marked off and studied while still part of undisturbed forest.
After clearing takes place, the reserves are studied on a
long-term basis as the species loss process ensues. The pre-
isolation data provide one basis for comparison, as does a single, large ca. 10,000 ha reserve which will presumably experience the species loss process so slowly relative to the small
reserves as to be equivalent to an unaffected stretch of forest
for comparative purposes. (Terborgh's estimate (1975) that a
neotropical forest reserve of 1000 mi^2 would lose 1% of its
original species complement per century, would suggest this).
The tiny reserves can provide quick and simple insights into
the ecosystem decay process, while the larger ones will yield
deeper and more sophisticated understanding which will be more
slow in coming.

Fig. 1 was proposed (Lovejoy 1980) as a simple hypothetical view of what takes place. After initial experience, we
would add to this a factor representing the considerable change
in physical conditions (temperature and relative humidity)
resulting from modification of the surrounding area. Both from
the theoretical point of view, and from the practical aspects
of designing and managing national parks, there are two critical (and obviously related) questions:

1. Are species lost in some sort of predictable order?

2. Will forest fragments of similar size end up with
    similar final species compositions?

The answers to these questions, although likely (because of
species with large area requirements) to be in the affirmative
to some extent, must await further results. By May 1983 only
two small reserves, one each of 1 ha and 10 ha had been isolated (fig. 2), providing an insufficient basis for strong gen-
eralities. This paper provides the second overview of results
emerging from the project (see Lovejoy et al. 1983). Detailed

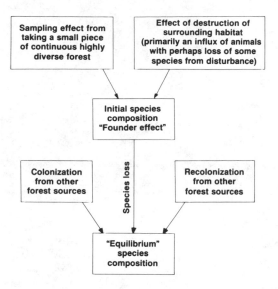

FIGURE 1. The initial hypothetical model of the consequences of fragmentation at the species level (Lovejoy 1980). This mode does not take into account the effects of altered temperature and relative humidity conditions observed in the isolated reserves in the Central Amazon.

methodology and results will appear in a series of papers on the work of the individual scientists.

BIRDS

Birds have been primarily studied by mist netting and banding (Bierregaard, ms.), and thus focus primarily on understory species.

The first notable result was the dramatic increase in capture rate in mist nets of understory birds (fig. 3), a statistically significant difference (t-test: for the 10 ha reserve, t=4.23 with 14 d.f. and p<.001; for the 1 ha reserve t=3.03 with 13 d.f. and .005<p<.01). This increase in bird activity could have stemmed from some resident birds having had their foraging areas truncated, as well as from the influx of birds

FIGURE 2. Aerial view of the first two isolated rain forest reserves, 1 ha on the left and 10 ha on the right. The reserves are square but distorted in this perspective. The thin strips of forest are required by Brazilian law to be left along stream courses. The forest is being cleared to create cattle pasture.

from the surrounding destroyed understory. This effect represents the addition of an overpopulation problem and change in community composition imposed from outside upon the area effect itself, with all its own changes in population and species composition. It is a consequence of habitat destruction rather than the isolation of the fragment.

Subsequent to isolation in October 1980, notable change has occurred in the bird communities of the two isolated reserves. Comparison of the birds sampled in the two communities with those sampled from nonisolated reserves indicates

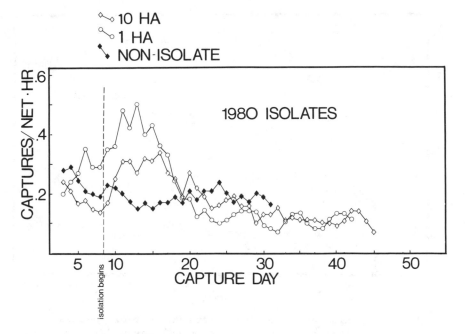

FIGURE 3. Bird activity as measured by capture rate
(birds/net-hour) (running three point averages) from December
1979 to January 1983 in 1 and 10 ha reserves of Central Amazon
forest near Manaus. Capture days occur at three week intervals
in each reserve. The two isolated reserves experience elevated
capture rates subsequent to isolation, an unisolated reserve
does not. Solid points from representative non-isolated 10 ha
reserve.

that the two isolated communities have become more similar to
one another and less similar to nonisolated reserves since isolation (Bierregaard, ms.). Species encounter functions (number
of species encountered with increasing number of individuals
sampled) calculated from post-isolation bird data from the 10
ha reserve (fig. 4) climb more slowly the later the initial
date of the sample. Thus for an equivalent number of individuals, later samples always consist of fewer species. This indicates that the bird nets were sampling an increasingly impoverished bird community and confirms that species loss was taking

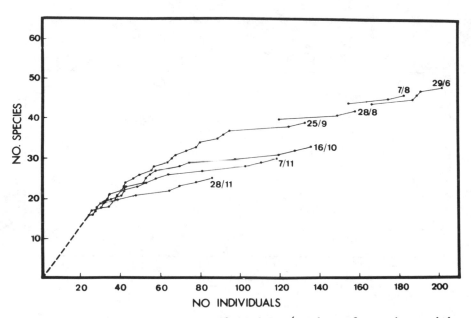

FIGURE 4. Species encounter functions (number of species with increasing number of individuals sampled) for understory birds in the 10 ha reserve after isolation in May 1980. The later the initial date (day/month) used to calculate a curve, the lower the rate of species encountered with increasing sample size. The earliest curves are not plotted all the way to the origin for ease of interpretation. These data indicate the understory bird community was declining in species number.

place. In comparison, such curves from reserves not yet isolated fall atop one another (Bierregaard, ms.).

The details of the change in the bird community are presented in figs. 5 and 6. The data are presented both in terms of percent individuals represented by a species in a sample, and the percent captures represented by a species in a sample. Percent individuals can be skewed to some extent by a vagrant species, e.g., when canopy birds like toucans happen to be caught by nets set in the understory. Percent captures can be skewed by differences in activity levels between species, differences in fundamental catchability (net avoidance, Lovejoy 1975) and net shyness (which develops from contact with nets).

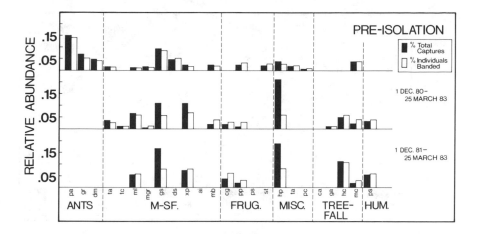

1 HA RESERVE

FIGURE 5. Data for some more abundant bird species netted from
the 1 ha reserve. First set of data is prior to isolation.
Second set of data is for a period from December 1, 1980 (six
months after isolation) to March 25, 1983. Third set of data
is from December 1, 1981 to March 25, 1983. Left hand bar for
each species equals percent individuals out of all birds
sampled. Right hand bar equals percent captures for that
species out of all captures. ANTS = ant followers, M-SF. =
mixed species flock, FRUG. = frugivores, MISC. = miscellaneous,
TREE-FALL = tree-fall foraging specialists, and HUM. =
Hummingbird. pa = Pithys albifrons, gr = Gymnopithys rufigula,
dm = Dendrocincla merula, ta = Thamnomanes ardesiacus, tc =
Thamnomanes caesius, ml = Mymotherula longipennis, mgr =
Mymotherula gutturalis, gs = Glyphorynchus spirurus, ds =
Deconychura stictolaema, xp = Xiphorhynchus pardolatus, ai =
Automolus infuscatus, mb = Myiobius barbatus, cg = Corapipo
gutturalis, pp = Pipra pipra, ps = Pipra erythrocephala, st =
Schiffornis turdinus, hp = Hylophylax poecilonota, ta = Turdus
albicollis, pc = Platyrinchus coronatus, ca = Cyphorhinus
arada, ga = Galbula albirostris, hc = Hypocnemis cantator, mc =
Microbates collaris, and ps = Pheathornis superciliosus.

Net avoidance can be a biasing factor in computations based on
individuals as well. Net shyness can also be a factor in such
calculations when a time period is selected for analysis out of
a long run of banding data; an individual of a previously

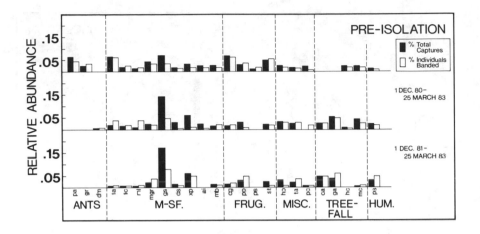

10 HA RESERVE

FIGURE 6. Data for some more abundant bird species netted from the 10 ha reserve. First set of data is prior to isolation. Second set of data is for a period from December 1, 1980 (six months after isolation) to March 25, 1983. Third set of data is from December 1, 1981 to March 25, 1983. Left hand bar for each species equals percent individuals out of all birds sampled. Right hand bar equals percent captures for that species out of all captures. The key appears in figure 5.

banded net shy species which is still present in the limited period is less likely to be caught than one less net shy.

The data represented in figs. 5 and 6 are only for selected, representative species from the sample. For the 1 ha reserve, there were 39 species totalling 99 individuals and 125 captures prior to isolation. For the post-isolation period of December 1, 1980 to March 25, 1983, the sample consisted of 36 species, totalling 81 individuals in 179 captures. This post-isolation period was separated by six months from the actual moment of isolation. A post-isolation period commencing even later, i.e., December 1, 1981 to March 25, 1983, provided a sample of 18 species, 36 individuals in 53 captures. Comparable figures for the 10 ha reserve include a pre-isolation

sample of 48 species, 124 individuals and 155 captures, the
longer post-isolation sample with 54 species, 207 individuals,
and 454 captures, and the shorter post-isolation sample with 38
species, 84 individuals and 117 captures. The species
encounter functions (fig. 4) indicate the progressive decline
in species number must be attributable in part to the impover-
ishment of the community as well as to sample size.

Birds which habitually follow swarms of army ants (principally Eciton burchelli) were present in both the reserves prior
to isolation but dropped out almost immediately. Interest-
ingly, an ant colony persisted in the 10 ha reserve longer than
the ant-following birds, indicating that a single colony is
insufficient to support ant-following birds, which is what
would be expected (Lovejoy 1980) from the ant/ant follower
relationship (Willis and Oniki 1978). Five "professional" followers (sensu Willis and Oniki 1978) dropped out of the bird
community (Pithys albifrons, Gymnopithys rufigula, Dendrocincla
merula, Dendrocolaptes certhia, and D. picumnus). Two non-
obligates, Hylophylax poecilonota and Percnostola rufifrons
remained.

Ants were again recorded in the 10 ha reserve on November
28, 1980 and January 10, 1981, the burn having taken place
October 31st. It is possible that the ants had been present
all along but we suspect that a colony had returned. Interest-
ingly on November 28, 1980 the ants were again attended by
birds, but only of the three large species (Hylexetastes
perrotii, Dendrocolaptes certhia and D. picumnus) one of which
had been banded in the same location. It is unlikely that the
birds had been in the reserve in the antless interval. They
almost certainly had returned, crossing the intervening open
area to do so. In unbroken forest these species travel long
distances in search of ants in a swarming state.

Flocks of understory birds appear to have notably changed
subsequent to isolation of the two reserves. Seven regular
understory flock species either dropped out or decreased in
numbers or activity (Thamnomanes ardesiacus, T. caesius,
Myrmotherula gutturalis, M. axillaris, M. longipennis,
Deconychura longicauda and D. stictolaema, Automolus infuscatus
and Philydor erythrocercus). A non-obligate understory flock
species, Pipromorpha macconnelli, also was adversely affected,
dropping out of the 10 ha reserve, and appearing to decline in
the 1 ha reserve. In one sense this latter is the reverse of
what one might expect. Yet, if there is a measurable probability of a species going extinct in an isolated reserve of a
given size, it can only be measured by an adequate sample of
reserves of different sizes. Until more reserves have been
isolated and the changes in their bird communities documented,
it is impossible to say whether these changes in the
Pipromorpha population are representative or not.

Generally speaking, canopy birds seemed, if anything to
increase with isolation, although this is based on small and
casual observations and not on netting data. Nonetheless, from
Karr's (1982) Barro Colorado analysis, it might be expected
that canopy birds could ignore habitat fragmentation to some
extent. Darkness is not a possible environmental cue as it is
for birds of the forest interior. Further they might well
benefit from the newly created edge (Amadon 1966). It is
interesting in view of Terborgh and Winter's (1983) findings
about body size that one fairly large (37.3 g) bird,
Xiphorhynchus pardolatus has persisted in both isolated
reserves. Based on auditory and visual observation, subcanopy
flocks appear to have dropped out.

Recapture rates for a reserve still part of surrounding
forest rises asymptotically to a value of about 47% (fig. 7)
(Bierregaard, ms.). Recapture rates in the isolated reserves

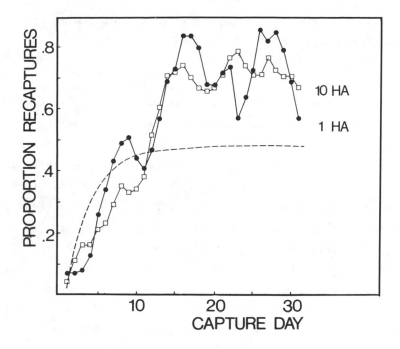

FIGURE 7. Recapture rate of understory birds in the two isolated reserves. The dashed line represents recapture rate as experienced in non-isolated reserves, leveling off at 47%. Capture days are at three week intervals. Recapture rate increases in the two reserves until isolation after which there is a brief decline followed by an increase. The decline coincides with increased capture rate as birds from destroyed forest crowd into the reserve. The subsequent increase is the result of netting in a relatively closed community. After the appearance of second growth vegetation in the surrounding fields, recapture rate declines suggesting the understory bird community had become less isolated.

are depressed somewhat immediately following isolation at the time of the influx of birds from the surrounding destroyed area. They then begin the climb again as would be anticipated from banding in a relatively closed community. The eventual later fall off in recapture rate coincides with growth of secondary vegetation in the surrounding pasture, presumably

making it easier for understory species to come and go from the
forest fragments.

BUTTERFLIES

Keith Brown of the University of Campinas has sampled
Ithomiine, Satyrine and other butterflies in a number of
reserves including the two isolated reserves. The local
species pool is estimated to be in excess of 500; of this 258
have been recorded as of September 1982. Table 1 summarizes
those results. Butterfly sampling efficiency was increased
with bait, Heliotropium (for Ithomiinae) and fermented bananas
(for Satyrinae). Whether just these two groups of butterflies
are sampled, or a larger number, there seems to be surprisingly
little difference in species number between 1 and 10 ha
reserves (fig. 8). The Satyrinae are rather uniformly distributed, with almost any reserve under normal conditions containing between 10 and 17 species. In accordance with other studies of the group (Brown and Benson 1974), the Ithomiinae are
much more patchy in distribution, some 1 ha reserves holding a
representative community of 7 to 10 species (e.g., 2108, 2107,
1110, 1113), while other 1 ha reserves (e.g., 1111) and even 10
ha reserves (1207, 3209) holding a smaller number. For Ithomiinae, only 100 ha plots can be certain to contain a representative community.

The above holds for plots within continuous forest. What
is the consequence of isolation? Species number for all butterflies follows a course apparently the reverse of that for
bird activity (and probably bird species number) (fig. 9). The
initial effect of burning, perhaps primarily a consequence of
smoke from the fires set to the felled forest to make way for
pasture is to greatly depress species number. Subsequently
there is a significant increase in species number, mostly a
consequence of penetration of the remnant patch by edge

TABLE 1. Occurrence of Rhopalocera in forest reserves

RESERVE #	SIZE	# OF DAYS SPENT COLLECTING	MONTH	MORPH/ BRASSOLINIDAE	SATYRINAE	ITHOM	OTHER NYMPH	PIER	PAPILIONIDAE	TRECLINAE	RIONIDAE	TOTAL	# OF BORDERS ISOLATED	# OF EDGE SPECIES ENCOUNTERED
1104	1 ha	4*	XII	0	1	3	3	2	0	1	4	14	4*	2
1104	1 ha	2**	XII,IX	1	10	5	11	0	1	7	15	50	3**	14
2107	1 ha	3	XII,I,VII	3	14	10	7	1	1	5	14	55	1***	6
2108	1 ha	1	XII	2	10	9	0	0	1	2	10	34	-	0
1110	1 ha	3	XII,V,VII	3	11	9	4	0	0	2	11	40	1****	0
1111°	1 ha	1	IX	2	6	4	4	1	0	5	18	40	1°°	6
1113	1 ha	1	IX	5	8	8	5	0	0	5	21	57	1**	2
1202	10 ha	4*	XII	1	6	6	14	3	0	3	10	43	4*	8
1202	10 ha	2**	XII,IX	4	15	10	22	4	1	15	32	103	4**	20
2206	10 ha	2	XII,I	4	12	7	0	0	0	1	9	33	-	0
1207°	10 ha	2	V,IX	5	8	3	8	0	0	7	22	53	-	0
3209	10 ha	1	VIII	2	11	5	5	0	0	9	18	50	-	1
1301	100 ha	6	XIII,I,IX	7	15	12	20	3	1	11	41	110	1/4	17
2303	100 ha	4	XII,I,VII	4	16	9	12	1	2	4	22	70	1	13
3304	100 ha	3	VII,VIII	7	19	14	10	4	0	15	50	119	2x1/2	12
3304	100 ha	1/2	VIII	3	12	3	3	0	0	7	32	60	-	0
1401°°°	1000 ha	6	II,VIII	9	19	11	31	3	1	17	54	145	1	22

* : sampled soon after isolation and burning; four sides without any green vegetation.

** : sampled one or two years after burning; four sides with second growth

*** : continuously growing; 110A had one side with very tall second growth.

**** : with a field camp located about 100m from the north side of the reserve, and much penetration of light.

**** : with a field camp less than 300m from the southern border and some penetration of light. Both are near a large gulley.

° : experimental reserves (with some manipulation).

°° : one side has been felled and borders the top of a hill (very changed).

°°° : encompasses previous reserves 1101, 1102, 1103, 1201, and one reserve borders.

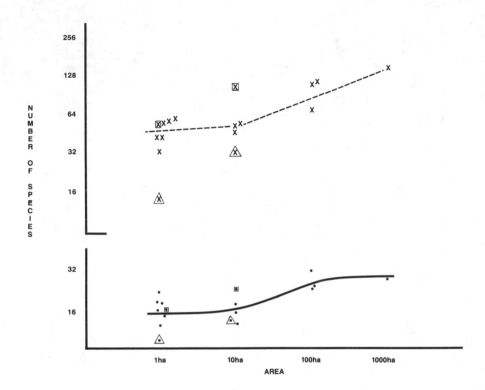

FIGURE 8.   Number of species of butterflies in different size
reserves.   Curves   fitted   by   eye.   (x) = Brassolinae,
Ithomiinae,   Morphinae,   other   Nymphalinae,   Papilionidae,
Pieridae,   Riodinidae,   Satyrinae,   and   Theclinae;   (o) =
Ithomiinae and Satyrinae; (△) = sampled   soon   after   isolation
and   burning;   four   sides   without   any   green   vegetation;   (□) =
sampled one or two years after burning; four sides with   second
growth continuously growing.

species; deep forest species adapted to shade and high humidity
become very rare and some disappear altogether.

      Butterflies of the edge, or ones of forest glades are nor-
mally rare in undisturbed forest, but increase in number in the
isolates (Brown, in prep.). This relates to increased light,
outside the forest but also within where it penetrates
laterally when the sun is low in the sky. These light conditions are favorable to both their activity and to many of their

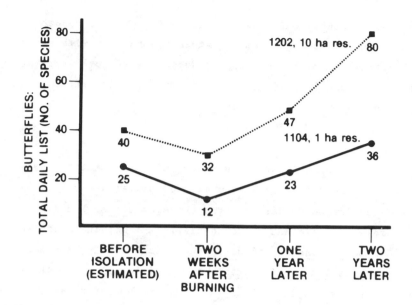

FIGURE 9. Number of butterfly species sampled daily in the first two reserves isolated.

food plants, such as <u>Solanum</u>, <u>Aristolochia</u>, <u>Passiflora</u>, Leguminosae and other families in the forest and to a greater extent in the surrounding pastures. Light stimulated butterflies penetrate into the reserves. Mostly newly recorded species are concentrated within 100 m of the edge, but are still observable at 200 m, and even occasionally (especially on ridges and small clearings) they appear 300 m from the edge. Canopy species (<u>Morpho</u>, Nymphalinae, Thechlinae, Pierinae) normally not observed in continuous forest appear in the regrown edges. Both canopy and edge species can compete with resident understory species for all types of resources (e.g., space and tranquility necessary for mate location, courtship, mating and oviposition).

The loss of shade loving species in favor of light loving ones proceeds until the primal forest butterfly community persists only in reserves of 100 ha or larger. Even in the 100 ha reserves, probably only the central 25 to 30 ha have such an assemblage. In reserves smaller than 100 ha, but with extensive regrowth around them which reduces the effects of light penetration and isolation, the primal forest butterfly community might become reconstituted.

MAMMALS

The only mammal data both prior and subsequent to isolation which are so far available are for primates and were largely collected by Marcio Ayres (Lovejoy et al. 1983). The 10 ha reserve contained three species: the golden-handed tamarin (Saguinus midas) which disappeared immediately, the saki (Chiropotes satanas chiropotes), two individuals of which persisted for a while, and the folivorous red howler monkey (Alouatta seniculus), a band of which has maintained itself and has produced young. There were some observations of mammals prior to isolation of the 1 and 10 ha reserves, but they could not be characterized as systematic.

In 1982 Louise Emmons collected baseline data on non-flying mammals and their relative densities in various project reserves including the two isolated ones. Her data differ from the rest presented in this paper by being solely from unisolated and isolated reserves, rather than the same reserves before and after isolation. A description of the regional fauna and discussion of its characteristics will be published elsewhere (Emmons, in prep.).

Baseline data from undisturbed forest indicated small mammal populations to be extremely low. In contrast populations of some large species, such as howler monkeys, acouchys, agoutis, pacas, peccaries and armadillos are quite high.

At the time the reserves were surveyed for mammals they had been isolated for two years. With a poor burn after the surrounding forest had been felled, the surrounding vegetation

had grown into a thicket of shrubs 1-3 m tall. This could well
have provided cover under which animals could cross from neighboring forest, or habitat where a few forest species could survive.

Table 2 compares the results of mammal surveys in intact
forest and the two isolated reserves. Small nocturnal canopy
mammals were not adequately surveyed by the methods used and
their abundances cannot be inferred from this data set.
Nonetheless, of roughly 20 mammal species present in reserves
still part of more extensive forest, only seven were encountered in the two isolated reserves. Of those that persisted,
Oryzomys capito and Dasypus novemcinctus can live in secondary
vegetation, Mesomys hispidus is a primary forest species that
favors areas of disturbed vegetation such as tree falls, and
Didelphis is a nomadic species that also thrives in secondary
vegetation (the one captured in the 1 ha reserve was certainly
a transient). Three of the four species classed as very common
in continuous forest persisted in the 10 ha reserve.

The most unexpected result was that Proechimys, a small
rodent which completely dominates the nocturnal mammal fauna of
undisturbed forest in number of individuals, was extinct in
both isolated reserves. Its high densities and very small home
range in all localities where it has been studied (Emmons 1982,
Guillotin 1982) would make Proechimys seem the most likely
species to persist in small isolated reserves. The mouse,
Oryzomys capito, was very rare in intact forest; by percentage
capture it was more common in the isolated reserves, although
the numbers are very small. It is possible that Oryzomys densities are higher in the absence of Proechimys, but since O.
capito can live in secondary vegetation, its presence in the
fragments may simply be due to lack of isolation.

For birds, proneness to extinction from forest fragments
has been shown to be related to initial density in the original

TABLE 2. All species of non-flying mammals observed and/or trapped in isolated reserves, or observed more than once during the study in un-isolated reserves, and their approximate relative densities in each habitat surveyed.

SPECIES	INTACT FOREST	10 HA	1 HA
Marmosa parvidens	+	-	-
Didelphis marsupialis	++	-	+
Metachirus nudicaudatus	+	-	-
Pithecia pithecia	+	-	-
Chiropotes satanus	++	-	-
Alouatta seniculus	+++	+++	-
Cebus apella	+	-	-
Saguinus midas	++	-	-
Tamandua tetradactyla	+	-	-
Dasypus novemcinctus	+++	+?	-
Sciurus gilvigularis	+	+	-
Oryzomys capito	+	+	+
Agouti paca	++	-	-
Dasyprocta agouti	+	-	-
Myoprocta acouchy	+++	+	-
Proechimys app.	++++	-	-
Mesomys hispidus*	-	-	+
Potos flavus	+	-	-
Tapirus terrestris	+?	-	-
Tayassu tajacu	++	-	-
Mazama americana	+	-	-

```
+++ = very common      - = not observed
 ++ = common           ? = only sign observed
  + = uncommon         * = only trapped once
```

forest (Terborgh and Winter 1980; Diamond, this volume). The preliminary results of the mammal surveys reported here indicate likewise the importance of high original densities, with

the exception of Proechimys. The failure of the latter to persist in a reserve large enough to contain several adult home
ranges, while larger species with larger home ranges (Alouatta,
Myoprocta) have survived, is an enigma meriting detailed study.
The low densities for populations of small mammal species compared to parts of Amazonia with higher species diversity (e.g.,
Dept. of Madre de Dios, Peru), such as at Manu, suggest that
for a given size of reserve there would be comparatively more
extinctions in the Manaus region.

AMPHIBIA

Surveys for amphibia carried out by Barbara Zimmerman both
before and after isolation suggest a reduction in species
number (table 3). Most of the decrease involves three species
of Phyllomedusa, frogs which require standing water for reproduction. All three were calling near the edge of the 1 ha
reserve in 1980. It may be inappropriate to include them on
the reserve list in that they were outside the perimeter when
recorded. The possibility notwithstanding that they may have
included a portion of the reserve in their home range, the
story is sufficiently interesting to merit mention.

The requisite standing water was provided by a white-
lipped peccary (Tayassu albirostris) wallow. This wallow along
with the reserve itself, was abandoned by the peccaries after
isolation. It consequently filled in and dried out rendering
the habitat unsuitable for breeding of the three species of
Phyllomedusa as well as one species of Colosthetus. If still
present, they are not calling and will be unable to breed. It
is reasonable to expect a number of extinctions linked between
groups, such as this example and that between ant followers and
army ants.

WOODY PLANTS

The previous summary paper (Lovejoy et al. 1983) cited the
dramatic change in physical conditions occasioned by isolation.
At the edge of a reserve, where previously temperature and
relative humidity conditions were relatively constant, such
conditions become highly fluctuating. For example, hot dry air
can move into the forest from the newly created pastures. The
effects of the wind itself are dramatic on the shallow rooted
trees particularly on the windward edge of a patch.

Figs. 10, 11 and 12 document the dramatic increase in tree
mortality and tree falls which have occurred since isolation in
the 10 ha patch (Rankin, in prep. a). In the first year after
isolation there were nine standing dead trees (fig. 10) and 65
in the second year (fig. 11). Trees broken by wind or the fall
of another tree numbered eight in the first year and 12 in the
second. Trees badly burned numbered two in the first year and
19 in the second. These latter were all concentrated in the
southeast corner within 1 ha with about 600 trees of dbh 10 cm
or greater. A fire started by the ranchers to burn back weeds
in the surrounding fields later flared up and entered the
reserve at that point. The difficulty of lighting a fire in
intact rain forest even at the height of the dry season indicates what a major change there had been in the understory of
the isolated 10 ha reserve. Within the reserve, the number of
trees uprooted by another tree or by wind numbered a single
individual in the first year and 11 in the second. The effects
of the wind are shown in fig. 12 where the vast majority of
tree falls in the buffer zone area are on the side of the pre-
vailing winds.

Added to these effects is that of the invasion of secondary plant species at the margin (Rankin, in prep. b). They
create a band of secondary vegetation among the skeletal trunks
of dead and fallen trees (fig. 13). Many of the light loving

TABLE 3. Amphibia recorded before and after isolation in the first two isolated reserves.

Species	SPECIES RECORDED 1980		SPECIES RECORDED 1983 (May/June)	
	10 ha Reserve	1 ha Reserve	10 ha Reserve	1 ha Reserve
Osteocephalous sp.	X	X	X	X
Eleutherodactylus fenestratus		X	X	X
Adenomera andreae	X	X	X	X
Leptodactylus pentadactylus	X		?°	?
Phyllobates femoralis	X		?	?
Colostethus marchesianus	(X)†	(X)		
Phyllomedusa bicolor		X*		
P. tarsius		X*		
P. tomopterna		X*		
Leptodactylus amazonicus	(X)		?	?

*Not immediately in the reserve, but at the edge and probably there because of the peccary wallow
†Parentheses indicate that the species were observed, but were not recorded calling
°Question mark = species which are possibly still in the reserves but had not been observed by June of 1983

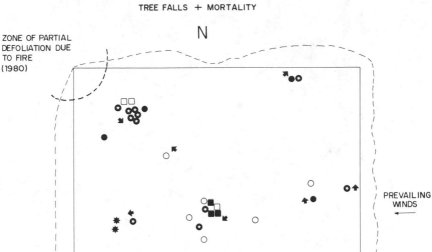

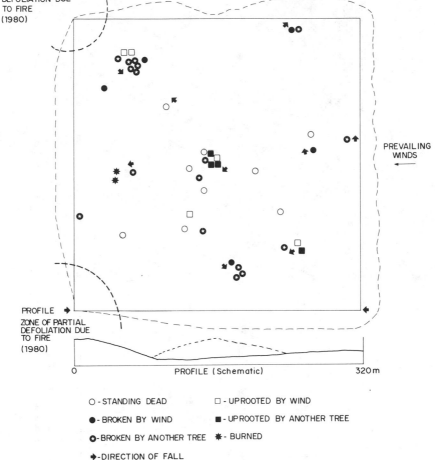

FIGURE 10. Tree (10 cm dbh or greater) falls and mortality   in
the 10 ha isolated reserve occurring during the first year of
isolation.

species already present in the reserve before isolation are now

well established in the pasture and along the reserve margin

and are entering reproductive maturity, providing an enlarged

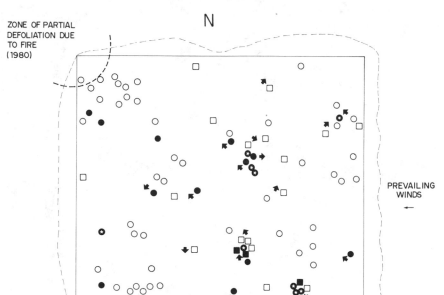

RESERVE 1202 POST — ISOLATION 1982
TREE FALLS + MORTALITY

O - STANDING DEAD   □ - UPROOTED BY WIND

● - BROKEN BY WIND   ■ - UPROOTED BY ANOTHER TREE

◉ - BROKEN BY ANOTHER TREE ✱ - BURNED

→ - DIRECTION OF FALL

FIGURE 11. Tree (10 cm dbh or greater) falls and mortality in the 10 ha isolated reserve occurring during the second year of isolation.

seed source. Taxonomic changes are also taking place: in August 1983 the first species of a family not before present in the 10 ha reserve (<u>Trema</u> sp. of the Ulmaceae) was discovered in

RESERVE 1202 POST — ISOLATION 1982
TREE FALLS + MORTALITY (RESERVE MARGIN ONLY)

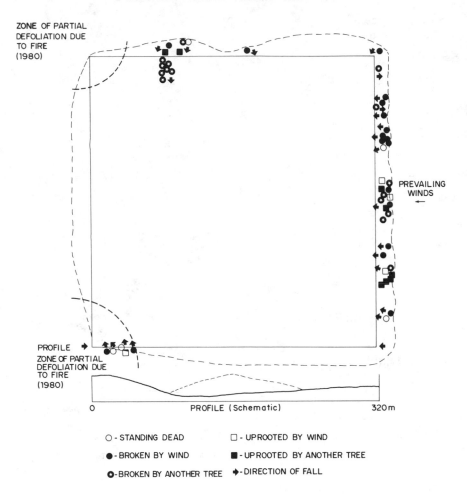

O - STANDING DEAD   □ - UPROOTED BY WIND

● - BROKEN BY WIND   ■ - UPROOTED BY ANOTHER TREE

◉ - BROKEN BY ANOTHER TREE   ➤ - DIRECTION OF FALL

FIGURE 12. Tree (10 cm dbh or greater) falls and mortality associated with the margin of the 10 ha isolated reserve. Note the concentration on the windward margin.

the heavily burned southeast corner. This is already reproducing in the surrounding pasture and seedlings are present inside the reserve fence.

FIGURE 13.   View of the forest margin in the vicinity of the
experimental reserves. Some primary forest trees have died at
the edge and second growth is coming up amongst them.

        How far the physical effects and invasions of secondary
species will eat into the primary forest fragment is yet to be
determined. Presumably at some point an equilibrium will be
established at the edge with the secondary vegetation providing
the insulating effects and restoring temperature and relative
humidity conditions to a state akin to that of undisturbed
forest. This will depend on reserve size. The above cited
trends suggest the isolated reserves of 1 and 10 ha will be
stands of primarily secondary succession species within a
decade.

CONCLUSIONS

The results obtained so far show predominantly effects associated with the newly created edge. As such, they are likely to loom largest in significance in small forest fragments, and to dwindle in importance the larger a reserve may be. The influx effect can probably be avoided by clearing from the margin of a reserve away from the reserve. The physical edge effects can be lessened by replacing the surrounding destroyed forest with arboreal vegetation such as rubber trees. The area effects themselves are likely to have been observable, in slow motion at least, during past climatic periods when rain forest vegetation is thought to have been fragmented (Haffer 1969).

This provides, in any case, a second glimpse of the dynamics of forest fragments in the Amazon, and is, of necessity, only preliminary. More reserves are being isolated in 1983. More replicates and additional size classes should provide greater precision of results and a better measure of predictability. Future data should provide more insight into change in the primary forest of the isolates rather than changes induced by the edges.

ACKNOWLEDGEMENTS

Funding for this project has come from the World Wildlife Fund-U.S., and the U.S. Man and the Biosphere Program, the National Park Service, the A. W. Mellon Foundation, and the Weyerhaeuser Family Foundation. Institutional support and encouragement has been provided by INPA (Instituto Nacional de Pesquisas da Amazonia). We are grateful to Barbara Zimmerman for the information on amphibia, and to Doug Stotz for analysis of bird data. Donna Bowles and Pieter de Marez Oyens made important contributions to the preparation of this paper.

LITERATURE CITED

AMADON, D. 1966. Birds around the world. Nat. Hist. Press, New York. 175 p.
BIERREGAARD, R. O. In prep. Analyses of community structure in understory birds of the central Amazonian Terra Firme forests based on an extensive mist-netting program.
BROWN, K. S., JR. In prep. Butterfly communities of fragmented and undisturbed Central Amazon forest.
BROWN, K. S., JR. and W. W. BENSON. 1974. Adaptive polymorphism associated with multiple Mullerian mimicry in Heliconius numata (Lepid. Nymph.). Biotropica 6(4):205-228.
CURTIS, J. T. 1956. The modification of mid-latitude grasslands and forests by man. In W. L. Thomas, Jr. [ed.]. Man's role in changing the face of the earth. Univ of Chicago Press, Chicago.
DIAMOND, J. M. 1972. Biogeographic kinetics: Estimation of relaxation times for avifaunas of southwest Pacific islands. Proc. Nat. Acad. Sci. 69:3199-3203.
DIAMOND, J. M. and R. M. MAY. 1976. Island biogeography and the design of natural reserves. p. 163-186. In R. M. May [ed.]. Theoretical ecology: Principles and applications. Saunders, Philadelphia-Toronto.
EMMONS, L. H. 1982. Ecology of Proechimys (Rodentia, Echimyidae) in southeastern Peru. Trop. Ecol. 23:280-290.
EMMONS, L. H. In prep. A survey of nonvolet mammals in fragmented and undisturbed Central Amazon forest.
FORMAN, R. T. T., A. E. GALLI and C. F. LECK. 1976. Forest size and avian diversity in New Jersey woodlots with some land use implications. Oecologia (Berl.) 26:1-28.
GUILLOTIN, M. 1982. Place de Proechimys cuvieri (Rodentia, Echimyidae) dans les peuplements micromammaliens terrestres de la foret guyanaise. Mammlia 46:299-318.
HAFFER, J. 1969. Speciation in Amazonian forest birds. Science 165:131-137.
KARR, J. R. 1982. Avian extinction on Barro Colorado island, Panama: A reassessment. Amer. Nat. 119:343-352.
LEVENSON, J. B. 1980. The southern-mesic forest of southeastern Wisconsin: Species composition and community structure. Contrib. Biol. Geol. Milwaukee Co. Public Museum, Milwaukee, Wisconsin.
LOVEJOY, T. E. 1975. Bird diversity and abundance in Amazon forest communities. Living Bird 13:127-191.
LOVEJOY, T. E. 1980. Discontinuous wilderness: Minimum areas for conservation. Parks 5(2):13-15.

LOVEJOY, T. E., R. O. BIERREGAARD, J. M. RANKIN and H. O. R.
    SCHUBART. 1983. Ecological dynamics of forest fragments,
    p. 377-384. In S. L. Sutton, T. C. Whitmore, and A. C.
    Chadwick [eds.]. Tropical rain forests: Ecology and
    management. Blackwell Scientific Publications, Oxford, U.
    K.
LOVEJOY, T. E. and D. C. OREN. 1981. The minimum critical
    size of ecosystems. p. 7-12. In R. L. Burgess and D. M.
    Sharpe [eds.]. Forest island dynamics in man-dominated
    landscapes. Springer-Verlag, New York.
LYNCH, J. F. and D. F. WHIGHAM. 1983. Effects of forest frag-
    mentation on breeding bird communities in Maryland. Biol.
    Cons. 26: in press.
OEDEKOVEN, K. 1980. The vanishing forest. Environ. Law and
    Policy 6(4):184-185.
RANKIN, J. M. In prep. a. Tree mortality and replacement
    rates in fragmented and intact Central Amazon rain forest.
RANKIN, J. M. In prep. b. Woody plant colonization and
    regrowth in large slash and burn tracts in the Central
    Amazon.
TERBORGH, J. 1974. Preservation of natural diversity: The
    problem of extinction prone species. Bioscience 24:715-
    722.
TERBORGH, J. 1975. Faunal equilibria and the design of
    wildlife preserves. p.369-380. In F. B. Golley and E.
    Medina [eds.]. Tropical ecological systems: Trends in
    terrestrial and aquatic research. Springer-Verlag, New
    York.
TERBORGH, J. and B. WINTER. 1983. A method for siting parks
    and reserves with special reference to Columbia and Equa-
    dor. Biol. Consv. 27:45-58.
WHITCOMB, R. F., C. S. ROBBINS, J. F. LYNCH, B. L. WHITCOMB, M.
    K. KLIMKIEWICZ and D. BYSTRAK. 1981. Effects of forest
    fragmentation on avifauna of the eastern deciduous forest.
    p. 125-205. In R. L. Burgess and D. M. Sharpe [eds.].
    Forest island dynamics in man-dominated landscapes.
    Springer-Verlag, New York.
WILCOX, A. B. 1980. Insular ecology and conservation. p.
    95-117. In M. E. Soule and B. A. Wilcox [eds.]. Conser-
    vation biology. Sinauer Associates, Inc., Sunderland,
    Massachusetts.
WILCOX, A. B. and D. D. MURPHY. Conservation strategy: The
    effects of fragmentation on extinction. Submitted to Am.
    Nat., Spring 1983.
WILLIS, E. O. 1979. The composition of avian communities in
    remanescent woodlots in southern Brazil. Papeis Avulsos
    Zool. 33(1):1-25.
WILLIS, E. O. and Y. ONIKI. 1978. Birds and army ants. Ann.
    Rev. Ecol. Syst. 9:243-263.

WILSON, E. O. and E. O. WILLIS. 1975. Applied biogeography.
    p.522-534. In M. L. Cody and J. M. Diamond [eds.]. Ecol-
    ogy and evolution of communities. Belknap Press of Har-
    vard University, Cambridge, Massachusetts.

APPENDIX -- ABSTRACTS OF PAPERS

PATTERNS OF EXTINCTION IN THE FOSSIL RECORD OF VASCULAR PLANTS
Andrew H. Knoll

     On the basis of fundamental attributes of tracheophyte
morphology and physiology, it can be hypothesized that vascular
land plants should be vulnerable to extinction resulting from
competition and/or climatic change (when no migration routes to
refugia are available), but relatively invulnerable to mass
extinctions resulting from catastrophic mass mortality. The
fossil record supports these hypotheses. There is no evidence
for globally synchronous mass extinctions in the evolutionary
record of vascular plants, but the influence of competition on
extinctions can be documented throughout tracheophyte history.
Both stratigraphic/bedding plane analyses of fossil assemblages
and comparative anatomical and morphological studies of
relevant taxa indicate that successive radiations of newly
evolved families precipitated the decline and extinction of
previously dominant groups in the Devonian Period. Comparable
evidence documents a similar phenomenon in the late Cretaceous
when angiosperms began their rise to ecological dominance.
Major climatic and geographical changes at the end of the
Paleozoic Era occasioned the extinction of many pteridosperm
and pteridophyte families and the concomitant expansion of

conifers and other gymnosperm groups, but floral transitions
were not globally synchronous. They occurred on a continent by
continent basis over a period of some 25 million years.

Extinction patterns reveal fundamental differences between
the evolutionary history of plants and animals. Mass extinctions have played a major role in determining large scale patterns of animal evolution, but in vascular plants, competition
seems to have been the major determinant of large scale change.

MARINE MASS EXTINCTIONS: A DOMINANT ROLE FOR TEMPERATURE
Stephen M. Stanley

Several lines of evidence suggest that temperature change
has been a prominent cause of mass extinction in the marine
realm, whereas areal effects of regression have not. The tiny
Hawaiian Islands and narrow Panamic-Pacific shelf support enormous provincial benthic faunas on much smaller areas of shallow
sea floor than have fringed continents during mass extinctions
of the past. Also, in Eocene/Oligocene and Plio-Pleistocene
times, climatic cooling caused mass extinction, but dramatic
global events of sea level lowering did not. Many earlier global regressions also failed to cause mass extinction, contrary
to the prediction that a universal relationship between diversity and area of sea floor has accounted for mass extinction by
regression.

Neogene extinctions have been regional (North Atlantic)
rather than global, reflecting irregular propagation of cooling
from high to low latitudes. In contrast, tropical taxa suffered preferentially on a global scale in most ancient mass
extinctions (Cambrian "biomere events", terminal Ordovician,
Late Devonian, terminal Permian, terminal Cretaceous, and
Eocene-Oligocene). For most groups of marine animals,

ecological specialization (stenotopy) is principally a matter
of stenothermy. Thus, the geographic pattern of ancient mass
extinctions suggests that global rather than polar cooling was
the agent: equatorial zones were affected most severely
because, while other climatic zones migrated equatorward, fully
tropical zones temporarily disappeared. Additional support for
thermal causation comes from (1) independent evidence that some
mass extinctions coincided with climatic cooling and (2) evidence that during some of the events nontropical biotas
migrated equatorward, to replace tropical biotas. The fact
that many extinction events spanned more than a million years
and were episodic in nature is consistent with the idea that
different taxa disappeared sequentially during pulses of cooling, as their respective thermal limits were exceeded.

EXTINCTION IN HOMINID EVOLUTION
Alan Walker

    This account deals with the robust species of
Australopithecus that was endemic to Africa and became extinct
a little over one million years ago. Scenarios attributing
this extinction to other hominid species activities are difficult to assess using the record from East Turkana, Kenya,
because it can be demonstrated that geologically contemporaneous hominid species need not necessarily have been sympatric in
life. The extinction of this Australopithecus species was not,
apparently, coincident with major changes in either the morphology or the behavior of the contemporaneous Homo. However,
the East African large carnivore guild changed three times in
composition in ways that may be related to this extinction: at
about 2, 1.5, and 1 million years ago. The robust lineage survived the first two faunal changes, but became extinct at the

third. Homo species, on the other hand, underwent marked
behavioral and morphological change coincident with the first
faunal change, but showed no obvious changes with the others.
The assessment of these changes is based in part on the
archaeological literature and in part on a new method of
evaluating and measuring changes in cranial shape. Possible
links between the changing adaptations of Homo, the faunal
changes, and the extinction of the robust Australopithecus are
suggested.

CATASTROPHIC EXTINCTIONS AND LATE PLEISTOCENE BLITZKRIEG:
TWO RADIOCARBON TESTS
Paul S. Martin

    Late Pleistocene extinctions involved 100 genera of large
land mammals and perhaps an even larger number of oceanic
island endemics of various sizes. In North America the
radiocarbon dating revolution of the last three decades as well
as recent stratigraphic studies indicate extinction of megamam-
mals around 11,000 yr B.P. In Eurasia megafaunal extinction was
more gradual and less sweeping. Several thousand years
separate the time of megafaunal extinctions on different continents, eliminating any possibility of "instantaneous" or
"simultaneous" extinctions. Presumably no worlds collided.
    Avian losses on oceanic islands in the late Holocene, such
as the moas of New Zealand, the elephant birds of Madagascar
and flightless geese of Hawaii, occurred within a few centuries
following the arrival of prehistoric people. Massive extinction of island faunas can be attributed to fire storms, land
clearing, and introduction of alien animals as well as to the
hunting activities of Neolithic societies. The possibility of

climatic change as a cause of Holocene insular extinction is
remote.

The pattern of extinction on the continents is less
clearly related to human impacts. Australia and America lost
many more large mammals than Eurasia and Africa. The giant
extinct marsupials of Australia and the ground sloths of America appear to have been especially "huntable". In both continents remains of extinct megafauna are seldom found in
archaeological sites, unlike the case in Africa and Eurasia.
Thus, for the Americas and Australia, a gradual attrition of
large mammals by human impact can be eliminated and only a sudden severe human impact ("blitzkrieg") remains as a testable
model.

"NORMAL" EXTINCTIONS OF ISOLATED POPULATIONS
Jared M. Diamond

Dramatic extinction waves arising from catastrophes, such
as asteroid collisions or arrivals of human hunters, have been
superimposed on a background of "normal" extinctions due to
fluctuations in the environment. This paper summarizes studies
of such "normal" extinctions and tests theoretical predictions
about them.

Simple theoretical considerations lead to six predictions
about lifetimes of populations in a fluctuating environment.
Lifetimes should increase with population size, hence with (1)
inhabited area (e.g., island area) and (2) population density;
with (3) generation time or individual life-time; with (4)
intrinsic rate of increase; and with (5) the ratio of birth
rate to death rate. Population lifetimes should decrease with
(6) temporal variability in population size.

These predictions are tested against four types of studies.

First, studies of turnover of populations on islands or census plots at equilibrium yield numerous examples of extinctions on a year-to-year time scale. Such studies are available for birds on European and North American islands, and for some other groups of organisms.

Second, a net preponderance of extinctions over the course of a century has been observed in several studies of habitats undergoing fragmentation. Examples include bird censuses in forests of Brazil, Ecuador, Barro Colorado Island, eastern North America, and New Zealand's Bank Peninsula.

Third, a new preponderance of extinctions over the course of 10,000 years has been documented or inferred for land-bridge islands severed from mainlands by late-Pleistocene rises in sea level. Among well-studied cases are the mammal faunas of Bass Straits and the Sunda Shelf; avifaunas of the Solomon Islands, New Guinea satellite islands, and other land-bridge islands; and lizard faunas of California land-bridge islands. An analogous study is of mammals on western North American mountains whose boreal habitats were formerly continuous but were sundered by late-Pleistocene warming.

Finally, extinction rates in evolutionary or geographical time can be inferred from the proportion of species in a fauna that are endemic at the species or genus level. The reason is that if populations go extinct quickly, few survive long enough to evolve into an endemic species or genus.

All four types of studies, at these four very different time scales, confirm the theoretical prediction that population lifetimes should increase with population density, measured directly or through its correlates such as trophic level and body size. Several studies confirm the predictions that population lifetimes should increase with individual life-times and decrease with temporal variability in population size. The two predictions concerning intrinsic rate of increase and the ratio of birth rate to death rate have yet to be tested.

In short, the dependence of extinction rates on population size (= inhabited area x population density) is so overwhelming that it must first be removed (e.g., graphically) before one can hope to detect other correlates of proneness to extinction.

MAMMALIAN EXTINCTION AND BIOGEOGRAPHY IN THE
SOUTHERN ROCKY MOUNTAINS
Bruce D. Patterson

The current distributions of montane species in the American Southwest are products of climatic changes during the Quaternary. A detailed reconstruction of events responsible for currently disjunct distributions has emerged from a variety of studies. This reconstruction is examined by reducing it to a collection of more-or-less discrete, testable hypotheses. The hypotheses are tested against patterns of distribution and divergence of montane mammals in the Southern Rocky Mountains, supplemented by appropriate paleontological and palynological evidence.

Support for the distributional hypotheses is abundant and convincing. Paleobotanical studies indicate expansions of montane vegetation to lowland areas between mountain ranges during glacial advances. Extralimital fossils of several boreal mammal taxa in southern lowlands indicate faunal interchange took place through these lowland corridors. That there is no current colonization of isolated ranges by these species is demonstrated by their absence in lowland habitats. Fossils document the post-glacial extinction of some montane mammal populations on two southern mountain ranges. That post-glacial

extinctions were widespread and selective is suggested by: 1)
the significant association between the occurrences of each
species and montane area, 2) correlations between body size and
trophic habits with the number of mountain ranges that different species occupy, 3) changing proportions of carnivores
and kinds of herbivores on isolated ranges with progressively
depauperate biotas, and 4) patterns of taxonomic diversification among montane species. Differential extinction of boreal
habitat specialists is suggested by trivariate plots of species
occurrences, montane area, and elevation.

Although support for hypotheses relating to evolutionary
divergence is considerably weaker, existing data are broadly
consistent with proposals that endemic forms originated on the
largest mountain ranges during interglacial intervals, and
spread from these to neighboring ranges during the succeeding
glacial advance. Deviations from these patterns refute the
contention that common patterns of divergence should characterize all elements of boreal montane communities.

ECOSYSTEM DECAY OF AMAZON FOREST REMNANTS
Thomas E. Lovejoy, Judy M. Rankin, R. O. Bierregaard, Jr.,
Keith S. Brown, Jr., Louise H. Emmons, and Martha E. Van der
Voort

Species loss, from isolated fragments of formerly continuous habitat, is an ecosystem decay process leading to less
diverse communities. This tendency is an almost universal
threat to efforts to conserve species and protect representative natural ecosystems, since so many protected areas are, or
are likely to become, isolated habitat fragments. It is a dominant theme in our effect on the biology of the planet.

Questions abound about this process. How predictable is
the order of species loss, i.e., local extinction? Do similar
sized fragments end up with similar species composition? A
joint Brazilian/United States research program is studying this
problem in the central Amazon where a size series of forest
reserves is being left in the course of development. This is
one of the few instances where the biology of a remnant will be
known before its isolation, and where the process rather than
the results can be studied.

The project has been underway for three out of a projected
minimum of 20 years duration. Almost 30 reserves have been
marked off, but only two have been isolated to date. First
insights into the species loss problem focus on questions associated with newly created habitat edge. They include an influx
of birds from the surrounding destroyed forests, the invasion
of secondary succession species of butterflies and plants, and
major changes in the woody plant community.

AUTHOR INDEX

A

Addicott, W. O.   85, 109, 116
Ahlquist, J. E.   240, 241, 245
Alford, J. J.   169, 185
Alvarez, L. W.   2, 4, 5, 8, 9, 12, 15, 17, 18, 58, 63, 104, 109, 154, 185
Alvarez, W.   2, 4, 5, 18, 58, 63, 104, 109, 185
Amadon, D.   306, 323
Anderson, E.   155, 156, 157, 158, 159, 160, 161, 168, 173, 187
Andrews, H. N.   39, 64
Angstadt, D. M.   90, 109
Antevs, E.   256, 289
Armentrout, J. M.   87, 88, 109
Armstrong, D. M.   249, 251, 262, 269, 289
Arthur, M. A.   71, 73, 111
Asaro, F.   18, 63, 109, 185
Aubry, M. P.   86, 88, 109
Austin, J. A.   109
Avcin, M. J.   66
Axelrod, D. I.   47, 49, 63
Ayer, M. Y.   260, 289

B

Bader, O. N.   166, 185
Bakker, R. T.   60, 63
Bambach, R. K.   68, 115
Banks, H. P.   35, 37, 39, 40, 41, 63, 64

Bardner, J. V.   113
Barnard, P. D.   100, 109
Barrett, S. F.   68
Barron, E. J.   109
Barton, C.   115
Baum, G. R.   113
Bè, A. W. H.   113
Beck, C. B.   42, 43, 63
Belau, D. E.   186
Benson, R. H.   85, 109
Benson, W. W.   308, 323
Benton, M. J.   43, 60, 61, 63
Berger, R.   178, 179, 180, 181, 187
Berger, W. H.   72, 116
Berner, R. A.   107, 109
Berry, W. B. N.   95, 109
Betancourt, J. L.   258, 290
Bierregaard, R. O., Jr.   295, 299, 301, 302, 306, 323, 324, 334
Bormann, F. H.   28, 63
Boucot, A. J.   95, 109
Boulter, M. C.   110
Bourliere, F.   134, 136, 150
Brace, C. L.   119, 150
Brain, C. K.   140, 145, 150
Braman, D. R.   50, 51, 63
Brenchley, P. J.   95, 109
Broom, R.   140, 150
Brown, J. H.   220, 223, 243, 249, 261, 262, 263, 265, 266, 286, 287, 290
Brown, K. S., Jr.   295, 308, 310, 323, 334
Buffler, R. T.   109
Bystrak, D.   324

C

Campbell, L. D.   81, 82, 83,
    116, 159, 189
Carlquist, S.   40, 42, 50,
    54, 63
Carlson, J. B.   167, 186
Carlson, S. S.   246
Carr, T. R.   79, 106, 109
Case, T. J.   233, 234, 243
Cerling, T. R.   143, 150
Chaloner, W. G.   35, 39, 63,
    65
Chamberlin, T. C.   72, 110
Chinzei, K.   116
Choi, D.   112
Cifelli, R.   86, 101, 110
Cinq-Mars, J.   167, 188
Clark, F. E.   170, 186
Clark, J. D.   132, 150
Clark, W. E., Le Gros   122,
    150
CLIMAP   71, 75, 83, 85, 110
Clisby, K. H.   258, 290, 292
Cockrum, E. L.   249, 251,
    262, 290
Cody, M. L.   234, 243
Cole, K.   257, 258, 259, 290
Collinson, M. E.   87, 90, 110
Connor, E. F.   265, 285, 290
Conway, G. R.   245
Coppens, Y.   120, 151
Copper, P.   96, 110
Corliss, B. H.   85, 86, 110
Cox, A. V.   64
Crosbie, J. R.   90, 111
Cuppy, W.   3, 18
Curtis, J. T.   295, 323
Cushing, J. E., Jr.   260, 290
Cuvier, L. C. F. D.   13, 14,
    18
Cvancara, A. M.   101, 110

D

Dalquest, W. W.   257, 290
Damon, P. E.   187, 189
Darwin, C.   13, 15, 61
Dawson, M. R.   112
Day, M. H.   146, 150
Denham, C. R.   114

Devereaux, I.   87, 110
Dhondt, A. V.   104, 110
Diamond, J. M.   ix, 3, 10,
    191, 196, 197, 199, 200,
    201, 202, 222, 224, 225,
    227, 229, 230, 232, 233,
    239, 240, 243, 244, 245,
    274, 290, 296, 314, 323,
    331
Dickens, J. M.   98, 110
Dilcher, D.   58
DiMichele, W. A.   51, 63
Dincauze, D. F.   167, 186
DiPeso, C. C.   163, 186
Donahue, D. J.   189
Dorman, F. H.   87, 110
Douglas, R. G.   102, 110
Doyle, J. A.   53, 54, 64, 65
Duncan, D.   94, 112
Durrant, S. D.   249, 251,
    262, 290

E

Eaton, R. L.   139, 142, 145,
    146, 150
Edwards, D.   39, 64
Eisenmann, E.   205, 246
Ekman, S.   76, 110
Emiliani, C.   256, 263, 290
Emmons, L. H.   295, 312, 313,
    323, 334
Ericson, D. B.   256, 263, 290
Everitt, B. L.   258, 292
Ewer, R. F.   138, 140, 150
Ewing, M.   290

F

Fabricius, F.   100, 110
Farmer, H. G.   114
Fassett, J. E.   66
Fenner, G. J.   186
Findley, J. S.   249, 251,
    256, 259, 260, 261, 262,
    263, 264, 269, 273, 275,
    284, 290, 291
Finks, R. M.   97, 111
Fischer, A. G.   18, 71, 72,
    73, 103, 111, 114
Fisher, J. B.   114

Flessa, K.   22, 64, 73, 111
Foppe, T.   189
Forbes, E.   211, 244
Forman, F.   292
Forman, R. T. T.   295, 323
Foster, C. B.   47, 49, 52, 64
Fowler, K.   110
Frakes, L. A.   102, 111
Frederiksen, N. O.   49, 50, 64
Frenzel, B.   26, 64
Friis, E. M.   26, 48, 64
Frison, G. C.   163, 186
Frizell, U. A.   116

G

Galli, A. E.   323
Galloway, R. W.   256, 291
Gardner, J. V.   113
Garrels, R. M.   109
Gartner, S.   72, 111
Gauss, G. F.   120, 150
Gensel, P. G.   39, 64, 65
Gerow, B.   189
Gierlowski, E. H.   68
Gilmore, J. S.   66
Gilpin, M. E.   224, 233, 244
Gingerich, P. D.   163, 186
Glass, B. P.   90, 111
Goel, N. S.   193, 245
Goldberg, D. E.   24, 64
Gothan, W.   22, 45, 64
Gould, S. J.   72, 111
Graham, R. W.   159, 161, 186
Grayson, D. K.   183, 186, 261, 262, 291
Greville, T. N. E.   125, 151
Guilday, J. E.   181, 186
Guillotin, M.   313, 323

H

Haffer, J.   322, 323
Haila, Y.   210, 244
Hall, C. A.   100, 111
Hall, E. R.   262, 275, 291
Hallam, A.   71, 72, 74, 98, 99, 100, 105, 111
Hambrey, M. J.   93, 111
Hansen, R. M.   170, 186, 290

Hardenbol, J.   116
Harland, A. B.   93, 111
Harland, W. B.   28, 29, 49, 64
Harper, J. L.   24, 64
Harris, A. H.   256, 259, 290, 291
Harris, G. A.   25, 64
Harris, J. M.   137, 138, 143, 151, 152
Harris, W. K.   47, 67
Harrison, C. G. A.   109
Hartman, C. M.   41, 64
Hassell, M. P.   245
Hay, R. L.   132, 144, 150, 151
Haynes, C. V.   163, 164, 166, 182, 186
Hemmer, H.   140, 141, 151
Hendey, Q. B.   140, 141, 142, 143, 144, 151
Hennings, D.   284, 291
Hester, J. J.   168, 169, 186, 187
Hickey, L. J.   53, 55, 56, 58, 64, 65, 102, 103, 111, 112
Hickman, C. S.   87, 112
Hills, L. V.   50, 51, 63
Ho, T. Y.   178, 187
Hoffmann, R. S.   284, 291
Holloway, J. D.   240, 244
Hope, J. H.   213, 214, 215, 244
House, M. R.   95, 112
Houston, D. C.   133, 151
Howard, E. B.   260, 292
Howell, F. C.   140, 142, 151
Hueber, F. M.   63
Hughes, N. F.   53, 65
Humboldt, A. von   25, 65

I

Imbrie, J.   22, 64
International Study Group   165, 187

J

Jablonski, D.   77, 112

James, H. F.   238, 245
Janzen, D. H.   155, 187
Jarvinen, O.   197, 201, 244, 246
Jelinek, A. J.   166, 187
Jelinek, J.   166, 187
Jenkyns, H. C.   73, 112
Johanson, D. C.   120, 151
Johnston, W. B.   206, 244
Jones, C.   290
Jones, H. L.   196, 197, 199, 200, 201, 202, 244
Jones, R.   167, 182, 187
Jorgensen, C. D.   261, 293
Judd, F.   290
Jull, A. J. T.   189

K

Karr, J. R.   205, 206, 210, 232, 244, 245, 287, 291, 306, 323
Kauffman, E. G.   101, 104, 112
Kay, E. A.   77, 112
Keany, J.   72, 111
Keen, A. M.   77, 112
Keigwin, L. E.   77, 86, 110, 112
Keller, G.   86, 88, 112
Kelson, K. R.   249, 291
Kendeigh, S. C.   197, 244
Kennett, J. P.   87, 115
Kershaw, A. P.   47, 67
Kevan, P. G.   44, 65
Kidston, R.   40, 65
Kiernan, K.   166, 183, 187
Kipp, N. G.   113
Kitchell, J. A.   79, 106, 109
Klein, J.   165, 187
Klein, R. G.   138, 139, 151, 153, 155, 166, 187, 188
Klimkiewicz, M. K.   324
Knight, J. D.   66
Knoll, A. H.   7, 21, 22, 30, 36, 65, 66, 93, 117, 191, 327
Kollmann, H. A.   102, 112
Krassilov, V. A.   54, 65
Kruuk, H.   142, 151

Kuchler, A. W.   249, 250, 251, 281, 291
Kurtén, B.   141, 151, 155, 156, 157, 158, 159, 160, 161, 168, 173, 179, 187

L

Lang, W. H.   40, 65
Lasaga, A. C.   109
Laughnan, P. F.   66
Leakey, M. D.   132, 133, 147, 151
Leakey, M. G.   140, 151
Leakey, R. E. F.   119, 150, 152
Leakey, R. E. G.   120, 152
Leck, C. F.   204, 244, 323
Leclercq, S.   63
Lee, M. R.   290
Leigh, E. G., Jr.   193, 195, 244, 245
Leopold, E. B.   48, 65
Lerman, J. C.   187
Levenson, J. B.   295, 323
Lewin, R.   ix, 30, 65
Likens, G. E.   28, 63
Lipps, J. H.   28, 45, 67
Llewellyn, P. G.   64
Lochman, C.   94, 112
Long, A.   170, 171, 173, 187, 189
Loutit, T. S.   90, 113
Lovejoy, T. E.   11, 61, 65, 192, 203, 210, 295, 296, 297, 298, 299, 302, 305, 312, 316, 323, 324, 334
Lowther, G. R.   133, 139, 146, 152
Lundelius, E. L., Jr.   159, 161, 186
Lyell, C.   14, 15, 18, 80, 81
Lynch, J. F.   197, 245, 246, 295, 324
Lyuber, A. A.   66

M

MacArthur, R. H.   73, 113,
    163, 187, 193, 196, 224,
    232, 245, 263, 265, 266,
    291
MacDonald, D. W.   146, 152
MacDonald, G.   174
MacNeish, R. S.   167, 187
Mamay, S. H.   49, 66
Marasti, R.   83, 113
Marcus, L. F.   178, 179, 180,
    181, 187
Martin, P. S.   9, 10, 153,
    154, 155, 159, 165, 168,
    170, 171, 173, 182, 183,
    187, 188, 189, 191, 258,
    259, 291, 292, 330
May, R. M.   193, 196, 244,
    245, 296, 323
Mayr, E.   224, 225, 244
McCoy, E. D.   265, 285, 290
McElhinny, M. W.   106, 113
McGhee, G. R.   97, 113
McIntyre, A.   86, 113
McLaren, D. J.   16, 18, 37,
    61, 65
McWilliams, M. O.   106, 113
Mead, J. I.   169, 170, 172,
    182, 188, 261, 262, 292
Meltzer, D. J.   169, 170,
    172, 182, 188
Metcalf, A. L.   284, 292
Meyen, S. V.   49, 52, 65
Michel, H. V.   18, 63, 109,
    185
Miller, K. G.   86, 88, 113
Minikh, M. G.   66
Mitchum, R. M.   116
Monechi, S.   104, 113
Moores, E. M.   105, 117
Morlan, R. E.   167, 188
Mosimann, J. E.   165, 181,
    183, 188
Mulcahy, D. L.   54, 65
Muller, J.   31, 33, 54, 65
Murphy, D. D.   296, 324

N

Naeser, C.   116

Neff, N. A.   148, 152
Neustrueva, I. Yu.   66
Newall, G.   95, 109
Newell, N. D.   72, 113
Newell, N.   21, 65
Niklas, K. J.   22, 28, 29,
    36, 42, 65, 66

O

Obonitskaya, E. K.   66
Ochev, V. G.   66
O'Dean, W. A.   186
Odum, E. P.   134, 152
Oedekoven, K.   295, 324
Olson, E. C.   46, 49, 66, 238
Olson, S. L.   238, 245
Olsson, A. A.   80, 113
Olsson, R. K.   90, 113
O'Neil, J.   150
Oniki, Y.   305, 324
Opik, E. J.   263, 292
Opler, P. A.   246
Oren, D. C.   296, 324
Orth, C. J.   58, 59, 66
Ouyang, S.   49, 68
Oxnard, C. E.   124, 152

P

Palmer, A. R.   21, 66, 94,
    113
Parker, W. C.   68
Parrish, J. T.   68
Patterson, B. D.   10, 192,
    220, 222, 247, 264, 265,
    270, 274, 275, 277, 282,
    283, 284, 285, 286, 287,
    292, 333
Payen, L. A.   167, 189
Pedder, A. E. H.   95, 114
Peppers, R. A.   63, 66
Perch-Nielsen, K.   101, 114
Percival, S. F.   103, 114
Petter, G.   140, 142, 151
Phillips, A. M.   175, 188,
    292, 293
Phillips, T. L.   50, 63, 66
Pickton, C. A. G.   64
Pillmore, C. L.   66
Pomerol, C.   87, 90, 92, 114

Ponomarenko, A. G.   66
Popper, K.   168
Potts, R. B.   133, 143, 145, 152
Prell, W.   113
Preston, F. W.   73, 114
Primoli-Silva, I.   104, 114
Prothero, D. R.   90, 114

R

Radczenko, G. P.   49, 66
Raffi, S.   83, 113
Ralph, E. K.   187
Rankin, J. M.   295, 316, 324, 334
Ranson, D.   187
Raup, D. M.   1, 18, 19, 21, 29, 33, 34, 36, 40, 43, 44, 56, 57, 61, 62, 66, 87, 93, 98, 99, 114, 157, 188, 191
Raymond, A.   68
Read, C. B.   49, 66
Reed, T.   202
Regal, P. J.   54, 66
Reid, C.   26
Reid, E. M.   26
Retallack, G. J.   47, 49, 67
Rice, G.   55, 58, 67
Richter-Dyn, N.   193, 245
Rinaldo, J. B.   186
Robbins, C. S.   246, 324
Robinson, J. T.   122, 123, 152
Romanovskaya, G. M.   66
Root, R. B.   120, 134, 152
Rosenkrantz, A.   101, 114
Roth, E.   290
Rothwell, G. W.   22, 65
Ruddiman, W. F.   113
Russell, D. A.   55, 58, 67
Russell, D. E.   158, 188

S

Sabels, B. E.   188
Saidakovsky, L. A.   66
Savage, D. E.   158, 188
Savage, R. G.   140, 152
Savile, D. B. O.   65

Savin, S. M.   55, 67, 102, 110
Schaller, G.   133, 139, 143, 145, 146, 148, 152
Schilpp, P. A.   168, 188
Schindewolf, O. H.   16, 19
Schoener, T. W.   202, 245
Schopf, T. J. M.   72, 76, 79, 80, 114, 117
Schubart, H. O. R.   324
Schuchert, C.   72, 114, 115
Schultz, C. B.   260, 292
Schultz, P. H.   6, 19
Scotese, C. F.   94, 96, 115
Sears, P. B.   258, 290, 292
Sepkoski, J. J., Jr.   18, 19, 21, 22, 29, 34, 35, 36, 44, 45, 60, 66, 67, 68, 73, 87, 93, 94, 97, 98, 99, 111, 114, 115, 157, 188
Shackelton, N. J.   87, 115
Sheehan, P. M.   95, 115
Sheerin, A.   35, 39, 63
Shipman, P.   133, 145, 152
Shutler, R., Jr.   171, 188
Sibley, C. G.   240, 241, 245
Siegel, S.   266, 273, 292
Signor, P. W.   28, 45, 67
Silver, L. T.   6, 19
Simberloff, D.   30, 72, 115
Simpson, G. G.   168, 188
Skevington, D.   95, 115
Sloan, A. J.   233, 245
Sloan, J. L.   103, 109
Sloan, R. E.   117
Sluiter, I. R.   47, 67
Smartt, R. A.   257, 292
Smiley, C. J.   55, 67
Smit, J.   101, 115
Smith, A. G.   64
Smith, C. A. F.   114
Sohl, N. F.   102, 115
Soule, M.   233, 245
Southwood, T. R. E.   245
Spasskaya, I. S.   66
Spaulding, W. G.   170, 188, 258, 292, 293
Stafford, D.   163, 166, 189

Stanley, S. M.   7, 8, 61, 67,
  69, 76, 77, 80, 81, 82, 83,
  93, 115, 116, 159, 189,
  191, 328
Stanton, T. W.   102, 116
Steneck, R. S.   67
Stitt, J. H.   94, 116
Stokes, R. B.   101, 116
Surlyk, F.   104, 116

                    T

Tappan, H.   97, 116
Taylor, M. E.   94, 116
Taylor, R. E.   167, 177, 189
Terborgh, J.   203, 204, 205,
  217, 232, 236, 245, 296,
  298, 306, 314, 324
Thierstein, H. R.   72, 116
Thompson, R. S.   189, 261,
  262, 292
Thompson, S.   116
Tiffney, B. H.   54, 65, 66,
  67
Tobias, P. V. T.   120, 152
Todd, R. G.   116
Toft, C. A.   201, 245
Traverse, A.   49, 67
Triplehorn, D. M.   116
Truswell, E. M.   47, 49, 67
Tschudy, R. H.   66
Turbott, E. G.   ,206, 207,
  246
Turner, D. L.   88, 116

                    U

Ungrady, T. E.   113
Urey, H. C.   16, 17, 19

                    V

Vail, P. R.   79, 88, 89, 90,
  97, 99, 100, 116
Vaisanen, R. A.   197, 244,
  246
Vakhrameev, V. A.   100, 116
Valentine, J. M.   28, 67
Valentine, J. W.   85, 105,
  116, 117
Valkenburgh, B. Van   67

Van der Voo, R.   115
Van der Voort, M. E.   295,
  334
Van Devender, T. R.   189,
  258, 259, 290, 292, 293
Van Valen, L.   103, 117
Vidal, G.   93, 117
Voigt, E.   101, 117

                    W

Walker, A.   7, 8, 119, 120,
  133, 147, 149, 150, 152,
  191, 329
Walker, D. H.   186
Wallace, A. R.   211, 217
Walters, R.   64
Ward, P. D.   104, 117
Waterhouse, J. B.   98, 117
Webb, S. D.   159, 168, 186,
  189
Webster, D.   165, 189
Wells, P. V.   257, 259, 261,
  293
Werner, P. A.   24, 64
West, F. H.   167, 182, 189
West, R. M.   112
Weyland, H.   22, 45, 64
Whigham, D. F.   295, 324
Whitcomb, B. L.   324
Whitcomb, R. F.   197, 208,
  209, 211, 245, 246, 295,
  324
White, T. D.   120, 143, 151,
  152
White, T. J.   246
Whittaker, R. H.   134, 152
Wiedemann, J.   104, 117
Wilcox, A. B.   295, 296, 324
Wilcox, B. A.   217, 219, 233,
  234, 235, 246
Williams, G.   206, 207
Williamson, M.   197, 246
Willis, E. O.   203, 204, 205,
  246, 295, 296, 305, 324,
  325
Wilson, A. C.   241, 246
Wilson, D. E.   290

Wilson, E. O.   73, 113, 163,
    187, 193, 196, 205, 245,
    246, 263, 265, 266, 291,
    296, 325
Winter, B.   204, 205, 232,
    236, 245, 296, 306, 314,
    324
Wise, K. P.   76, 79, 80, 117
Wolfe, J. A.   49, 68, 87, 88,
    102, 103, 117
Wollin, G.   290
Wolpoff, M. H.   119, 123, 152
Wood, B. A.   150
Wood, C. E.   26, 68
Wright, H. E.   155, 188
Wright, R. C.   113
Wright, S. J.   201, 205, 206,
    210, 246
Wyman, J.   163, 189

Y

Yao, Z. Q.   49, 68

Z

Zabel, T. H.   189
Zeimens, G. M.   186
Ziegler, A. M.   49, 68, 115
Zimmerman, B.   315
Zimmerman, M. R.   152
Zinsmeister, W. J.   87, 117

SUBJECT INDEX

A

acritarchs   93, 97, 106
Aden Crater   174
Albian   29
altitudinal zonation   266,
    270
American chestnut   27
amino acids   178, 179, 180,
    181, 182
ammonites   98, 104, 106
amphibia   315ff, 317
angiosperm   28, 30, 34, 35,
    53ff, 87, 103
angiosperm diversification
    55
anoxic events   73ff
ants   305
Aptian   29
Aquilapollenites province
    55, 56
area   201, 236, 239
area effects   295
arthropods   94
artiodactyls   156
Ashgillian   94
asteroid   37, 53ff, 58, 183,
    184
asteroid impact   2, 4, 5, 6,
    8, 12, 16, 17, 168
Atlantic   80, 81, 86, 99
Australia   155, 183, 184,
    212, 213, 215, 218, 228,
    240

Australopithecus   8, 119,
    120, 121, 122, 123, 126,
    127, 128, 129, 143, 144,
    149
Australopithecus afarensis
    120
Australopithecus boisei   119,
    121
Australopithecus robustus
    119, 121, 122, 138, 149

B

Bajocian   99
banteng   217
Bardsey Island   196, 197,
    198, 199
Barremian   29
Barro Colorado   205, 206,
    209, 210, 242, 297, 306
Bass Strait   213, 214, 215
bats   155, 225, 226
benthic community   37
benthic diversity   78
Berriasian   29
bioclimatic law   249, 281
biogeography   44ff
biogeography historical fac-
    tors   247
biogeography island   248
biogeography mammals   247ff
biogeography nonequilibrium
    insular   286, 287
biogeography provinces   78

biogeography theory   248
biomass   134, 135, 143
biomere   94, 95
biota montane   285
biota tropical   72, 100
bird   184, 192, 202ff, 212,
    224, 226, 230, 232, 233,
    234, 235ff, 239, 241,
    299ff, 305, 313
bird activity   301
bird canopy   302, 306
bird captures   301, 302, 303,
    304, 306, 307
bird communities   300, 302,
    306
bird distributions   208
bird isolation   304
bird large   205
bird populations   196ff,
    222ff
bird relict   226
bird understory   306, 307
birth rate   195, 201, 241,
    242
bison   166, 178, 182
bivalves   61, 97, 98, 99,
    101, 104
Blancan   156, 158, 160, 161
blitzkrieg   153ff, 161, 163,
    165, 166, 167, 168, 169,
    173, 181, 182, 183, 184
body size   266, 268
boreal   101, 102
boreal-tropical transition
    100
bovids   137
brachiopod   97, 98
breeding census   198
British Islands   197
bryozoans   98
Bucatunna Formation   91
burning   308, 310, 311
burro dung   170
butchery site   145, 147
butterflies   308ff, 311

                    C

calamitalean   51
Calico Hills   167

California Channel Islands
    196, 200, 201
Callixylon   43
Callovian   99
Calvin cycle   23
Cambrian events   94
camels   181
Campanian   29
capture rate   299, 301
Carboniferous   28, 29, 38,
    50, 51, 92
Caribbean   80
carnivore   179, 201, 205,
    216, 222, 223, 268
carnivore guild   120, 138ff
carnivore large   140, 216
carnivore small   155
catastrophe   2, 13, 14, 17,
    37
catastrophic events   27
catastrophic mass mortality
    23
catastrophic models   184
catastrophic overkill   169
cave fauna extinct   260
cave fauna extralimital   260
Cenomanian   29, 99
Cenophytic flora   22
Cenozoic   71, 74ff
chance   44
cheetah   142, 144, 145
Chickasawhay Formation   91
Chihuahuan desert   257
Cladoxylopsida   39
cladoxylopsid   42
clams   61
climate   7, 8, 9, 10, 11, 25,
    52, 55, 62
climate change   23, 44ff,
    155, 163, 169
climate conditions   25ff
climate model   173
climate shift   257
Clovis   163, 166, 182, 183
Clovis hunters   169, 177,
    179, 181, 182
Clovis sites   168
coextinction   184
colonization   229, 237, 260,
    299

colonization glacial   261, 281
colonization route   259
community benthic   37
community closed   307
community composition   300
community montane   211ff
community structure   60
community terrestrial   37
competition   23, 24, 35ff, 40, 54, 61, 62, 74, 163, 193
competition interference   145, 146
competitive displacement   40
competitive exclusion   120
conifer   46, 49, 100
conodonts   98
coral   95, 96, 98, 104
coralline   61
cordaites   46
cow dung   170
Cowboy Cave   174
craters   see asteroid
Cretaceous   2, 3, 5, 8, 11, 27, 28, 29, 53ff, 73, 98, 100, 101, 102, 104, 153, 168, 191
Cretaceous diversification   31, 33
Cretaceous-Tertiary boundary   28, 37, 53, 54, 56, 58, 59, 184
crinoids   98
culture   167
cut-marks   145
cycads   46, 54
C^{14} dates   172

D

Danian   101, 102
death rate   195, 201, 242
density compensation   288
Devonian   16, 28, 35ff, 38, 39, 95ff
dinoflagellates   101, 105
dinosaurs   2, 4, 5, 6, 154, 183, 184
disjunct distributions   213, 219, 247

dispersal   25
divergence taxonomic   282ff
diversification   22, 35
diversification plant   36
diversity   37, 52, 78
diversity invertebrate   36
diversity pattern   28ff, 30
diversity Permian   45, 46
diversity Permo-Triassic   45
diversity plant   31, 33
diversity standing   156, 157, 158, 160, 161
diversity taxonomic   22
diversity tracheophyte   29
diversity Triassic   45, 46
Djulfian   98
dog hunting   143, 144

E

earth's albedo   107
ecological time   62
ecosystem critical size   297
ecosystem decay   295ff
Eifelian   36
elephant   217
Emsian   36
endemic avifauna   239
endemic species   239
endemism   237ff, 240, 241, 242, 282
endentates   156
environmental fluctuations   192, 193, 195
environmental perturbations   26
environmental stress   26
Eocene-Oligocene   90
Eocene   5, 85ff, 101
equids   137
equilibrium   196ff, 199, 201
eustatic fall   89
Eutamias quadrivittatus   284
evolution   2, 3, 4, 7, 8, 9, 13, 15, 17
evolution carnivore   138ff
evolution hominid   119ff
evolution human   8
evolution pattern   60, 62
evolution plants   53
evolution rates   123, 124ff

evolution theory   13, 15, 17
evolutionary divergence   288
evolutionary faunas   22
evolutionary floras   22
evolutionary potential   275,
    276
evolutionary time   237ff
extinction abundance   203
extinction background   192
extinction baseline   157
extinction catastrophic
    153ff, 165, 182
extinction chronology   169
extinction cumulative   270
extinction differential   214,
    215, 219, 222, 223
extinction extraterrestrial
    causes   18
extinction gradual   179
extinction hominid   119ff
extinction local   263
extinction mammals   247ff
extinction marine   7
extinction mass   see mass
    extinction
extinction pattern   28
extinction periodicity   18
extinction post-glacial   263
extinction probability   194,
    199, 277ff
extinction progressive   270
extinction rates   233
extinction record   169
extinction resistance   214
extinction risk   202, 204,
    228, 234, 242
extinction selective   271
extinction susceptibility
    275
extinction threshold   277
extinction tropical   92

                    F

Fammennian   36, 37, 95
Farnes Islands   196
fauna bivalve   80, 81, 82
fauna cave   260
fauna composition   271
fauna endemic   282ff
fauna evolutionary   22

fauna molluscan   80
fauna relict   248
fauna size   271
fauna total   160
fauna tropical   95
felids   137
fern   46, 59
Fiji   239
First American Bank site   181
flora   102
flora Cenophytic   22
flora evolutionary   22
flora Mesophytic   22, 46, 49
flora Neogene   48
flora Paleophytic   22, 46, 49
flora transitional   49
Florida   83
food web   74, 105
foraminifers   85, 86, 88, 98,
    101
forest Amazonian   192, 203,
    204, 295ff, 301
forest bird   207
forest continuous   308
forest deciduous   207ff
forest diverse   299
forest expansions   258
forest fire   316, 318, 319,
    320
forest fragments   313, 322
forest habitats   257
forest herbivores   268
forest intact   313
forest islands   203
forest patches   209
forest primary   321
forest remnants   296
forest reserve   300
forest undisturbed   298, 312
fossil   260
fossil land plants   21ff, 30,
    61
fossil preservation   22, 30
fossil record   21ff, 43, 44
founder effect   299
fragmentation   210, 295
Fraser Cave   166
Frasnian   36, 95
Frasnian-Fammennian boundary
    37

Frasnian-Fammennian crisis
    96, 97
fusulinids   98

G

gastropods   98, 101, 102
Gauss hypothesis   120
Gedinnian   36
generation time   196, 202,
    241
geographic range   259
giant beavers   155
giant lemurs   175, 183
gibbon   217
gingkos   46, 54
giraffids   137
Givetian   36
glacial colonization   261,
    281
glacial episodes   79, 92
glacial event   93
glacial interval   83
glacial maximum   71
glaciation   95, 98, 106
glaciation Ordovician   94ff
glaciers Pleistocene   260
globigerines   86, 101
Gondwana relicts   240
gradualism   12, 14, 17
Great Basin   220
greenhouse effect   107
ground sloth   154, 170, 173,
    184
grouping behavior   146
Guadalupe Mountains   170, 175
Guadalupian   98
gymnosperms   54
Gypsum Cave   170, 171, 174

H

habitat area   204
habitat changes   197, 202
habitat destruction   3, 9,
    11, 295, 299
habitat forest   257
habitat fragmentation   202ff,
    209, 223, 242, 295, 296
habitat generalists   222, 223
habitat montane   192

habitat specialists   216, 222
habitat specialization   266
habitat trophic   268
hare   222
Hauterivian   99
Hawaiian archipelago   77
Hawaiian Province   78, 106
Hemphillian   159
herbivores   134, 143, 163,
    214, 216, 222, 223, 268,
    275
hippopotamids   137
Holocene   163, 164, 173, 182,
    263
hominid   137
hominid evolution   119ff
hominid phylogeny   120ff
hominid speciation   144
Homo erectus   119, 121, 122,
    127, 128, 129, 130, 131,
    132, 133, 138, 143, 144,
    147, 148, 149
Homo habilis   121, 122, 126,
    128, 129, 130, 131, 132,
    133, 142, 145, 148
Homo sapiens   121, 122, 123,
    125, 127, 128, 131, 132,
    148, 154, 215, 216
homogeneity   134
homology   125
Hopkin's law   249, 281
horse   178, 181
human activity   9, 11
human evolution   8
human impact   163
human species   8
humidity   298, 299, 316
hunter   133, 142
hyalosponges   97
hyena   137, 141, 142, 143,
    144
hypervitaminosis   147

I

Ice Age   79, 80
Illinoian   160, 161
immigrants   240
immigration   197, 203, 213,
    237
inoceramid   104

insectivores   155, 268
interglacial persistence
    283ff
invertebrates   36, 154
iridium   5, 18, 59, 168
Irvington   161
Irvingtonian   156, 160
island area   196, 214, 215,
    228, 239
island biogeography   248, 296
island montane   220, 221, 223
island oceanic   232
isolated population   191ff
isolated reserves   306, 307,
    308, 313, 314, 317, 318,
    319
isolation   239, 241, 262,
    295, 296, 297, 298, 300,
    301, 302, 303, 304, 305,
    306, 307, 308, 310, 311,
    312, 313, 315, 316, 317,
    318, 319
Isthmus of Panama   77

J

Jurassic   98, 99, 100

K

Kikuyu crania   126

L

lagomorphs   155
land bridge   211, 224, 226,
    236, 237
land bridge islands   211ff,
    222ff, 228, 229, 232, 233ff
land connections   228
latitude   201
latitudinal temperature gra-
    dients   75
Lehner   166
leopard   142, 144, 217
lion   143, 144
living space   72ff
lizards   192, 233ff, 239
lycopods   39, 191
lycopsids   50, 51
Lyellian percentage   80, 81

M

Maastrichtian   29, 101, 103,
    104
macrofloras   49
macrofossils   35, 36
Madagascar   155, 184
Malay bear   217
Malvinokaffric Province   96
mammal   184, 192, 205, 211,
    212, 213, 214, 216, 217,
    219, 222, 230, 233, 234,
    235ff, 239, 312ff
mammal biogeography   247ff
mammal biomass   135
mammal fauna   219
mammal flightless   215, 219,
    220
mammal large   135, 136, 137,
    155, 157, 161, 162, 163,
    217, 218, 222
mammal megafauna   181
mammal montane   219, 220, 252
mammal non-flying   312, 314
mammal populations   211ff
mammal small   155, 157, 158,
    159, 161, 162, 163, 218,
    222, 223
mammal survey   314
mammal terrestrial   155, 159
mammoth   163, 164, 166, 177,
    179, 181, 182, 183, 184
Manaus   297, 301
marine community   37
marine extinctions   7
marine invertebrates   44, 45,
    53, 61
marsupials   155, 214, 216
mass extinction   1, 4, 6, 8,
    15, 16, 18, 23, 27, 37, 43,
    44, 60, 61, 69ff
mass extinction biotic factors
    74
mass extinction Ice Age   79ff
mass extinction limiting fac-
    tors   70ff
mass extinction mammalian
    159
mass extinction marine   69ff
mass extinction temperature
    69ff, 105ff

mass mortality   23
mastodonts   154, 181
Meadowcroft   167
Mediterranean   82, 83, 85
megafauna   156, 164, 171,
   173, 183
megaspore   50, 51
mesic   268, 279ff
Mesophytic   22, 45, 46, 49
Mesozoic   53, 54, 98ff
metazoan record   43
meteorite   4
microfloras   49
microfossils   36
microspores   36
migrants   208
migration   25
minevaporal   256
Miocene-Pliocene boundary
   159
Miocene   159
moas   175
Modern Synthesis   15
mollusc   77, 80, 82, 87, 159
monkey   312
mountain lion   156
montane biota   285
montane islands   220, 221,
   223
montane satellites   283ff
montane vegetation   228, 248,
   250, 256, 278, 279ff
Muav Cave   174, 175
Murray Springs   166
mutualism   44, 193

N

Namurian   29
nannoplankton   88
natural selection   3
Neandertals   8, 9, 123, 127,
   128, 131
Neogene   47, 48, 159
Neolithic   145
neotropical rainforest   11
nested subset hypothesis   274
nested subset relationship
   273, 274
net shyness   302

New Guinea   228, 229, 232,
   237, 240, 242
New Zealand   206, 207, 240
niche partitioning   24
noeggerathiopsids   51
non-random distribution   266
non-randomness tests   267
Norian   98
North Sea   82, 85

O

Old Crow   167
olenids   94
Oligocene   85ff, 88, 89, 92
orangutan   217
Ordovician   94ff
origination   157, 158, 160
ostracodes   85
overkill   155, 165
overpopulation   300
oxygen isotopes   102
oxygen layer   73

P

Paleocene   101, 103
paleogeographic map   96
Paleolithic   154, 166, 183
Paleophytic   22, 45, 49
palynoflora   49
Panamic-Pacific Province   77,
   80, 82, 106
Panamic-Pacific realm   85
Panthera crassidens   140,
   141, 143
pathogens   44
Permian   16, 44ff, 47, 49,
   50, 52, 62, 97ff, 153
Permian event   97
Permo-Triassic   28, 45
Phanerozoic   35
phylogeny hominid   120ff
phytoplankton   74, 93, 97,
   105, 106
pin cherries   27
Pinecrest shell bed   84
plankton   103
plant distributions   25ff
plant diversification   36
plant diversity   31, 33

plant fossil record   21ff,
    30, 37
plant vascular   23ff
plant woody   316ff
Pleistocene   8, 10, 18, 26,
    76, 80, 81, 153ff, 156,
    158, 159, 160, 161, 162,
    163, 165, 175, 177, 191,
    192, 211ff, 217, 218, 219,
    220, 222ff, 225, 226, 227,
    229, 233ff
Pleistocene blitzkrieg   153ff
Pleistocene glaciers   260
Pleistocene habitat fragmenta-
    tion   223
Pleistocene Ice Age   159
Pleistocene mammals   160
Pleistocene megafauna   169
Pleistocene vicariance   287
Pliensbachian   99
Plio-Pleistocene   71, 79, 92,
    157, 158
Pliocene   7, 26, 80, 83, 159,
    160, 163
pluvial   256
pollen   53, 59
polytaxic interval   73
population area   241
population density   196, 201,
    204, 217, 228, 232, 241,
    242
population lifetime   193ff
population lizard   233ff
population relict   227
population size   196, 197,
    200, 201, 222, 228, 232,
    242, 266, 287
population variability   196,
    206, 232, 237, 287
pre-Clovis   164, 167, 173,
    175, 182
Precambrian   7, 93ff
predation   44, 61, 74
Pridolian   36
primates   137, 312
proboscideans   137, 156
progymnosperms   39, 42, 43
pseudoextinction   8, 9
Psilophyton   41
psychrosphere   85
pteridophytes   46

pteriodosperm   40, 42, 46

R

radiocarbon   165, 169
radiocarbon dates   177, 178,
    179, 180, 183, 184
radiocarbon tests   153ff
rain forest   2, 11, 18, 300
rainfall   134, 135
Rampart Cave   170, 171, 174,
    175
Rancho la Brea   175, 177,
    179, 180, 181
Rancholabrean   156, 157, 160
rats   225
Recent   160, 161
recolonization   209, 210,
    235, 236, 299
reef   96, 101, 104, 106
regression   70, 72, 74, 75,
    76, 79, 85, 88, 90, 91, 92,
    94, 95, 107
relict   226, 227, 248, 262,
    282
reproductive isolation   241
rhinoceroses   137, 211, 217
rhodophytes   61
Rhopalocera   309
Rhynia   41
rhyniophytes   39, 40, 41
Rhyniopsida   39
Rocky Mountains   220, 247ff,
    251
rodents   155, 216, 313
rudist   101, 104, 106

S

sabretooths   141, 143, 149,
    175, 178, 184
salinity   72
Sandia Mountains   170
Sangamon   160, 161
Sao Paulo   295
scavenger   133, 142
sea level   8, 10, 13, 89,
    212, 217, 218, 225, 226,
    227, 230, 235
seismic stratigraphy   88, 99
shade species   311

shape analysis   124
Shasta ground sloth   170,
   174, 175, 176, 177, 178,
   181, 182
Shelter Cave   174
Siegenian   36, 39
Sierra Madre Occidental   251
Silurian   36, 39
sirenians   156
skunk   156
Smilodon   179
snails   154
solar "constant"   70, 106
Solomon Islands   224
species area   74, 90, 106,
   211, 263, 264
species area curve   296
species area effects   73,
   76ff, 79, 89
species area hypothesis   72,
   73
species area relationship
   219, 220, 227, 232
species canopy   311
species composition   299, 300
species death   1ff
species elimination   273
species encounter   302, 305
species equilibrium   299
species fragmentation   299
species loss   296, 297, 298,
   299, 301
species number   214
species occurrences   272
species regression   264, 265
species richness   28, 134,
   136, 137
species secondary   316, 321
species sedentary   204
species shade   311
species sympatric   133ff
sphenopsids   51
spider   201
sporophytes   35, 36
stenothermy   105
stenotopy   105
Stephanian   29
stromatoporoids   96
subspecies incidence   276
succession secondary   321
suids   137

Sunda Shelf   217, 218
Sungir   166
Sunnyvale   167
survivorship differential
   276
sympatry of species   133ff

                    T

tabulates   96
Tabun   166
taphonomy   134
tapir   217
Tasmanian wolf   216
Tasmania   212, 213, 214, 215,
   216
taxonomic divergence   275ff,
   283
taxonomic diversity   22
taxonomic richness   22, 35,
   156
tektites   16
temperature   71ff, 75, 87,
   90, 91, 97, 99, 101, 102,
   103, 105, 159, 298, 299,
   316
Tertiary   28, 29, 37, 144,
   159, 168
Tethyan   101, 102
Tethys   100
tiger   217
Tithonian   98
Toarcian   99
tools   132
Tournaisian   29
tracheophyte   29, 37, 38, 57,
   61
tree fall   316, 318, 319, 320
tree mortality   318, 319, 320
Triassic   33, 44ff, 49, 52,
   62, 98
trigoniid   101
trilobite   94
trimerophyte   40, 41, 42
Trimerophytopsida   39
trophic habitat   268
trophic interaction   163
trophic level   123, 206, 266
tropical benthos   102
tropical biota   72, 100
tropical realm   104

tropical seas   95
tropical taxa   98, 105
turnover   196ff, 201, 209,
    242

                    U

ungulates   156
Upper Sloth Caves   174, 175

                    V

Varangian event   93ff
vascular plants   21ff, 34,
    35, 46, 56
vegetation displacements
    256, 258
vegetation disturbed   313
vegetation montane   228, 248,
    250, 256, 278, 279ff
Vendian   93
vertebrates   154
vicariance   285ff
Visean   29
volcanic islands   76
vultures   133

                    W

wallaby   215, 216
Westphalian   29, 51
Williams Cave   174
wind effects   316, 318, 319,
    320
Wisconsin relicts   282
Wisconsin   160, 161, 162
woodland   197257
World Wildlife Fund   297

                    X

xeric   268